The Perils of Protest

THE PERILS OF PROTEST

State Repression and Student Activism
in China and Taiwan

Teresa Wright

University of Hawai'i Press
Honolulu

Library of Congress Cataloging-in-Publication Data
Wright, Teresa.
    The perils of protest : state repression and student activism in China
and Taiwan / Teresa Wright.
        p.   cm.
    Includes bibliographical references and index.
    ISBN 0–8248–2348–6 (alk. paper) — ISBN 0–8248–2401–6 (pbk. : alk. paper)
    1. Students—Political activity.   2. Students—China.   3. Students—Taiwan.
I. Title: State repression and student activism in China and Taiwan.   II. Title.

LB3610.W74   2001
378.1'981'0951—dc21   00–064928

University of Hawai'i Press books are printed on acid-free
paper and meet the guidelines for permanence and
durability of the Council on Library Resources.

Designed by Nighthawk Design

Printed by The Maple-Vail Book Manufacturing Group

Contents

Acknowledgments

I am grateful to many people and institutions for their support of this project. My research could not have been conducted without the funding of the Jacob K. Javits Fellowship, the Simpson Fellowship, University of California, Berkeley's Vice Chancellor's for Research Fund, and a summer stipend from California State University, Long Beach. In addition, the Department of Sociology at Taiwan's Academia Sinica, under the directorship of Michael Hsin-Huang Hsiao, kindly took me on as a visiting scholar, providing me with work space, resources, and a great deal of helpful advice.

The manuscript benefited immensely from the guidance of Elizabeth Perry, Lowell Dittmer, Thomas Gold, Dorothy Solinger, Andrea Roberts, Marcus Kurtz, and many others. I also am thankful for the words of encouragement given by colleagues, friends, and family. Finally, I express my gratitude toward the student and intellectual activists who took the time to share with me their thoughts and opinions. Their courage and vision are inspirational, and I wish them the best in their current and future endeavors.

Chapter 1

Introduction

For three long months in the spring of 1989, the unfolding Democracy Movement in mainland China entranced the world. When former Party General Secretary Hu Yaobang died on April 15, students and citizens poured into the streets in mourning, soon transformed into more organized calls for an end to party corruption and increased political and economic reforms.[1] By April 24, the students had established an all-Beijing student federation—the first citywide student organization free of any Party sponsorship or control in the communist era. Almost daily, ever-growing protests, marches, and rallies took place in Beijing. On April 27, over a hundred thousand students defied police blockades and official condemnation, marching for miles to Tiananmen Square. On May 4, over a million students and citizens flocked to the Square.

Yet the Party remained intransigent. Frustrated, on May 14 a group of students began a hunger strike, soon drawing thousands of participants. Students now occupied Tiananmen Square continually, setting up an encampment. Due to this occupation, on May 15, gala plans to welcome Mikhail Gorbachev for the first meeting of top Chinese and Soviet leaders since the Sino-Soviet split had to be canceled.

Incensed by these bold actions, on May 19 the party declared martial law. Yet when the army then attempted to enter the city and clear out the Square, hundreds of thousands of city dwellers spontaneously blocked the soldiers. Making no use of force, the army simply turned back. Jubilant at this successful act of resistance, students continued to occupy the plaza. Early in the morning of June 4, however, the movement ended abruptly. The army again entered the city to clear out the square, but this time it would not be stopped. Those who attempted to block the soldiers and their tanks and trucks were forcefully moved—or shot. In the end, between two hundred and two thousand were dead, and thousands injured.

These gripping events were a watershed in post-Mao Chinese politics. With the movement's tragic end, the post-Mao cycle of political opening and constriction has been broken; since June 1989 Chinese Communist Party (CCP) officials have unswervingly and decisively repressed any and all attempts at autonomous political organization.[2] Earlier hopes that China might make decisive moves in the direction of Western-style democracy have been abandoned. Thus, it is crucial that we understand the causes of this movement's sad conclusion. After so many weeks of growing popular support and international attention, why did the protests go awry? Scholars have not shied away from these questions; indeed, a profusion of academic studies have sought to provide answers. Interestingly, in many of these analyses, responsibility is placed not only on ill-intentioned ruling elites but also on the student protestors themselves. Had students behaved in a more mature and thoughtful manner, many suggest, the movement's terrible outcome might have been averted, or at least ameliorated.[3] This book calls these assessments into question by drawing on new data and a novel methodology.

Despite the prevalence of works that treat student behavior in 1989, one important source of information has not been emphasized in most studies: the student leaders themselves. Concerned that this may have produced gaps in our understanding of student motivations and actions, I conducted lengthy personal interviews with students representing all of the major factions and groups that formed.[4] In the course of these interviews, I came upon revealing information from the transcription of a 1991 Paris conference where key student leaders discussed in detail their thoughts and actions during the movement.[5] Taken together, these interviews and transcripts comprise the most complete and representative compilation to date of the thoughts and opinions of movement leaders in Beijing in 1989.[6] To buttress this information, and to check for any distortions or misrepresentations, I consulted virtually all available student-produced documents from the movement in Beijing, as well as all major secondary sources on the movement.[7]

To further enhance our understanding of the movement of 1989, I have chosen an explicitly *comparative* perspective. Up to now, only Craig Calhoun's *Neither Gods Nor Emperors* has taken such an approach. Unlike Calhoun's work, however, this book focuses on a specific comparative case study: the Month of March movement of 1990 in Taiwan.[8]

Like that of 1989, the Month of March movement was the largest and most sustained student protest action in the history of the region. It arose as a response to an internal Kuomintang (KMT) conflict over the choice of a new president, whose selection was scheduled for March 21, 1990. This conflict had it roots in the political structure that had been in place in Taiwan since the KMT government fled to the island in the wake of the Communist victory in mainland China in 1949. Two years earlier, while the KMT was still nominally in control of the mainland, elections had been held for the National Assembly (Guomin Dahui), the body charged with ratifying the party's choice of president.[9] The assembly was comprised of representatives from China's provinces; each was to serve a six-year term. However, following the KMT's final defeat on the mainland in 1949, it became impossible to hold new elections once the original six-year term expired. Thus, these original representatives simply remained in office.

This body of elderly statesmen continued to ratify the president every six years, yet this was little more than a formality, as there was only one real choice for president: Chiang Kai-shek. Shortly after Chiang's death in April 1975, his son Chiang Ching-kuo rose to the position, holding the presidency uncontested until his death in 1988.[10] After the younger Chiang's death, then Vice President Lee Teng-hui, a party member of Taiwanese rather than mainland descent, became the acting president. In 1990, Chiang Ching-kuo's final six-year term expired; thus, according to the constitution, the National Assembly was required either to reconfirm Lee or to choose a new president. The general public would have no voice.

Internal KMT conflict over the matter began in February 1990. Aware that Lee Teng-hui was virtually assured the presidency, the nonmainstream (*fei zhuliu*) party faction had hoped to handpick a nonmainstream vice-presidential candidate. Instead, Lee purposely bypassed any consultation with powerful nonmainstream party members and chose a mainstream loyalist to be his vice president. Angered, the nonmainstream faction countered with an alternative ticket. Subsequently, throughout the early months of 1990, these two factions maneuvered to strengthen support within the National Assembly for their candidates.

The original ascent of Lee Teng-hui to the presidency had been widely heralded as a major symbol of the "Taiwanization" of the KMT and proof of the KMT's commitment to political reform. Thus, the spectre of renewed domination by conservative and military party elites caused great anxiety among many members of the public. As the factional conflict over the presidency unfolded, they were reminded daily that true political democracy still was not a reality in Taiwan, and that future political reform was far from assured.

To protest this situation, in mid-March students began an open-ended sit-in at the Chiang Kai-shek Memorial, the central square in Taipei. Their reformist goals were expressed on banners inscribed with Four Big Demands: (1) reelect the National Assembly; (2) abolish the old Constitution; (3)

present a schedule for political reform; and (4) convene a National Affairs Conference to discuss political reform. The following morning, military police emerged from the nearby Presidential Office and proceeded in formation to the Memorial, where they noisily awakened the sleeping students. The police did not use force to disperse the students, however, and soon retreated. Emboldened by this mild police action, hundreds of students and city folk flocked to the Memorial in the days that followed.

Despite these activities, the government did not officially respond to the students' demands. Frustrated, on March 19 a group of ten students began a hunger strike. By March 20, over five thousand students had gathered at the Memorial and close to sixty had joined the hunger strike. On the morning of March 21, Lee Teng-hui was elected president by the National Assembly. That evening, Lee met with student movement leaders at the Presidential Office, agreeing to convene a National Affairs Conference to discuss the students' demands. Presented with this compromise, the student protestors reluctantly agreed to evacuate the square; by the afternoon of March 22, the Memorial was virtually empty. In June and July, the National Affairs Conference was held, and in 1991 the Constitution was revised and the National Assembly completely reelected.

In many ways, this series of events provides an ideal case for comparison with China's Democracy Movement of 1989, for students in both movements behaved in strikingly similar ways. In each case, for example, student leaders maintained a strict separation between student and nonstudent participants. Further, student organizations in both movements were unstable and conflict-ridden. At the same time, however, the Month of March movement ended very differently from its counterpart on the mainland. Whereas the movement of 1989 ended with violent repression, this student action ended peacefully, voluntarily, and successfully, having all of its demands addressed by the government. Given this similarity in behavior yet difference in outcome, these cases provide an ideal opportunity to assess the origins and impact of student behavior in 1989.[11]

With regard to the causes of student behavior in 1989, many analyses suggest that student elitism contributed to the students' problems with broad-based organization as well as to their insistence on remaining separate from other social groups. In their search for a source of this elitism, some of these studies refer to the Chinese historical tradition of placing intellectuals—the moral conscience of society—in a privileged position to criticize and monitor the government.[12] Others argue that the more recent Chinese Communist tradition of glorifying radicalism and intolerance fed the students' tendencies toward disorganization and separatism.[13] At the same time, however, some note the improvisational nature of student behavior during the movement, emphasizing its constant flux and indeterminacy.[14]

In contrast, this book suggests that, at its root, student behavior in 1989 was both predictable and rational. In both China and Taiwan, the students' behavior largely reflected the political environment they faced.[15] In particular, sustained single-party monopolization of state institutions, party–state domination of the media, party penetration of social organizations, and a high propensity toward harsh state repression all exerted a profound influence on student actions and choices. Student difficulties with organization followed from their knowledge that their activities might be severely punished, as similar actions had been in the past. This fear of punishment made them hesitant to compromise with other students of whose intelligence, competence, or loyalty they were unsure. Interestingly, prior student organization may have heightened this tendency, for many student movement participants were suspicious of those who had previously been active in groups with which they were unfamiliar. Compounding this problem, students who had previously been active felt that their prior experience of activism made them more worthy of making decisions during the later movement. In the end, the strongest organizations were those based on friendship and that had few ties to previous organizations. Student concern with maintaining the "purity" of their ranks also derived from their fear of repression. Knowledge of past accusations of movement infiltration by "outside influences" in the party-controlled media, as well as the party's discriminatory use of force to quell dissent by certain social groups (workers, in the case of China; the Democratic Progressive Party, in the case of Taiwan), made students hesitant to allow nonstudents into their protest ranks.

What effect did student behavior have on the outcome of each movement? If student behavior was the key reason for the failure of the movement of 1989, then the movement of 1990 in Taiwan also should have ended in failure. Yet, this was not the case. Evidence suggests that growing organizational conflict and instability did impede the success of both movements. In the case of Taiwan, however, student unity finally (albeit weakly) was achieved before these organizational problems seriously derailed the movement. What of student efforts to remain separate from nonstudent demonstrators? Many existing analyses argue that this strategy may have hindered student success in 1989. In particular, some suggest that the students' failure to unite with workers deprived the movement of a mass base with sufficient power to bring about real change.[16] While this may be true, this theory tends to downplay the fact that a separatist strategy was the students' only choice if they wished to avoid repression. In reality, more broad-based mobilization probably would have sparked either earlier repression or revolution—neither of which was the students' goal.[17] The same appears to be true in the case of Taiwan. Overall, then, this suboptimal strategy was the students' only reasonable option.

More broadly, these findings add to our general understanding of the success and failure of social movements in nondemocratic societies. Current social movement theory grew largely out of cases of popular protest in Western countries, where the state has been much more open and pluralist in nature. This work is part of a new wave of scholarship that broadens this focus by looking at cases of protest in more overtly illiberal and repressive political systems.

Many prominent theorists of collective action note that political context, or the "political opportunity structure," is crucial to understanding protest organization, mobilization, and strategy. In specifying the concept of political context, scholars stress the relative openness or closedness of political institutions to opposition, the state's capacity for and propensity toward repression, and the relation of the media to the state and political parties.[18] Expanding these conceptions, this book details the influence of single-party monopolization of state institutions, party–state domination of the media and social organization, and harsh state repression in China and Taiwan.

Following this path, the book concludes that it may be useful to envision political context as a spectrum ranging from the most oppressive environments to those that are the most open and pluralistic. Although organization and mobilization are difficult even in the least dangerous and restrictive situations, the limitations on these social movement resources will be much more severe as the risk involved in protest increases. Indeed, in the most repressive, intolerant, and closed political environments, such as existed in China in 1989, effective reform-oriented political protest may be close to impossible.

In its exploration of these themes, the book proceeds as follows. Chapter 2 focuses on the key variable in the argument: the political environment of students in China and Taiwan. The chapter begins with a description of national political structures, which in both cases were characterized by long-term domination by a single party. Next, the more localized environment of the college campus is examined. In each instance, the ruling party presence on college campuses was pervasive. At the same time, however, the political environment in Taiwan was relatively less repressive and restrictive. The chapter concludes by investigating the internal conflicts among more conservative and relatively reform-oriented party elites in the period preceding each movement.

Chapter 3 begins the detailed examination of case studies. Due to the lengthy duration of the 1989 movement in China, this discussion is broken into two portions. Chapter 3 focuses on student organization and mobilization from the beginning of the movement in mid-April through the initiation of the hunger strike in early May. In particular, this chapter details the origins and development of student organization at Beijing University and Beijing Normal University, the two earliest and most influential campuses to organize. The chapter also looks at the rise of China's first autonomous cross-campus group, the all-Beijing Secondary Students' Autonomous Federation. Chapter 4 continues with an analysis of student behavior throughout the period of the hunger strike, the visit of Gorbachev, the declaration of martial law, and the June 4 massacre. Chapter 5 provides a comparative review of student behavior, protest development, and movement outcomes in Taiwan.

The final chapter ties together the lessons of this study. After summarizing the specific influence of political context in China and Taiwan, Chapter 6 examines the wider applicability of these findings, taking a comparative look at student movements in other places and at different world-historical times. Finally, the chapter presents new hypotheses regarding the impact of political context on social movement processes and outcomes, discussing the implications for successful, reform-oriented protest in nondemocratic regimes.

Chapter 2

The Political Environment
of Students in China and Taiwan

The outcomes of China's Democracy Movement of 1989 and Taiwan's Month of March movement of 1990 could hardly have been more different. In China, the student protests were brutally crushed, initiating a period of harsh repression toward any and all attempts at autonomous or dissident organization. Across the straits, in contrast, student demonstrators met with a conciliatory official response, resulting in the acknowledgment and implementation of their demands and the subsequent democratization of the political system. Yet student protestors in both movements exhibited strikingly similar behaviors.

How can we explain this likeness in behavior yet difference in result? A key part of the answer may be found in the political environment within which the students acted. Overall, commonalities in the political opportunity structure bred similar student protest behavior. Students in both cases reacted to single-party domination of the state, the media, and social organization, as well as to a high likelihood of harsh state repression. These realities combined to create an environment of great danger and risk for student protestors, causing them to be extremely hesitant to compromise and exceedingly careful in choosing their allies. Oddly, this atmosphere also led students to place a premium on courage as a leadership credential and to see any calls for moderation as suspect. At the same time, the relatively less threatening environment in Taiwan made such behavior less extreme in the Month of March movement.

What relation did student behavior have to the outcome of each movement? In general, the less disruptive the students appeared, the greater chance they had of succeeding in their goal of reform. For, in both cases, the ruling elites were split into two major factional groupings, one more reform-oriented, and the other more conservative. When the student protests began, each party faction hoped to use the demonstrations to buttress its power. In general, party hard-liners gained when protestors were disorderly, thus providing evidence that the country would fall into turmoil if reforms proceeded too quickly. Conversely, organized and moderate actions on the part of the students supported the more reformist faction's claim that the populace was "ready" for further political loosening. At the same time, protest mobilization that did not include groups which the regime found threatening made it less likely that the hard-line faction would insist on repression. Concurrently, however, if the demonstrations included only "nonthreatening" sectors (such as students), the hard-liners could feel safe in ignoring the protestors' demands, as doing so likely would not expose the party to the risk of widespread unrest.

Nondemocratic Political Environments

Although there is no general agreement as to the proper definition of "democracy," most identify it as a type of rule with meaningful elections, and that it protects basic civil liberties such as legal rights to a fair trial and freedom of expression, assembly, organization, and the media.[1] Nondemocratic, or "illiberal" regimes, lack these characteristics. At the same time, scholars have long stressed the great variation among nondemocratic forms of rule, especially regarding the extent to which a regime attempts to permeate and suffocate all independent social interaction.[2] With this in mind, I suggest that it may be useful to envision a spectrum of regime types extending from the most democratic to the least, based on the degree of: (1) single-party monopolization of state institutions; (2) party–state domination of the media; (3) party penetration of social organizations; and (4) harsh state repression. On this continuum, by 1989 and 1990 China and Taiwan had moved away from the more extreme oppressiveness of their pasts, with Taiwan having made notable strides in the direction of liberalization (and having started from a less severe position). Yet, in each case a single party continued to dominate and penetrate society, and a legacy of repression remained fresh in the minds of the population.

To what extent did China in 1989 and Taiwan in 1990 exhibit the four features listed above? To begin, in each case a single party had completely dominated the governmental structure for over forty years, with virtually no viable challenges to its power. At the same time, by the late 1980s the KMT's grip was much looser than that of the CCP. In China, single-party rule was justified by an ideology that claimed the Communist Party embodied the will of the masses. In the post-Mao period, however, party efforts to mobilize the population in a struggle for ideological rectitude diminished dramatically relative to the strict controls that had been evident earlier. At the same time, the party continued to claim that opposition to the CCP amounted to opposing the will of "the people." Consequently, political parties not under party control were banned and basic civil liberties denied. In Taiwan, single-party rule also was legitimated by an ideology, yet one far less illiberal in nature. Under the rubric of Sun Yat-sen's Three Principles of the People, the KMT claimed that democracy was its ultimate goal, but that a "tutelary" period of single-party rule was necessary to eradicate imperial rule and the communist threat, as well as to create a "foundation" for democracy. As a result, as of the early 1990s, the most powerful organs of the government remained firmly under the control of the KMT. At the same time, the KMT's controls over political expression had become far weaker than was the case in China. Partly because this more flexible ideology made it possible (but more as a consequence of international pressure), the KMT legalized opposition parties and street demonstrations in the mid-1980s.

The CCP and KMT also dominated virtually all areas of the media throughout their rule. By the late 1980s, these controls had become somewhat relaxed under both regimes but were far looser in Taiwan. In the post-Mao period in China, unsanctioned journals and newspapers were sometimes tolerated, and even official media outlets occasionally deviated from the official party line. At the same time, all official and unofficial media outlets remained under the watchful eye of the party and quickly met with repression if they became perceived as a threat. In Taiwan, by 1990 the media had been liberalized to a much greater degree, so that nonparty newspapers and journals enjoyed legal circulation and a small but substantial readership. Still, virtually all major newspapers, as well as radio and television stations, remained under KMT control.[3]

The ruling regimes in both Taiwan and China also worked to penetrate and dominate social organization, though in Taiwan these controls were more relaxed. Looking at university life, in each case the party-controlled Ministry of Education designated key administrative figures, such as university presidents. Such positions in the most prestigious institutions often required consultation with the highest party leaders.[4] Via the same mechanisms, the party centrally dictated curricular content and admissions quotas.[5] Further, in both cases students were tested on party ideology on national college entrance exams and were required to continue this study in their undergraduate years.[6]

The party also penetrated and dominated student organizations. In both China in 1989 and Taiwan in 1990, students legally were allowed to form organizations only under the sponsorship and oversight of the party. The student campus government, for example, acted only under the guidance of the party, and student officers typically were selected by party-controlled student groups. Further, official campus newspapers were controlled by the ruling party, and student-produced publications had to be submitted to a party-dominated committee for prior screening.

In China in the post-Mao period, controls over education had been relaxed to such a degree that unsanctioned student groups occasionally appeared, particularly at the ultra-elite Beijing University. Yet these groups were never tolerated for long. In Taiwan, by the end of the 1980s autonomous student organization was far less regulated. Many independent students had openly flouted campus regulations, not only running for campus offices, but often winning. Subsequently, the ruling authorities tolerated the appearance of reformist student governments at many universities. In addition, other students with a more leftist bent had been allowed to organize autonomous groups focused on social and economic justice. Nonetheless, at most campuses the KMT maintained a party branch, and each student was assigned a KMT-sponsored "counselor" (*jiaoguan*) who lived with the students in the dormitory and kept close tabs on their actions and behavior.

Finally, in both Taiwan and China, the ruling party displayed a high propensity for harsh repression of students who disobeyed official regulations. At the same time, cooperation with, and loyalty to, the party were often rewarded with desirable employment contracts and, in the case of Taiwan, scholarships. Typically, punishment would involve expulsion or the entry of unfavorable remarks in a student's permanent record (coupled in the PRC with being required to write a "self-criticism" to be aired publicly).[7]

To understand the severity of these punishments, one must appreciate the immense obstacles faced by students seeking university admission in China and Taiwan. In both cases, entrance to university was available to only a tiny percentage of the population, based on scores on a national entrance examination. Passing this examination required years of rigorous study, beginning with a student's primary school experience. In each region, students from an early age hotly competed for slots in "priority" schools known to pass higher percentages of students. To gain entrance to an elite institution required much more than simply a passing score, and thus even more uncompromising diligence. Overall, in the mainland, the possibility of admission was exceedingly low: less than one-half of one percent of Chinese citizens were admitted to university, amounting to a slim two hundred university and college students per hundred thousand mainland Chinese citizens.[8] Moreover, in the decade preceding 1989, the percentage of Chinese students moving up the educational ladder actually decreased.[9] In Taiwan, the figures were more favorable, yet entrance to a degree-granting university or college remained intensely competitive.[10] In addition, in both regions admission to study popular fields in the humanities was extremely difficult to gain.[11]

In each case, a student who was expelled could not simply enter another university. In the mainland, expulsion meant that a student would be forever unable to achieve a college education, despite his or her tireless years of devotion toward that goal. In Taiwan, an expelled student also would face immense difficulties in gaining acceptance to a different university, as changes in institution generally were not allowed.[12] Even if such a student was eventually admitted to an alternative institution, it was virtually guaranteed that the new institution would be of inferior status in the strictly defined educational hierarchy.

Should a student not be expelled but still accrue unfavorable notes in his or her official record, the consequences could be equally traumatic—especially in the case of China. As of 1989, the vast majority of university graduates in China were still placed in jobs by state assignments. Thus, a "blackened" record was almost certain to have a devastating effect on one's future livelihood, including possible exile to a post in a remote and undesirable region. In Taiwan, a sanctioned student would have more freedom in job choice, but his or her alternatives nonetheless would be limited by the tainted record. In addition, in Taiwan all males were required to serve two years in the military; in this service, an imperfect political record typically would lead to an undesirable posting and rank.[13]

Even more ominously, in each case the threat of imprisonment and physical violence was quite real. In China, persons designated as "traitors" to the socialist cause often faced years of imprisonment, forced labor, and excruciating torture, despite the party's half-hearted attempts to emphasize the rule of law in the post-Mao period. Although China's 1982 judicial code stipulated that detainees had to be tried and sentenced within sixty days, in reality public security staff widely ignored this regulation. Indeed, individuals routinely remained in detention for many months, or years. During this time, prisoners typically would have no contact with the outside world, leaving their families tormented about their whereabouts and well-being. Those who eventually were tried faced slapdash and arbitrary proceedings, leading to almost certain conviction and lengthy prison terms. Throughout this process, prisoners suffered brutal physical and mental torture as well as forced labor. For most, even the completion of one's sentence did not result in freedom. Although their formal status changed, many were required to remain in "Reeducation through Labor" camps or other forms of forced job placement. Those fortunate enough to escape this fate continued to experience official surveillance and occasional harassment once they rejoined the outside society. Under this cloud, few were able to eke out more than the most basic existence.[14] In Taiwan, such harsh treatment of opposition activists had become far more rare by the late 1980s, yet students and citizens vividly remembered similar violence done to dissidents in the very recent past.[15]

Overall, then, by the late 1980s students in both China and Taiwan labored under regimes that had loosened their controls to a degree, yet still retained ponderous elements of their more repressive pasts. At the same time, the KMT in Taiwan had moved much further in the direction of liberalization. As will be shown, these varying degrees of social and political controls created unique constraints on collective action resources in the student protest movements that arose in 1989 in China and 1990 in Taiwan. At the same time, because the political environment in Taiwan was relatively less oppressive than that in China, the obstacles faced by students in Taiwan were less considerable.

The Political Opportunity Structure and Student Behavior

These realities exerted a great influence on students, creating an environment of fear and uncertainty among student protesters in both movements. As involvement in student protest activities entailed great risk, students were exceedingly careful in their choice of codissidents and were highly suspicious of those who appeared suspect. More concretely, student leaders in both cases were extremely fearful of infiltration by student party spies, or by party spies posing as students. This fear was far from paranoiac, as both the CCP and the KMT had used this tactic in the past and again attempted to do so during both movements. As a result, in each case student leaders trusted only those with whom they were well acquainted prior to the movement and were hesitant to compromise with anyone whose competence or loyalty they had not personally verified. Thus, although students who were members of autonomous groups prior to each movement did trust those who had been part of their particular group, student members of different autonomous groups did not fully trust one another.

In this environment, the risks involved in miscalculation were quite high. A bad decision could result in very negative consequences for student participants, and as a result individual student leaders were hesitant to compromise with one another. Many students feared that yielding to the will of the majority could result in an action that would incur the wrath of the authorities; consequently, dissenting student leaders often opted to "exit" a group rather than bow to majority rule or negotiate a compromise. Subsequently, competing student movement leadership groups arose, each adhering to its own principles of decision making. This was true in both Taiwan and China, although the relatively less severe atmosphere in Taiwan lessened the intensity of these reactions among student protestors there. Stated simply, whereas student leaders in China feared that a bad decision would render them "criminals of history," student leaders in Taiwan worried that poor judgment would brand them "incompetents of history." Thus, in both cases compromise and unified organization were hindered, though slightly less so in Taiwan.

In addition, this environment made students extremely hesitant to welcome unorganized or unruly elements into their ranks, or to fully unite with groups that had been the target of state repression in the past. Students knew that any appearance of disorder (*luan*) or serious threat likely would provoke negative media coverage and/or a severe response by the authorities; consequently, they felt that their only safe and reasonable option was to exclude from their ranks nonstudent groups and individuals. At the same time, in Taiwan, due to the relatively relaxed atmosphere, these limitations on mobilization were less extreme.

Finally, in both cases these illiberal political realities gave rise to unique notions of legitimacy. Given official prohibitions against and punishment for autonomous student actions, any student willing publicly to flout these rules immediately gained the respect of other students. As a result, those students who were the first to act during the movements of 1989 and 1990 enjoyed a great deal of charismatic legitimacy due to the perceived courageousness of their action. Yet, at the same time, during each movement, these primarily charismatic student leaders were often confronted with doubts regarding their representative or rational-legal legitimacy. In some cases, these leaders subsequently sought to supplement their charismatic legitimacy by holding elections. In other cases, student leaders claimed that charisma and courage alone were enough to legitimize their authority.[16]

Overall, then, the political environment of China in 1989 and Taiwan in 1990 showed many important similarities, engendering commonalities in student protest behavior. At the same time, as the political environment in Taiwan was relatively less oppressive than that in China, in Taiwan these aspects of student behavior were somewhat muted.

Intraparty Conflict

In general, student behavior that revolved less around charisma was exclusive of unorganized elements and groups that the party deemed threatening, and was relatively organized and open to compromise raised each movement's chances of successfully bringing about reform. To understand the mechanics of this process, it is necessary to review the larger political developments in the societies within which the students were acting, especially at the elite level. Perhaps most important, within each party two major factions existed, one that was relatively reform-oriented, and one that was more conservative. These factional divisions were exacerbated as each faction vied for control of the party. When students took to the streets in 1989 in China and 1990 in Taiwan, in each case one party faction was more sympathetic to the student demonstrators while the other was less so. At the same time, each faction hoped to use the student demonstrations as a vehicle to enhance its own power. The more reform-oriented elites hoped that the demonstrations would prove that society was indeed "ready" for further reform, whereas more conservative leaders sought to show that further opening would lead only to chaos. Consequently, more moderate and loyal student behavior tended to strengthen the hand of the reformist faction, whereas more radical and confrontational student behavior buttressed the position of the conservatives.

Elite Divisions in the CCP

To better understand this dynamic, one must grasp the nature and relative power of these party factions immediately prior to each movement. In the PRC, the main factional division did not exist within the ranks of the top tier of the party elite, which included (roughly in order of most powerful to least): Deng Xiaoping, Chen Yun, Yang Shangkun, Wang Zhen, Li Xiannian, Peng Zhen, Bo Yi-Bo, and Sun Renqiong. Despite the fact that many of these men no longer held formal positions within the party, they remained extremely influential. Although these eight party elders often disagreed, they did not split into factional groupings. Rather, disagreements typically were settled when the more influential leader insisted upon his views after listening to and weighing the opinions of the others.[17]

Instead, the main factional division within the CCP in 1989 existed among its second and third tiers. This division revolved around both power and policy: each faction wished to become the heir to the first-generation leadership, and each held different views regarding the proper pace and extent of reform.

Prior to the movement of 1989, Zhao Ziyang, a proponent of accelerated economic reform, was Deng's chosen successor. Zhao was appointed premier of the government in 1980 and was raised to the position of Party General Secretary in 1987, following the demise of Hu Yaobang. Throughout the 1980s, Deng gradually withdrew from the daily operations of the CCP, allowing Zhao greater discretion over the pace and extent of reform. As this transpired, Zhao began to recruit and promote many younger technocrats and reformers to influential positions within the party. These cadres showed great allegiance to Zhao and served as the core of the relatively liberal faction that formed around him. Nonetheless, Deng remained the final arbiter of all major decisions. Thus, Zhao's position and power remained completely dependent upon Deng's continued good favor.[18]

Shortly after Zhao became General Secretary in October 1987, he presented his plan for reform at the 13th Party Congress. In the plan, Zhao identified expansion of China's productive forces as the primary goal of reform, arguing that all party work would be evaluated according to this criterion. Concretely, Zhao proposed that productivity be increased through the support and expansion of exports from China's coastal regions, coupled with national price reform.[19] Perhaps most important, Zhao argued that increased productivity would require "emancipation of thought."[20]

What did Zhao mean by this statement? To begin with, it must be remembered that throughout Deng Xiaoping's rule, the party had insisted on adherence to the Four Fundamental Principles: uphold the socialist road, uphold the dictatorship of the proletariat, uphold the leadership of the Chinese Communist Party, and uphold Marxism–Leninism–Mao Zedong thought.[21] Thus, despite Deng's promotion of privatizing reforms in the economy, as well as his acceptance of the greater social complexity and diversity of views resulting from these reforms, he continued steadfastly to insist on unchallenged leadership by the Communist Party.

Even leaders known as "liberals," such as Zhao Ziyang, agreed on this point. For example, in his report to the 13th Party Congress, Zhao argued that China was in a "preliminary stage of socialism," requiring the leadership of the CCP and adherence to the Four Fundamental Principles in order for economic development to occur and China to become a prosperous modern socialist country.[22] As Edward I-hsin Chen notes, this theory, which subsequently was adopted at the 13th Party Congress, "provides an ideological justification of the party's endorsement of economic reform but not of other reforms."[23] Indeed, Zhao believed that China should be governed by a "New

Authoritarianism." As encapsulated by Wu Jiaxiang, a researcher at a party-sponsored think-tank with ties to Zhao, the New Authoritarianism rests on the belief that "without authority, the healthy development of liberty is impossible."[24] Similarly, Shanghai Teachers' University professor and New Authoritarianism proponent Xiao Gongqin argues that a "new despotism" under the rule of the CCP "is a 'necessary evil' for China, if economic reforms are to be pursued."[25] Many liberal Chinese theorists, such as Yan Jiaqi and Su Shaozhi, have harshly criticized this notion as antithetical to democratic reform.[26] Nonetheless, as of early 1989 even the most reform-oriented members of the CCP elite, such as Zhao, embraced it.

After the 13th Party Congress, great debate erupted between Zhao and the leader of the more conservative faction, Premier Li Peng. Not only had Li been eschewed by Deng as the successor to party leadership, but Li also believed that reform must occur slowly, and that macroeconomic controls should be eased only gradually. In this round, however, Zhao was victorious: in January 1988 Deng approved Zhao's plan, and in February the Politburo accepted it. At a speech for the Spring Festival, Li emphasized that this policy was Zhao's and voiced concern with the plan.[27] Consequently, a great deal of Zhao's legitimacy became staked on the success of his plan.

Unfortunately for Zhao, the plan did not bring about its promised effects, at least in the short run. By mid-1988, inflation had spiraled out of control, leading to widespread public dissatisfaction. In July 1988, Zhao fell under severe criticism. More important, his economic decision-making powers were taken over by Li Peng and Vice-Premier Yao Yilin. Immediately, Li and Yao proposed that the pace of economic reform be slowed in an effort to restore economic stability. In September, the 3rd Plenary Session of the 13th Central Committee approved the plan.[28] Around the same time, party elders Chen Yun and Wang Zhen expressed dissatisfaction with Zhao's policies. Reportedly, Chen admonished Zhao, saying to him, "socialism is planned and orderly development. Now, how many socialist ingredients does our country still have?"[29] In March 1989, Li Peng capitalized on Zhao's apparent loss of status; in Li's Government Work Report given at the 2nd Session of the 7th National People's Congress, he chastised Zhao for "fail[ing] to take into consideration the country's vast population, the shortage of natural resources, and the prevalent pattern of unbalanced economic development, the lack by many of full understanding of the complexity of these reforms, the lack of good supporting measures, and the failure to pay enough attention to whether price reforms were acceptable to business enterprises and the people."[30] Thus, by the spring of 1989, Zhao was in a precarious position. He remained the appointed successor to Deng, yet his leadership abilities were in doubt. At least two prominent Party elders had begun to question his policies, and Li Peng relentlessly spoke of Zhao's failings.

In many ways, the outcome of this party infighting would be determined by factors beyond the students' control. And indeed, throughout the movement of 1989 students insisted that their actions were not aimed at supporting one faction or another. Nonetheless, each faction looked to the student movement as an opportunity to strengthen its hand within the party. For, as the members of both factions well knew, the student movement could either provide fuel for Li's assertions that Zhao's policies were creating disorder or support Zhao's claim that his policies were necessary and appropriate. Consequently, even though students did not wish to become involved in intraparty struggles, their behavior helped to shape this battle. Overall, it appears that more moderate, organized, and loyalist student behavior helped Zhao's cause, whereas more radical, disorganized, and confrontational student behavior increased the leverage of his detractors. Inasmuch as the results of the movement were dependent on the outcome of this factional struggle, organized and nonthreatening behavior was in the interest of the reform-oriented students.

Elite Divisions in the KMT

Prior to the Month of March movement in Taiwan, factional divisions had also appeared within the KMT. As in the case of the PRC, these divisions centered on two issues: leadership succession and the pace of reform. As noted in Chapter 1, in 1984 Chiang Ching-kuo took a momentous step toward liberalization by choosing Lee Teng-hui, a native-born Taiwanese technocrat, to be his vice president. With Chiang's death in January 1988, Lee ascended to the presidency. In March 1990, when Chiang's original six-year term expired, observers widely expected that Lee would be appointed president for another six years. If this transpired, it would affirm the dominance of technocratic reformers and native Taiwanese within the KMT.

This situation gave rise to the formation of two factions within the party, partly based on policy differences, but mostly revolving around conflict between mainstream leaders associated with Lee, and nonmainstream leaders whose future party power was not fully institutionalized. The most powerful figures in the nonmainstream faction were Hao Po-ts'un and Lee Huan. Hao was the minister of defense, and, like most of the other members of the nonmainstream, was also a mainlander who feared that political reforms were being implemented too hastily. Lee Huan, though also a main-lander, was simultaneously a technocrat and a reformer, and thus actually quite similar to Lee Teng-hui in terms of policy preference.[31] Instead, Lee Huan's opposition to Lee Teng-hui had its roots in a power struggle. At one time, Lee Huan had been Lee Teng-hui's superior, but upon Chiang's choice of Lee Teng-hui for the vice presidency, this situation was reversed. This was particularly aggravating to Lee Huan, as he had a much larger personal backing within the party than did Lee Teng-hui.[32] Consequently, by 1989, Lee Huan had joined the nonmainstream faction and begun to oppose Lee Teng-hui.

In early 1990, when the time came to choose Lee Teng-hui's vice presi-dent, conflict flared between these two factions. Given that Lee Teng-hui, a mainstream representative, was the sure choice for the presidency, most expected that the nonmainstream faction would be allowed to choose his running mate. In fact, on January 2, major papers such as the *China Times*, the *Central Daily*, and *Capital News* all featured front-page articles specu-lating that the vice presidency would be filled by either Lee Huan or Chiang Wei-kuo, Chiang Ching-kuo's half-brother.[33] Yet when the Central Com-mittee met in February, Lee Teng-hui announced that he had chosen Lee Yuen-tsu, a mainlander with little power, to be his vice president. The non-mainstream faction was irate: not only had Lee chosen a weak vice president, but he had not consulted with Lee Huan or Hao Po-ts'un before making this decision.[34]

Consequently, the nonmainstream launched a counteroffensive. First, some of its members proposed that the constitution be altered to replace the presidential system with a cabinet system.[35] Next, the nonmainstream agreed on a counterticket of powerful Taiwanese politician Lin Yang-kang and Chiang Wei-kuo to oppose the ticket of Lee Teng-hui and Lee Yuen-tsu.[36] Throughout the early months of 1990, the two factions maneuvered to strengthen support for their candidates. At one point, the Lin–Chiang com-bination was reported to have the support of over a hundred members of the National Assembly.[37]

Thus, when the students took to the streets in March of 1990, the main-stream faction of Lee Teng-hui was dominant but was under siege by the nonmainstream. As was the case in the PRC, each faction hoped that the students' actions could be used to strengthen its position within the Party. Whereas members of the nonmainstream hoped that the student movement would demonstrate that hasty reform under the unchecked leadership of Lee Teng-hui would lead to chaotic results, members of the mainstream hoped that the movement would affirm Lee's contention that the populace could be trusted, and thus that political liberalization could proceed at a relatively fast pace. Like the student protestors in the PRC, students in Taiwan insisted that their action was not intended to influence this internal Party struggle. Nonetheless, as was the case in the PRC, moderate and orderly student behavior lent credibility to Lee Teng-hui and the mainstream, whereas more radical, disorderly, and threatening actions buttressed the power of the nonmainstream. Thus, student behavior did in fact influence both the outcome of this factional struggle and the fate of the movement itself.

In sum, students in Taiwan and China in 1990 and 1989 confronted similar political structures and patterns. This illiberal environment bred fear among protestors, engendering disorganized, uncompromising behavior among student participants. At the same time, the less repressive atmosphere in Taiwan mitigated these tendencies somewhat. Simultaneously, factional divisions within both the KMT and the CCP made possible a variety of movement outcomes that were partly dependent on the students' protest behavior. The less threatening the students appeared, the stronger the case of party reformers; the more disorderly, the stronger the case of the conservatives. As the following chapters detail, these aspects of the students' political environment interacted to shape student behavior, and thus the process and outcome of both movements.

Chapter 3

Student Mobilization and Organization in China, April 15–May 10, 1989

Studies of the Democracy Movement of 1989 in China generally agree on the basic behavior of the student protestors: they insisted on a separation of students and nonstudents; their demands and actions were loyal and reformist in nature; and their organizations were marked by continual divisions and changes. To explain the students' exclusion of nonstudents from their protest ranks, a number of analyses point to a feeling of superiority in students, who were indeed the elites of Chinese society. Confident in their own intelligence and morality, they lacked faith in the competence and motivations of other social groups.[1] Some scholars also note that this separatist behavior reflected deeply rooted historical Chinese protest traditions.[2] In the same way, many suggest that the students' moderation and loyalism derived from the traditionally close relationship between intellectuals and the Chinese government. Chinese students felt that they had a special link with the regime, the argument runs, so they tended to remonstrate rather than rebel.[3] Finally, some intimate that the disorganization apparent in the movement of 1989 was related to Chinese political culture. Most notably, Liu Xiaobo argues that the Chinese Communist worship of "revolution" was so embedded in popular mentalities that student activists in 1989 valued radicalism and self-righteousness over compromise.[4] Without compromise, democracy and organizational stability were impossible.

Many of these analyses allude to China's nondemocratic political opportunity structure, yet few make this the centerpiece of their explanations. I do. In reality, I believe that the key to understanding these disparate, and sometimes perplexing, student behaviors can be found in China's oppressive political system. In an atmosphere characterized by extreme danger, students feared that compromise with misguided or ill-intentioned individuals could have devastating consequences. Thus, democratic decision making and stable organizational development were extremely difficult. Similarly, students consciously couched their demands in loyalist terms in order to reduce the threat of official repression. Finally, students feared that an alliance with unorganized or particularly threatening sectors of the population would elicit official charges that the protests were creating disorder and precipitate a crackdown.[5]

Underestimating the rational basis of this fear, many studies suggest that the movement might have had a more favorable outcome had the students behaved in a more inclusive manner. Indeed, Walder and Gong conclude that "future democratic movements will be crippled unless this obvious barrier between students and intellectuals on the one hand, and ordinary working people on the other, is broken down."[6] Yet, given the students' dangerous environment, this "barrier" between students and nonstudent groups was a quite practical protest strategy. In fact, had students united more fully with other social sectors, the movement likely would have ended more quickly, and possibly even more brutally. While it is true that a broader-based mobilization would have attracted more government attention, making it harder for ruling elites to ignore the protestors' demands, in the quasi-totalitarian political environment of China at the time, the students' primary concern was how to avoid repression.

This chapter provides a brief historical background of student protest in the post-Mao period, followed by a detailed analysis of the movement of 1989 from its inception (April 15) to the beginning of the hunger strike (May 10). Although these dates are in some sense merely convenient dividing points, this partition underscores the fact that the hunger strike intensified the movement in many ways, raising the feelings of conflict and fear among student leaders to a new level.

Student Organization before April 1989

Student behavior in the spring of 1989 can be understood only in the context of cyclical student unrest and repression in the post-Mao period. In the years following Mao's death in 1976, Deng Xiaoping ascended to the top ranks of the Communist Party with an agenda of economic pragmatism and political normalization. In this new atmosphere, citizens were hopeful that their long-standing grievances would finally be relieved. As party elites signaled support for greater freedom of expression and action, citizens held street marches, wrote wall posters, and published private periodicals to air their views. Yet, inevitably, the limits of official tolerance were reached, and the demonstrators punished. A period of relative public silence followed, as potential dissidents were jailed or otherwise scared into submission. As time passed, however, party elites would again signal their support for greater loosening and reform, and activists would again air their grievances. Once more, though, party elites would grow skittish and crack down on their activities. This cycle repeated itself at least twice prior to the movement of 1989, instilling in potential activists the knowledge that official support for reform was fragile and fickle, and could quickly change into repressive vengeance.

The first cycle of loosening, protest, and repression came with the Democracy Wall movement of 1978–1979. With clear indications of Deng's support, citizens produced wall posters and people's journals, airing grievances accrued during the Cultural Revolution and calling for greater political reforms. Swept up by this movement, students began to produce on-campus literary periodicals, and candidates for campus elections engaged in wide debates on democracy and freedom. More mundanely, students called for official attention to the abysmal state of on-campus housing and security. Yet, before long, Deng's tolerance had been stretched to its limits. One by one, the party announced bans on wall posters, the independent publication of journals, and finally any activities running counter to the Four Fundamental Principles. Prominent activists were publicly excoriated, detained, and imprisoned. The most famous, Wei Jingsheng, had worked as an electrician prior to his arrest. Brought to trial for publishing prodemocracy tracts, Wei "was portrayed in official propaganda as a chronic malingerer and troublemaker who had sold military secrets to foreigners."[7] He was imprisoned for nearly twenty years.[8] Simultaneously, "the press labored to identify the remaining activists as thugs and traitors and to argue that anyone who resorted to mimeographed newspapers, wall posters, and demonstrations wanted to restore the chaos of the Cultural Revolution."[9] Students remained relatively unscathed, yet the seriousness of the government's response—especially toward dissident workers such as Wei—impressed them.

Chastened, China's campuses remained silent for over half a decade. Finally, in 1985, Party hard-liners incited students to protest against the alleged "new Japanese economic invasion" stemming from China's opening to foreign trade. Unfortunately for the hard-liners, the student demonstrations quickly flared into more general political unrest, including demands for greater freedom and democracy along with familiar complaints about poor living conditions and rising costs for food and books. Before student activities got out of hand, provincial and city party secretaries were dispatched to leading universities to listen to student grievances and defuse the demonstrations.[10]

Not long after this party hard-liner-inspired debacle, key reformist party elites again signaled their support for greater reform. In the first half of 1986, Party General Secretary Hu Yaobang indicated that economic reform required a loosening and restructuring of China's higher education system. Authorities chose the University of Science and Technology (UST) in Hefei, China's leading institution in basic and applied science, to lead the experiment with more academic and administrative flexibility; in November of 1986, the *People's Daily* showcased the UST reforms.[11] Encouraged by such positive media reports, as well as the university's outspoken vice president, Fang Lizhi, students at UST began to question the legitimacy of provincial, local, and campus-level elections, calling for a more open nomination process. Soon, wall posters and demonstrations of thousands of students spread from UST to other leading universities. In Shanghai, then under the rule of Jiang Zemin, crowds of nearly a hundred thousand took to the streets.

Yet almost immediately ominous signs appeared, indicating a turn in Party support. In Shanghai and other cities, reports of beatings and arrests swirled. Local media "denounced disruptions caused by 'a small number of criminals and people with ulterior motives,' " warning "that anyone taking part in banned activities would be 'severely punished.' "[12] As the protests continued, "a number of articles made ominous comparisons between the student demonstrators and the Red Guards."[13]

Then came the crackdown: Fang Lizhi was removed from his post and expelled from the Party, and in mid-January of 1987 Hu Yaobang was forced to resign. To purify the public mind, the Party began an "antibourgeois liberalization" campaign, railing against the introduction of Western ideas in China. More seriously, countless students and workers were arrested. Yet, as with the Democracy Wall Movement of 1978–1979, workers were treated much more harshly. Although the protests had been primarily orchestrated by students, the number of workers arrested far exceeded the number of students.[14] In addition, most detained students were soon released, whereas their worker counterparts remained in custody. Further, television news reports showed "arrested workers looking downcast and beaten, [and] broadcasters referred to their criminal intent."[15] Once again, students were impressed by the danger involved in dissent, as well as the government's differential treatment of students and workers. At the same time, they were disheartened by the party's disparagement of their outspoken supporter, Hu Yao-bang.

In the fall of 1987, a few Beijing University (Beijing Daxile; hereafter, Beida) students tentatively made steps to renew discussion of reform. Under the guise of promoting scholarly interchange, a group of around ten students organized informal gatherings, enlisting notable figures such as U.S. Ambassador Winston Lord and Fang Lizhi to speak at various "Wednesday Forums" on the grassy hill surrounding the Cervantes statue at Beida. Later 1989 activists Wang Dan and Yang Tao were the most active in the group, but they purposely kept its structure loose. Anyone interested in attending the lectures was welcome, and when more famous speakers came to campus, fairly large numbers of students did attend. These gatherings—particularly those involving individuals with known dissident leanings, such as Fang Lizhi—quickly elicited the ire of campus authorities. After only a few months, school officials forced the group to disband.[16]

Mustering their courage to try again, at the end of the 1987–1988 school year some of these students joined with others to form a new informal group. Following a typical discussion gathering at Beida's "triangle" (*sanjiao*), eleven students (including Wang Dan and Yang Tao) decided to form a Committee of Action.[17] To demonstrate their commitment to publicly support the group, the students compiled a list of their names and signatures. The group made a successful appeal to a sympathetic professor, who allowed them to use an office at the philosophy department's branch of the Communist Youth League. Shortly thereafter, the group published a leaflet announcing its formation, feeling that it would be best always to air its demands through proper legal channels so as to lessen the likelihood of repression. Members of the committee soon decided to schedule a rally for June 8 and drafted a list of demands for the government.[18]

Still, the group dissolved before the scheduled rally was held. Members had been closely watched by school authorities since the group's public founding. Then, on June 7, representatives of the Communist Youth League expelled the committee from its office. Later that day, campus loudspeakers broadcast that "a small group" was manipulating students and "creating chaos." Around the same time, the Beijing branch of the Communist Youth League posted a list of the committee's members. Under fear, the group met one final time, and disbanded. In fact, the pressure from school authorities was so intense that the members decided to suspend all contact with each other. Nonetheless, school authorities forced the group's members to write self-criticisms to be entered into their permanent records.[19]

In the middle of the fall semester of 1988, these students and others cautiously began to form new extraparty groups. To avoid the negative experiences of earlier groups, these new organizations explicitly claimed to be academic rather than political entities. In autumn 1988, the Olympic Institute and the Democracy Salon formed almost simultaneously at Beida. The seven-member Olympic Institute, founded by one-time Committee of Action member Shen Tong, met at various places to discuss academic and scientific matters. The group also researched and wrote essays, sending them to newspapers and official organs. Perhaps most notably, the group submitted an essay on educational reform to the National People's Congress (NPC). The Democracy Salon, founded by the familiar duo of Wang Dan and Yang Tao, was a more political organization and functioned in a way similar to the Wednesday Forum, inviting speakers to lecture at the May Fourth Monument at Beida. A few weeks after their formation, the Olympic Institute and the Democracy Salon held a joint meeting, where members decided that the two groups would remain separate yet cooperate on all events. The members also discussed important anniversaries coming up in the spring and summer, such as the seventieth anniversary of the May Fourth Movement and the bicentenary of the French Revolution.[20] Around the same time, other Beida students founded the Beida Education Society. Led by Chang Jin, this was a much larger group, with around fifty active members. Generally, the Beida Education Society organized students to participate in educational reform. More specifically, it conducted surveys on rural education and sent letters to the NPC.[21]

These groups, as well as several others, continued to function throughout the fall, winter, and early spring of 1988–1989. Members of these groups formed connections that would continue to be influential during the movement of 1989. Within these groups, students built mutual trust and common understandings. Accordingly, most studies of the movement of 1989 assume that these groups provided the basis for later organization during the movement.[22] Yet in reality these ties were not always beneficial. Indeed, in some ways these groups were the basis of cleavages that plagued student organization throughout the movement of 1989. In fact, Beida, the site of the most autonomous student organization prior to the movement of 1989, exhibited the most intense organizational conflict and division of any school during the movement of 1989. Further, these organizational problems hampered Beida's participation in the larger cross-campus movement organization that would form later. Indeed, the first cross-campus group to form in the spring of 1989 (and indeed the first such organization ever to appear in Communist China) was born, not at Beida, but at Beijing Normal University (Beijing Shifan Daxue; hereafter, Shida), where students had virtually no prior organizational experience free from state control.[23]

What accounts for this counterintuitive fact? When asked this question, one student whom I interviewed laughed and said, "Maybe Beida had too much democracy!" After some pondering, I realized that by using the word "democracy," this student did not mean elections and the like, but rather what is typically termed "civil society": group formation outside the sphere of the state. This student's point was that the preexisting extraparty groups at Beida actually may have hindered later movement organization there. For each previously active student felt that his or her prior experience of dissent and demonstrated devotion to the cause rendered him or her uniquely qualified to make important decisions for the movement. After further interviews and consultation with written materials, it became clear that the type of network that formed the basis of the various organizations was much more important than their mere existence. In the dangerous atmosphere surrounding the movement of 1989, personal bonds of friendship appear to have been virtually the sole means for attaining organizational strength and stability. This friendship could be built on social ties or derive from mutual involvement in the same group or organization. Yet when Beida students formed an autonomous group to lead campus activities during the movement of 1989, most of its members were unacquainted. Accordingly, they lacked a basic trust in the competence and loyalty of one another. Because its members feared that the group's efforts might be ruined by incompetence or conspiracy, Beida's campus-level movement organization exhibited constant conflict and immobility.

Autonomous Campus Groups Form: Beida and Shida

The first autonomous student groups to appear during the movement of 1989 were campus organizations. By the end of the movement, such groups existed at nearly every institute of higher education in Beijing. Yet each campus autonomous group was formed through a different process, each differed in its degree of development and organization, and each enjoyed different levels of student trust and support. Some formed spontaneously after the death of former Party General Secretary Hu Yaobang; others formed later, under the guidance of other campus autonomous groups or the All-Beijing Secondary Schools Autonomous Federation. Some campus groups established rigid and complex structures while others were almost completely fluid, existing in name only. Finally, some were highly democratic, whereas others were quite isolated from the students whom they were supposed to represent and lead.

An exhaustive description of the formation and operation of all of the campus autonomous groups established in the spring of 1989 would require more space than is here available. Thus, the description that follows focuses only on the campus autonomous groups at Beida and Shida. Many factors justify this choice. First, Beida and Shida were two of the first campuses to organize autonomous campus groups. Each of these groups organized spontaneously, with no guidance from outside groups or organizations. Second, the autonomous campus groups at Beida and Shida were the most influential formed during the movement. Third, the two campus groups provide a clear contrast with regard to their background, establishment, and functioning. Fourth, each had an important, yet contrasting, relationship with the All-Beijing Secondary Schools Autonomous Federation. Similarly, each had a unique relationship with the Hunger Strike Command.

It is important to note that these two campus groups initially were formed by only a handful of students. The main reason for this is quite clear: fear. In an environment where all student activity was closely scrutinized by campus authorities, and where any autonomous student organization would likely meet with repression, few students dared to publicly step forward and establish a nonparty group. After these first few students made this brave step, many others joined and supported these groups. However, precious few were willing to risk being charged with initiating such action. Consequently, those who were willing to take the first step earned an enormous amount of respect from their fellow, less courageous, students. Indeed, those students who were deemed to be the most "courageous" enjoyed the greatest legitimacy. Thus, in the earliest phase of the movement, legitimacy tended to be defined, not by the rational-legal criterion of representativeness, but by charisma. As the movement progressed, students seeking greater legitimacy competed for charismatic credentials by undertaking more risky actions. Consequently, the movement became characterized by a radicalizing trend in student behavior. At the same time, however, conceptions of representative legitimacy also came to compete with, and sometimes supplement, notions of charismatic legitimacy.

Students were jolted out of their cautious pursuit of reform by the death of Hu, who many felt not only had been deposed for his support of reform but also suffered medical problems as a result of his ill-treatment. Indeed, rumors spread that Hu had died as a result of a heart attack brought on by an argument in the Politburo over educational reform.[24] Almost immediately after new of Hu's April 15 death was announced, posters appeared on Beijing campuses mourning the dead leader. On April 17, students first marched to Tiananmen Square. Led by the University of Politics and Law, students at Beida and the People's University soon followed suit.

Initially, these marches were fundamentally displays of mourning for Hu and were not overtly political in nature. At Shida, for example, a three-

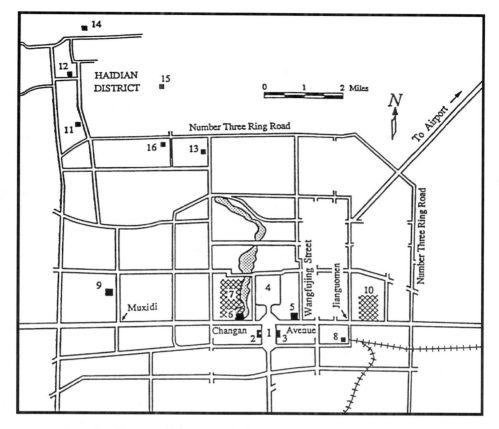

Map 1 Central Beijing and University District

1   Tiananmen Square
2   Great Hall of the People
3   Museums of the Chinese Revolution and Chinese History
4   Forbidden City
5   Beijing Hotel
6   Xinhuamen (rear entrance to Zhongnanhai)
7   Zhongnanhai (Chinese Communist Party compound)
8   Beijing Railroad Station
9   State Guesthouse
10   Embassy Area
11   People's University
12   Beijing University
13   Beijing Normal University
14   Qinghua University
15   Beijing Aeronautics Institute
16   University of Politics and Law

Source: Han Minzhu, ed., *Cries for Democracy* (Princeton, NJ: Princeton University Press, 1990).

thousand-person march to Tiananmen on April 17 included party officials, members of the Communist Youth League, and members of the official student government. Similarly, on April 17, Wang Dan organized students at Beida to collect donations for a floral wreath to bring to the square to memorialize Hu. On April 18, several schools again organized marches to the square, and some students began a sit-in in front of the Great Hall of the People. Along with simply expressing their sadness at Hu's death, protestors now began to include calls for an official reappraisal of his accomplishments and the party's mistakes; publication of official incomes; freedom of speech, press, and assembly; and more money for education and intellectuals.[25]

Although these activities quickly came to involve great numbers of people, and to include more overt political demands, in these first few days of protests, no clear student organization or leadership was operating. As one student activist notes, "everyone was playing by their own rules, making their own rules . . . people just did things, organized things."[26] Similarly, a student who helped lead the Beida contingent to the square on April 17 acknowledges that "We hadn't planned what to do once we arrived at the square."[27] In short, between April 15 and April 18, student actions were spontaneous and haphazard. Concerned that such unorganized action risked chaos and a government crackdown, by April 19 and 20, students at Beida and Shida separately began to organize autonomous campus groups.[28]

The Beida Autonomous Union

On the morning of April 19, a news brief posted at the Beida triangle announced an evening meeting to discuss the establishment of a campus-wide organization free from party control.[29] By dusk, hundreds of students milled about anxiously. A number spoke out about Hu Yaobang's achievements, but only a handful dared to call publicly for an autonomous student organization. Although the crowd shouted in affirmation, most everyone present was too afraid to speak out as an individual. After some time, a student named Ding Xiaoping asked for volunteers to lead a new campus organization. Yet all of the students were profoundly aware that anyone willing to volunteer was likely to be punished by the authorities, and that official spies almost certainly were in their midst. Consequently, according to one witness, Ding "three times called on people to come forth to lead, but each time received no answer. Then he said, 'OK, do we want to recall the official student government?' The crowd roared, 'Yes!' Ding continued, 'After its recall, what should be done? Do we want to establish our own organization?' Again the resounding reply was, 'Yes!' " Yet still no one volunteered. Finally, Ding suggested that the "brave" persons who had spoken earlier be the leaders.[30] Though many of the speakers were hesitant to do so, they felt that they had no choice but to back up their words and step forward.[31] Ten students volunteered: Wang Dan, Yang Tao, Xiong Yan, Feng Congde, Chang Jin, Ding Xiaoping, Ti Bo, Guo Haifeng, Zhang Boli, and Zhang Zhiyong.

This brave act, an act that the vast majority of the students at the gathering were afraid to undertake, engendered great respect for these students. At the same time, however, many of the students who had courageously volunteered to lead the group were not well acquainted with one another. Although some of them had been involved in previous autonomous organizations, few had been involved in the *same* groups. As a result, they lacked trust in the competence and dedication of the others and feared that some of them might be Communist Party infiltrators. Further, although these students enjoyed a great deal of charismatic legitimacy, the group had no true representative legitimacy vis-à-vis the general student body. In combination, these factors soon led to great conflict within the group.

The volunteers held their first meeting at the Cervantes statue on campus, as the triangle had become very crowded.[32] Soon after the meeting began, it became obvious that all of the members held strong views regarding the proper nature and organization of the group, and that many were suspicious of their fellow volunteers. In fact, Ding Xiaoping feared that the group had already been infiltrated by individuals sent by the Public Security Bureau, warning those present that they "must be extremely careful."[33] Similarly, Feng Congde worried that "opportunists" might "enter the movement for their own political benefit."[34] To counter this possibility, Feng notes that "because we didn't recognize each other, every new student that came had to be introduced by another student."[35] In this tense atmosphere, the members decided that each could speak for only two minutes at a time, and that Ding would act as the group's chair.[36] The group decided to call itself the Beida Preparatory Autonomous Student Union (BAU), to denote that the committee would serve as only a temporary leadership body during the movement. After the movement, a new Beida Autonomous Student Union would be elected.

As the students discussed these matters, a group of Qinghua University students interrupted the meeting, asking Beida students to join them in a march to Xinhuamen, the rear entrance to the main compound of the Communist Party. Feng Congde and Xiong Yan were appointed to be the group's official liaisons with Qinghua and accompanied the contingent.[37] With this, the remaining students decided to reconvene the following morning.

Events at Xinhuamen that night charged the tenor of the next meeting. From late in the night on April 18, students had begun to gather in front of Xinhuamen, demanding to speak with an official. Eventually, authorities allowed three student representatives to enter the compound and present their demands for reform. The students never reappeared. As tensions and frustrations mounted, in the early predawn hours broadcasts ordered the students to clear the area, and a large contingent of police arrived. Those who did not withdraw were then forced to do so; in the process, many students were beaten.

This so-called Xinhuamen tragedy raised the intensity of the movement to a new level. Not only had the police beaten unarmed students, but the official media claimed that it was the students who had initiated the violence. The Beijing Television and Central Government Television evening news reports ran a close-up of a soldier wounded by a soda bottle and warned of a dangerous group of protestors.[38] Similar charges were leveled in official newspapers, which claimed that "the students, yelling reactionary slogans, rushed out from Xinhuamen and assaulted many policemen."[39] The students reacted with great anger and indignation, resulting in the mobilization of many more students than had participated before. At the same time, the eruption of violence, as well the distorted reports printed in the CCP-controlled news media, demonstrated to many the importance of organization to control and protect student demonstrators and to lessen the possibility of official slander. This incident, then, raised the stakes for student leaders, causing them to become extremely concerned that the movement be led in the "proper" direction, by competent and loyal leaders. More negatively, events at Xinhuamen caused student leaders to be increasingly on the lookout for suspicious or incapable students seeking to participate in the leadership of the movement.

The second meeting of the BAU was filled with tension, as rumors circulated that school authorities had used a special infrared video camera to tape the committee's activities of the previous night.[40] Moreover, some members continued to fear that a representative of public security had already infiltrated the group.[41] Indeed, despite the precautions taken by the leadership, on the morning of April 20 a student member of the CCP informed the group that the school's party branch already knew of their planned activities for that evening.[42]

In this charged atmosphere, Wang Dan and Yang Tao announced that they would no longer be part of the group. Why? Some argue that Wang and Yang were frustrated by their inability to control the group.[43] But during the night of the nineteenth Wang and Yang had been under great pressure from school authorities to cease any organizing activities. In addition, an anonymous large-character poster had been posted at the triangle accusing the two of graft. Although most recognized that the poster likely was written by the authorities, it had a disconcerting effect.[44]

These developments, coupled with the eruption of violence at Xinhuamen the previous night, greatly heightened the fear felt by the group's members. Yet at the same time their anger propelled them to organize a march for that afternoon. For the march, the group designated five students to lead slogans, and two hundred to act as security marshals.[45] As the afternoon proceeded, approximately two thousand students met at Beida for the demonstration. As they gathered, a heavy rain began to fall. Determined to persist in their march, the students left the campus and walked to Qinghua University. The gate at Qinghua was closed, however, and an official car circled in front, broadcasting that Qinghua students were not participating in the march, and that the Beida students should return to their campus.[46] Disheartened but undaunted, the Beida contingent walked to the University of Politics and Law. Students there offered the Beida students bread and water but declined to join the march.[47] The marchers then traveled to Shida, where approximately nine hundred students joined them. Many students from smaller Beijing schools also participated.

After arriving at the Square that night, the students assembled around the Monument to the People's Heroes. A handful of students spoke to the group, including Chang Jin, Shen Tong, Wu'er Kaixi, Zhang Tiguo, Chen Mingyun, and Zhou Yongjun.[48] Most stressed that their collective purpose was to protest the eruption of violence at Xinhuamen. Some also suggested that the students should establish a national university organization to unite and lead the student movement.[49] Yet an argument broke out over how to set up such an organization, and in the end the students took no specific action. Moreover, by this time all of the students were thoroughly drenched and had begun to disperse. Many Beida participants became angry with the newly founded Beida Autonomous Union at this time, as no arrangements had been made to transport the chilled students back to campus.[50]

Indeed, some of the members of the Beida Autonomous Union had been holding a meeting on campus while the others were participating in the march.[51] When the members of the group who had participated in the march finally returned, they joined the others in the meeting, which lasted until dawn. First, the reassembled group decided to change the chairmanship of the group, as most of them felt that Ding had been unduly manipulative and domineering. As one member states: "Ding had a bad habit of insisting on his own opinion. If people did not agree with him, he would stop the

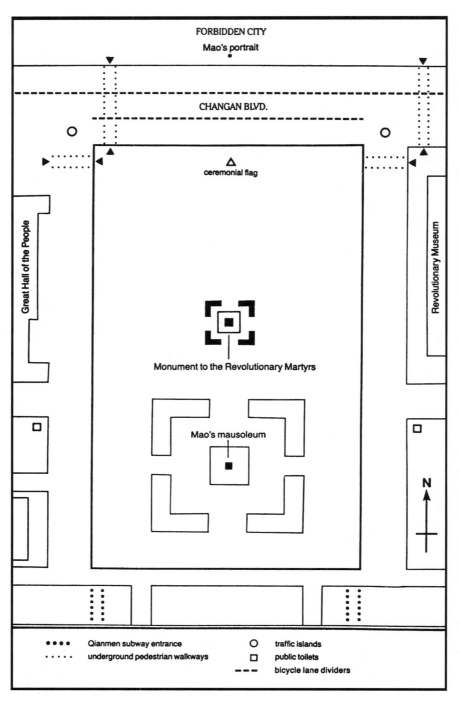

Map 2 Tiananmen Square

Source: Scott Simmie and Bob Nixon, *Tiananmen Square* (Seattle: University of Washington Press, 1989).

meeting and force them to agree."[52] Given the tense and risk-laden environment, the other members of the group felt it was essential that their opinions be considered as well; a wrong decision could lead to dire consequences. Thus, the members dismissed Ding from the chairmanship, choosing Guo Haifeng in his stead. Next, the group agreed to declare a class boycott and drew up a notice to be posted in every classroom.[53] Finally, the group discussed what action it should take regarding the official memorial service for Hu Yaobang, which was slated for the following day. As official reports indicated that all entrances to Tiananmen Square would be blocked by 5:00 A.M., the group decided to march to the square late that night.[54]

The Shida Autonomous Union

Concurrently, students at Shida were busy forming their own autonomous campus group. Yet unlike Beida, the Shida Autonomous Union (SAU) did not have its origins in any sort of public meeting. Rather, early in the morning on April 20, three Shida students who were close friends but had not been part of any previous autonomous organization—Wu'er Kaixi, Liang Er, and Zhang Jun—decided to form a campus-wide nonparty group.[55] To publicize their decision, Wu'er Kaixi suggested that the three simply write a wall poster. After drawing up and copying the announcement, the three placed copies on classroom and dormitory doors across campus. The poster read:

> (1) Students of Shida no longer acknowledge the role of the official student government, due to its lack of responsibility; (2) Shida has formed the Shida Autonomous Union; (3) Those departments which have not yet formed a departmental autonomous union, or joined the school autonomous union, should do so and register with the union; (4) The office of the autonomous union is in Northwest Dorm Room no. 339; (5) The president of the autonomous union has been elected, and his name is Wu'er Kaixi, the general secretary is Zhang Jun, and the deputy general secretary is Liang Er; (6) The Shida Autonomous Union obeys the leadership of the Temporary Student Union of Beijing.[56]

Of course, the poster represented the unilateral declaration of these three students and had no basis in reality. As of this time, the Shida Autonomous Union existed in name only; no department had registered with the group because no Shida student had heard of the union before they read the poster. Moreover, there was no Temporary Student Union of Beijing in existence. Further, there had been no real election for the offices of president, general secretary, and deputy general secretary; the three students had simply appointed themselves to these positions. Finally, the "union office" was located in Wu'er Kaixi's dorm room.[57]

Nonetheless, the claims made in the poster soon became a reality. Upon reading the poster, students were deeply impressed by the courage of the three students who had publicly posted their names as founders of an illegal group. Moreover, the vast majority of the student body agreed with the sentiments on the poster. In the end, students proved to be much less afraid of joining the group than they had been of initiating it. This fear was further eased as Liang Er met with official student leaders from each academic department. Liang easily gained the trust of these leaders, as he himself held a leadership position in the Communist Youth League.[58] Consequently, students not only began to organize and register for the group, but they did so with great haste, apparently out of concern that their department would be the last to register with the group (and would therefore be the least worthy of respect). By that evening, virtually every department on campus had sent a representative to Room 339 to register.

Although the members of this group had no connections with any previously existing activist group, and despite the fact that the group was not initiated through any sort of public discussion, the SAU was effective and stable because the three initiators knew and trusted each other. Moreover, when a city-wide student federation was formed to unite dissident students from all Beijing campuses, it was Shida that took the lead, while Beida remained mired in its own organizational conflicts.

The All-Beijing Secondary Schools Autonomous Federation

On May 19–20, the three self-appointed leaders of the SAU also composed and distributed another poster announcing that an All-Beijing Secondary Schools Autonomous Federation had been formed, and that its first gathering would be at 6:30 P.M. on April 21 at the soccer fields of Shida.[59] By 6:00 P.M. on April 21, some sixty thousand students had gathered for the meeting. In the meantime, however, Wu'er was on the run. When school authorities discovered the posters, Wu'er's father had been located and convinced to come to the campus to talk to his son. Having been tipped off to these events, Wu'er hid at various places on campus, with sympathetic students relaying information to help him stay one step ahead of the authorities.[60] Finally, at 8:00 P.M., Wu'er emerged in front of the crowd. Yet, as the three poster writers had not acquired any sound equipment (expecting only around a thousand to attend), Wu'er made only a short speech announcing the establishment of the Temporary Student Union of Beijing.[61] This was nothing more than a statement; at the time, the union had no organization, formal leadership, or clear membership. Wu'er had simply declared the group to be in existence. Until the group formally met to decide on principles of organization, leadership, purpose, and tactics, it would exist in name only.

Following this announcement, Wu'er called on the students to march to Tiananmen that night, so as to be prepared for Hu's funeral the following morning. To help organize the march, Wu'er asked the crowd to evacuate a large space in front of him. Next, he asked all Beida students to shout out the name of their school and go to this space. Within a few minutes, a group of Beida students had formed in front of him, unfurling a flag that they had prepared, reading "Beida." Interestingly, although many Beida students attended the meeting, and some had been organized enough to create a banner, the Beida Autonomous Union had sent no formal representative. After the Beida students were assembled, Wu'er asked some Shida students to lead the group to the main gate. One by one, school groups followed, forming an orderly procession.[62]

By the time the students were lined up to leave Shida, messengers brought news that students at Qinghua University, the University of Politics and Law, and Beida had organized separate contingents on their campuses and were beginning to march. Indeed, around 11:00 P.M., the Beida Autonomous Union had called students to gather in the Beida triangle for a march to the square. As the various campus contingents converged in the streets, they joined together in a long chain and marched in an orderly fashion to Tiananmen.[63] Students on the outside edge of each contingent joined hands to form a "human chain" to keep students neatly arranged, and to maintain a separation between student marchers and nonstudent onlookers.[64]

The Qinghua University students were the first to arrive at Tiananmen Square. Upon entering, the front line of the contingent (still holding hands) moved forward to clear a space for the students to sit. Each school group followed in the same manner, until the Square was filled with orderly rectangles of campus contingents, each ringed by its "security team" (*jiuchadui*) and demarcated by a poster bearing the name of its school.[65] In addition, participants wore various "marks" (*jihao*) to show their student status, displaying white flowers, black bands, school name-plates, and cafeteria coupons.[66] Student leaders had made no plans about what the students would do at the Square, though. After settling down, most simply rested and tried to sleep.

As dawn came, Wu'er called a meeting of representatives from each school.[67] Although the group called itself the Nineteen University Temporary

Coordinating Small Group, it never became a formally established body.[68] Nonetheless, those who attended later became active in the All-Beijing Secondary Schools Autonomous Federation.[69] Wu'er asked the representatives what they wanted to do. No one responded. Wu'er then suggested that they return to their school groups to elicit opinions and suggestions. Back and forth, this process was repeated three times and quickly became quite chaotic.[70] Finally, the representative group agreed on a seven-point petition that had been drafted by the Beida Autonomous Union. The petition called on the government to:

> (1) Reassess Hu Yaobang, recognizing his achievements regarding democracy and freedom; (2) Punish those who have beaten students and common people, and find those who are responsible; (3) Make the news law public and allow unofficial newspapers to exist; (4) Have officials make their incomes public; (5) Have a national discussion of education policy and fees; (6) Reassess the antibourgeois liberalization campaign; and (7) Truthfully and realistically assess this movement.[71]

In all, these demands were reformist, not revolutionary. Further, demands no. 2 and no. 7 were simply responses to the government actions of the previous few days.

With thousands of students at the Square, shortly after 8:00 A.M. officials began to appear for the memorial service. Around 9:30 A.M., authorities aired a live broadcast of the memorial service and the national anthem. By 10:00 A.M. the ceremony was over. A few minutes later, the funeral procession slipped out of the west gate of the Square, rather than circling the Square for the people to see, as was the usual protocol.[72] This hasty and secretive ceremony angered the students. As one student leader states, "after the memorial for Hu, when we realized that we wouldn't see the [funeral] car, we decided, 'Let's march.' "[73] Led by each school's "security team," students marched around the Square chanting "We want dialogue." The group halted in front of the Great Hall of the People, whereupon four students pushed their way through the police line in front of the hall, demanding to speak with Li Peng.[74] After some time, the students were told that Li would meet with them that afternoon.[75] As the students waited, they became increasingly impatient. Finally, three Beida students walked up the steps of the hall and knelt down, holding the seven-point petition above their heads. After forty minutes, there was still no official response. The student masses looked on in anger and pain, many of them weeping. In frustration, some then attempted to push their way into the hall. At this point, however, self-appointed student leaders convinced the group to hold hands for a moment and then return to campus.[76]

Campus-Level Activities

Back on campus, on April 23 the autonomous unions at Beida and Shida engaged in further organizational activities. At Beida, students set up a broadcast station in Shen Tong's room and designated a neighboring room as a reception area for visitors from other schools and journalists. Students reserved another room for meetings, and yet another for a publishing center (the group had garnered two mimeograph machines). Guards kept watch on the floor below to protect the news center from intruders. Before long, the news center was producing six separate pamphlets and a press packet. One reporter covered the Beida Autonomous Union, and a team of students asked liaisons at schools around Beijing to send representatives to the news center with daily reports. Concurrently, donations of money and supplies began to pour in. Student accountants kept track of donations, although they were soon overwhelmed.[77] Representatives of the Hong Kong College Student Union also visited the union, presenting it with a copy of their constitution. However, some members of the BAU were opposed to creating an allied organization, feeling that Beida still lacked sufficient basic-level organization.[78]

At Shida, students also plunged into further organizational activities. First, students erected a broadcast system and garnered equipment to print written materials. In addition, the SAU began to set up an electoral system. Each department elected its own officers and sent its president to attend campus-level meetings. Each department also established a few contingents to go out to other schools, as well as onto the streets and into factories, to spread information, propagandize, and solicit opinions.[79]

The highest official positions within the campus committee were to be elected by the departmental presidents. However, the selection process was not entirely democratic. As one of the original poster writers explains: "the three of us were already in the highest leadership positions, so no one else could compete with us. Thus, we automatically were elected by the departmental representatives."[80] Despite this flaw, the electoral process strengthened the legitimacy of the Shida Autonomous Union and its leaders. The strong departmental organizations gave students a sense of linkage with the union, and the attention devoted to representative qualifications gave students trust in the electoral process. On April 28, the Shida Autonomous Union began another movement to legitimate its position. The group collected signatures of support for the three main leaders, as well as for the campus autonomous organization. Out of a student body of seven thousand, over five thousand signatures were collected. Of these signatures, 95 percent supported the organization, and virtually all authorized Wu'er, Liang, and Zhang to represent and lead the campus.[81]

Thus, the Shida Autonomous Union enjoyed a substantial amount of legitimacy, despite the fact that its leadership had been largely self-designated. Although the legitimacy of the three highest leaders of the group was not based on a truly democratic selection, they did enjoy a great deal of charismatic legitimacy, deriving from their courageous decision to publicly found the union. Moreover, with the subsequent ratification vote, these leaders also gained a degree of representative legitimacy. Of equal importance, as these three leaders had been close friends prior to the movement, they trusted each other and had confidence in one another's abilities. As a result of these factors, throughout the movement, the Shida Autonomous Union was relatively stable and effective.

At Beida, in contrast, although the Autonomous Union enjoyed a great deal of charismatic legitimacy, the lack of any comparable election and ratification process detracted from the representative legitimacy of the group. Perhaps more important, the lack of trust among members of the union caused it to be plagued with internal conflict, rendering it unable to engage in grass-roots organizing. As Chai Ling states, "by April 24, many of us already felt that the Autonomous Union was very unstable, and was becoming separated from the masses."[82] To begin with, many members of the committee were dissatisfied with Guo Haifeng's chairmanship, feeling that Guo was abusing his power by spending large amounts of donated money on food, drinks, and expensive equipment (such as walkie-talkies and cassette recorders) for committee members. On April 24, a general conference of Beida students was called at the May 4th Memorial on campus. Although it is claimed that nearly two-thirds of all Beida students attended the gathering, some members of the Autonomous Union did not attend (apparently because they purposely had not been notified of the meeting).[83] At the gathering, Ding Xiaoping told students that the Autonomous Union was internally divided and unworthy of leadership. In addition, a student accused former union member Zhang Zhiyong of being a spy for the official graduate student union. The meeting quickly grew chaotic, and in the end the majority of the committee resigned. A poster later displayed at the triangle asked each of the twenty-nine campus departments to send two representatives to attend a meeting the following day.[84]

Accordingly, at noon on the twenty-fifth, students gathered to reconstitute the union's leadership.[85] However, meeting participants were not screened for representative qualifications, and some feared that there were CCP spies among them.[86] Indeed, Feng Congde relates that a "very suspicious person" attended this meeting, and that "everyone thought he was a CCP plant." When asked to present his student ID, this student did not, explaining that he was "a very unique student at Beida, studying some confusing trade . . . living off campus, and having no classmates."[87] Despite these grave concerns, a new five-person Standing Committee ultimately was elected. Zhang Yaoguo, Kong Qingdong, Feng Congde, Wang Dan, and Shen Tong became the group's new leadership.[88] That afternoon, the new committee decided that its primary goal would be to engage in a direct dialogue with the government to discuss the seven points raised in the petition drafted on April 21. In addition, the group continued to develop "executive" bureaus to carry out tasks such as propaganda and accounting, and decided to meet daily. Chai Ling (the wife of Feng Congde) acted as the committee's secretary, taking notes and informing members of upcoming meetings.[89]

Although the Standing Committee had been reelected, its membership remained unstable and its organization weak. First, the representativeness of the group was in question. With no clear department-level organization, and with no system for ascertaining representative credentials prior to a general vote, the Standing Committee could not really claim that it represented the views of the general student body. Moreover, within the Standing Committee itself, confusion and controversy impeded decision making and implementation. As one committee member notes, "there was conflict between the [Standing Committee] and the executive bureaus. At this time, the [Standing Committee] did not actually do anything—it just made decisions, without concern for whether or not they could actually be implemented."[90]

In an environment of threatened party repression, many members of the executive bureaus felt that such incompetence could lead to dire consequences. As a result, on April 29, the heads of the executive bureaus staged a coup: together, they announced that they would act as a supervisory committee to oversee the Standing Committee. Zhao Qiguo, a student who had proven quite capable at organizing security teams during various gatherings and demonstrations, was elected by the bureau heads to be president of the supervisory committee. Zhao's first official act was to call for the resignation of the Standing Committee. Alarmed by this, two influential postdoctoral students called a meeting of all members of the different bureaus (i.e., everyone involved with union activities, aside from the Standing Committee). At the gathering, those assembled elected five students to form a new Committee of Executive Directors to lead the union: Feng Congde, Wang Dan, Xiong Yan, Chang Jin, and Yang Tao.[91] After this, the group became temporarily stabilized. Perhaps most notably, it successfully organized a demonstration on May 4.

Yet, almost immediately following the May 4 demonstration, the group underwent another crisis. Still frustrated by its inability to implement its decisions, it decided to change the entire system. First, the Committee of Executive Directors was dismissed. The group then convened a general meeting so that a new election could be held. Yet, as usual, problems arose concerning the election process. As one student leader states: "With so many people participating in the meeting, many questions arose. Who will vote? Who will chair? Who will organize?"[92] Finally, participants agreed that Chang Jin, the student most generally recognized by the participants as both trustworthy and competent, should organize the meeting.

By the meeting's end, the entire Beida autonomous student organization had been restructured and clarified. To replace the Committee of Executive Directors, a president and two vice presidents were elected. The executive bureau heads were made directly responsible to these officers. Each bureau was led by one head, one associate head, and a body of executive members. The executive members were charged with finding students to carry out the actual work assigned to each bureau. Bureaus and their responsibilities also were clarified. The Secretary Department was responsible for preparing meetings, reception, collecting information from students, drafting documents, publishing brief reports of current information, overseeing printing and broadcasting subgroups, and assigning propaganda teams to go into the streets to make speeches and mobilize the city folk. The Security Team was responsible for organizing security team members, keeping order during demonstrations, and overseeing special tasks such as providing bodyguards should any prominent intellectuals come to campus. The Finance Bureau was to deal with fund raising and accounting. The Support Bureau was responsible for the acquisition and allocation of materials. Finally, two special task forces were created. One was called the General Election Task Force. As the leaders of the Autonomous Union had always been chosen through an internal election, this group was to prepare for a general election in order to increase the representative legitimacy of the organization. The other special group was responsible for establishing department-level unions.[93] At this point, campus organization at Beida stabilized somewhat. However, for the first three weeks of the movement, the Beida Autonomous Union had been almost completely paralyzed by internal divisions and organizational alterations, as students who did not fully trust one another reacted to the tense atmosphere created by CCP structures and behavior.

The All-Beijing Secondary Schools Autonomous Federation

Meanwhile, on April 24, students officially established the All-Beijing Secondary Schools Autonomous Federation (Beijing Gaoxiao Zizhi Lianhehui, BSAF). As the name implies, the organization was a federation of campus autonomous student groups. From the start, however, the extensiveness of the federation's constituency made it difficult for the group to choose leaders or make decisions that enjoyed firm, broad-based support. Moreover, student participants disagreed on the nature and power of the organization. Some believed that the organization should act as an overall director of the movement, whereas others felt that it should simply coordinate decisions made independently by campus-level groups. As a result, throughout the movement different groups clashed with the BSAF over matters of power and responsibility. In the atmosphere of fear arising from the threat of suppression—particularly after the publication of the April 26 *People's Daily* editorial—student leaders felt it imperative that the movement proceed in what they believed to be the "correct" direction. Consequently, they were extremely hesitant to compromise with or to cede power to any group over which they had little control. For in doing so, a student risked becoming a "criminal of history" by exposing the student masses to potential harm by the authorities. By early May, these conflicts and problems were so great that the movement had lost much of its momentum and legitimacy.

From the outset, various students had called for a united university student group. The April 22 meeting at the Shida soccer fields ostensibly had marked the first gathering of such a group. Yet the BSAF was not formally established until April 24. On that day, a group of thirty to forty students, representing approximately twenty Beijing schools, gathered. It is not clear exactly how students were notified of the meeting. It is certain, however, that Shida student activists were instrumental in the proceedings. In part, this was due to the fact that these leaders, such as Wu'er Kaixi, were the most vociferous proponents of an overarching organization. Yet perhaps more important at the time, the Shida Autonomous Union was the most effective and stable autonomous student organization in existence. True, other universities had established autonomous campus bodies, but these organizations were not as developed as that at Shida. Consequently, in this early stage, the federation used Shida Autonomous Union facilities for all of its printing, communication, and preparation. Shida also "loaned" hundreds of its students to the BSAF to aid in the formation of the federation's executive departments.[94] Moreover, before the BSAF established its own constitution, it utilized that of the Shida Autonomous Union.[95] As one student leader states, at this early stage, the Shida Autonomous Union was "more or less the executive of the BSAF."[96]

The Beida Autonomous Union, in contrast, had almost no involvement in the formation of the BSAF. This is somewhat surprising, as Beida had been the first campus to establish an autonomous body and also had the earliest and most highly developed communication system of any campus. Why was Beida so uninvolved? First, the BAU at this time was constantly undermined by controversy and instability. Cognizant of the immaturity of its organization, many members of the BAU were leery of participation in an overarching organization.[97] Second, the chaotic nature of the BAU made it unable to serve as the media center for the BSAF. Third, many Beida student leaders felt that the BSAF was bent on controlling rather than coordinating the campus autonomous groups.[98] Fourth, some claim that the BAU was purposely not notified of the BSAF founding meeting.[99] For these reasons, the BAU did not formally participate in the establishment of the BSAF and was not instrumental in any of the federation's early activities.[100] As time passed, tension between the BAU and the BSAF would increase.

Those who did attend the BSAF meeting on April 24 decided that the group would form a Standing Committee with seven seats: one for each of the "big four" universities (Beida, Qinghua, Shida, and People's University); one for the Central Minority Institute; one for the Beijing Motion Picture Institute (to represent the ten artistic schools of Beijing); and one for the Chemical-Industrial Institute (to represent the many schools in the "east corner" [*dongjiao*] university region).[101] Next, students elected the Standing Committee and its chair, or president. However, of the thirty to forty students attending, only fifteen felt that they could truly represent their school. Thus, only fifteen votes were cast for these important positions.[102] Zhou Yongjun, a student at the University of Politics and Law who had been active in establishing an autonomous campus union there, won over Wu'er Kaixi for the presidency by a vote of 9 to 6.[103]

Subsequently, the group debated over the proper frequency of its meetings. Many espoused the view of the "reform literature" of the 1980s, calling for shorter and less frequent meetings as an antidote to long, drawn-out party meetings where little actually was accomplished. Accordingly, these proponents argued that the group should meet perhaps once a month. Yet

Liu Gang, a prominent pro-reform intellectual who had been asked to attend the meeting, convinced the others that this would be a foolish decision. As the current situation was dire, he argued, the group had a responsibility to meet at least once a day. Convinced by this view, Wu'er and Wang persuaded the rest to agree to daily meetings.[104] Finally the group took its first concrete action: in protest against the beatings at Xinhuamen, an open-ended class strike would begin the following day.

Federation representatives gathered again on April 25, this time at the University of Politics and Law.[105] The Standing Committee was to meet at 5:00 P.M., prior to a general meeting scheduled for 6:00 P.M. However, at 4:00 P.M. the Central People's Radio broadcast the text of the *People's Daily* editorial that was to be published the next day. Entitled "It Is Necessary to Take a Clear-Cut Stand against Turmoil," the editorial read:

> During the past few days, a small handful have engaged in creating turmoil . . . some shouting, "Down with the CCP!" . . . beating, looting, and smashing . . . [and] calling for opposition to the leadership of the CCP and the socialist system. In some universities, illegal organizations have formed to seize power from student unions; some have taken over broadcasting systems, and begun a class boycott. . . . If we tolerate this disturbance, a seriously chaotic state will appear, and we will be unable to have reform, opening, and higher living standards. . . . Under no circumstances should the establishment of any illegal organizations be allowed. We must stop any attempt to infringe on the rights of legal organizations.[106]

The broadcast of this editorial marked Zhao Ziyang's first clear loss in the factional battle that was raging within the CCP. As noted in Chapter 2, Zhao did not favor autonomous political action. Thus, he had never argued that the party should concede to the students' demand that such action be legitimized. At the same time, however, Zhao also knew that if party elites came to view the students as a serious threat, Li Peng's more conservative rival faction likely would be strengthened. Thus, from the start of the movement, Zhao counseled moderation in the party's response to the students. With this editorial, though, it became clear that Deng disagreed. Indeed, given the violent police action at Xinhuamen on April 19–20, as well as the official interpretation of this event, Deng seems to have viewed the student movement as a serious threat from the start.

To make matters worse, on April 23, Zhao departed for North Korea. In his absence, Zhao's foes presented their views to Deng without challenge. On April 24, the Politburo Standing Committee called an emergency meeting, forming an ad hoc group to deal with the crisis. At the meeting, Li Peng,

Beijing Mayor Chen Xitong, and Beijing Party Secretary Li Ximing prepared a report calling the movement " 'an anti-Party and anti-socialist political struggle' and urging an immediate crackdown."[107] The following morning, Li Peng and Yang Shangkun personally met with Deng to express their agreement with the report. Party elder Chen Yun concurred, reportedly stating, "We must take strong action to suppress the student movement; otherwise it will only grow bigger, and if workers join in, the consequences will be unimaginable."[108] Apparently, however, Deng did not need convincing. In his official response, which was broadcast on radio and television that evening and repeated the following morning in the *People's Daily*, Deng declared:

> This is not an ordinary student movement, but turmoil. So we must have a clear-cut stand and implement effective measures to quickly oppose and stop this unrest. . . . Their motive is to overthrow the leadership of the Communist Party and to forfeit the future of the country and the nation. . . . The Four Basic Principles are indispensable. Comrade Yaobang was weak and retreated; he did not truly carry through the campaign against bourgeois liberalization. . . . This turmoil is entirely a planned conspiracy to transform a China with a bright future into a China without hope. . . . We must prepare ourselves to enter into a nationwide struggle and resolutely crush the turmoil.[109]

After making this statement, Deng reportedly placed the People's Liberation Army (PLA) on alert, ordering ten thousand troops to move closer to Beijing.[110] The next day, April 26, Party leaders announced to a gathering of ten thousand party cadres that the army was poised to enter Beijing if necessary.[111] Thus, Deng had clearly and unequivocally sided with the conservatives in seeing the movement as a serious threat. Further, party elites were extremely concerned about potential worker involvement in the protests.

Back at the BSAF gathering, intense emotion and debate followed the editorial's broadcast.[112] Feeling that the situation was now critical, federation representatives feared that their next move could have serious consequences. Moreover, rumors swirled that the federation's activities were under surveillance. As one participant reports, "not long after the meeting had begun, someone announced, 'We must immediately move to Building no. 3, as it seems the government knows of our meeting place. Everyone bring their student IDs; we will have security at the door.' "[113] In this tense atmosphere, when the meeting reconvened students erupted in a heated debate. Some argued that it would be dangerous and irresponsible to engage in provocative activity after such an unequivocal and threatening government statement. Others, however, argued that, as an illegal organization, the BSAF had to strengthen its position by demonstrating that it had great popular support. Proponents of this view suggested that the federation organize a major demonstration on April 28. In the final vote, these two opinions tied, 3 to 3 (one member abstained). The question was left to the general assembly, which by this point represented about forty schools. In the final vote, almost 99 percent were in favor. In fact, the general assembly decided to hold the demonstration one day earlier than had been suggested.[114] Students then drafted a resolution to be sent to every university in Beijing.[115]

Proponents of the less confrontational approach were not completely vanquished, however. Pointing out that the editorial claimed some had shouted "Down with the CCP!" in previous demonstrations, these Standing Committee members convinced the general body to chant "Long live the CCP!" during the April 27 demonstration.[116] In this way, the words of the party-dominated media clearly influenced the strategy choice of the BSAF.

The next day, confusion surrounding the impending demonstration reigned. Under great pressure from the authorities, and in the risk-laden atmosphere created by the April 26 *People's Daily* editorial, nearly every major student leader had second thoughts about holding the demonstration. At Beida, two members of the Autonomous Union met with school admin-istrators on the morning of April 26. The authorities said that if students refrained from demonstrating, there would be a good chance for a dialogue. The BAU leadership later held a meeting, and through a vote of 3 to 2 de-cided to cancel the demonstration. Fearing that this decision would cause the union to lose legitimacy, the group then presented the motion to the gen-eral student body at Beida. The students, however, remained determined, voting down the motion.[117] In the end, they settled on a compromise. Beida students would participate in the demonstration but would turn back at the Third Ring Road rather than continuing to Tiananmen Square.[118] At Shida, student leaders were under similar pressure to cancel the demonstration. One prominent Shida student, for example, reports that he was called to the chancellor's office and told that the primary school across the street con-tained a thousand soldiers waiting to meet any protestors.[119] Feeling a "very heavy responsibility," the student met with departmental leaders to express his confusion and fear.[120] He then went to Beida to persuade student leaders to call off the demonstration. Upon hearing that Beida students could not be thus swayed, he returned to Shida.[121]

Almost simultaneously, further confusion erupted: on the evening of the twenty-sixth, federation president Zhou Yongjun unilaterally announced that, due to extreme danger, the Standing Committee had decided to cancel the demonstration. In actuality, Zhou had consulted no one before announcing this change of plan.[122] Apparently, he too had been under immense pressure from school and government authorities, and felt that he could not bear the responsibility for placing students' lives in danger.[123] Thus, Zhou reasoned that he must act to protect the students, even at the cost of nullifying the majority decision of the federation.

Zhou's announcement created further turmoil. Because his declaration contradicted the decisions made by various campus autonomous groups, many students were confused as to which direction they should follow. Moreover, although most of the larger schools eventually heard of Zhou's announcement and began to demobilize, many smaller schools were completely unaware of the change in plan.[124] These contradictory and incomplete messages angered many students. For example, one Beida leader complains that, "When we later heard that the Federation had changed its mind on the march, we felt mad . . . we had already been preparing, making pamphlets, etc."[125] Similarly, a Central Minority Institute student reports that "on the dawn of April 27, we went to our school gate . . . then [a student leader] came and said that the Federation had decided to have a sit-in [rather than a street march]. . . . After this, I felt that the Federation didn't have much use."[126]

Despite this confusion, fear, and anger, the demonstration was held. Moreover, it was an overwhelming success: over one hundred thousand students, representing every school in Beijing, marched for hours, passing through numerous police blockades, to Tiananmen Square. Students from Beida quickly changed their plan to turn back at the Third Ring Road and continued on triumphantly to the Square. Hundreds of thousands of city folk lined the streets in support. As students marched, the tension and uncertainty of the previous two days turned to exultation as students realized that their action would not be repressed. As one participant relates,

> This hugely successful demonstration was one of the greatest events in history. . . . During the demonstration, we received tremendous help from the Beijing city people. The route . . . was mostly on Second Ring Road. . . . Second Ring Road has seven overpasses, and every time the students went through one, people were all over, shouting, 'Long Live the Students!' 'Long Live Democracy!' The students got especially excited every time this happened and walked in an even more orderly manner. I still get very excited talking about this today. Approximately one million people greeted us. We were out marching [all day], and were constantly surrounded by people supporting us. The government was extremely embarrassed. It was a huge, amazing success.[127]

Why did the police not make more of an effort to stop the student protestors, and why was the army not called upon? It appears that the party had hoped that its tactics of intimidation would convince the students to reconsider their action. Indeed, those official threats did come very close to succeeding. In addition, it seems that the party did not expect such a large number of students to join the march, or such a large group of onlookers to gather in support. Having these expectations, the party simply may not have deployed enough officers to block the march effectively.

The BSAF met again at the University of Politics and Law on the following day, April 28. Although the mood was triumphant, many were angered by Zhou's attempt to cancel the demonstration. Thus, as the first order of business, representatives forced Zhou to resign from the presidency (although he remained on the Standing Committee).[128] Wu'er Kaixi became the new president. In addition, Standing Committee members downgraded the power of the president, feeling that Zhou's abuse of power had endangered the movement. In the future, the president would have the authority only to call and chair meetings; he or she would have no other authority over the Standing Committee.[129] Finally, the group decided to hold its next demonstration on May 4, the seventieth anniversary of the May 4th Movement of 1919.[130]

On April 29, the government called for a dialogue with representatives of the official student governments on various campuses. When members of the BSAF attempted to participate in the meeting, they were told that they could attend but would not be allowed to speak.[131] Thus, the party continued to recognize only those groups that were officially sponsored. At the dialogue, even those students who were allowed to speak soon grew frustrated. Yuan Mu (spokesman for the State Council), He Dongchang (vice-minister in charge of the State Education Commission), and Beijing Municipality officials Yuan Liben and Lu Yucheng represented the government in the talks. Yuan Mu began the meeting by stating that students should return to classes, and that the editorial of April 26 had been directed, not against the broad mass of students, but rather against a "small handful" that was against the CCP. He also stated that, although most students were for democracy and reform, China needed stability to overcome its difficulties. Students then grilled the government officials with questions regarding the legitimacy of the official student government, political corruption, education reform, and constitutional provisions regarding freedom of expression. The officials responded with vague, rambling replies.

The meeting ended abruptly. In response to a student query regarding the April 20 "Xinhuamen incident" and the April 26 *People's Daily* editorial, Yuan Liben said, "The police were very restrained on April 20. Maybe one or two policemen lost control. . . . Further, in every student demonstration, there are some bad elements, and idlers." He Dongchang added, "There were also some perverts." Yuan Mu nodded in agreement, adding, "We love our children, even though we don't approve of some of your actions." With that, He Dongchang closed the meeting, saying: "We just have different views on some problems. Let's call it a day."[132] Students were outraged; the meeting immediately became known as the "fake dialogue."

The words of the Party officials reminded the students once again that the Party was determined to maintain the impression that the students had been infiltrated by "bad elements" with evil intentions, and that the movement was creating instability. At the same time, these words fueled student fears that the Party hoped to infiltrate the movement with its own spies so as to lend credibility to its accusations. Consequently, student leaders became even more convinced of the need to demonstrate that the student movement was both orderly and "pure."

In the face of this government intransigence, and in light of certain actions undertaken by student leaders, on April 30, the Federation underwent further organizational change. On April 28, Wu'er Kaixi and Wang Dan went into hiding, ostensibly out of fear that the Beijing police were searching for them.[133] On April 29, the two reappeared to hold their own press conference at the Shangri-la Hotel.[134] At the April 30 meeting of the BSAF Standing Committee, Wang Dan suggested that he hold only a nominal, or honorary, position on the committee, rather than an actual seat.[135] Wu'er Kaixi did not attend the meeting. Consequently, committee members agreed that Wu'er was not taking responsibility for his position and elected Feng Congde to the presidency. An office of vice presidency also was established, in case of a presidential absence in the future. Wang Chaohua, a graduate student at the National Institute of Social Science, was elected to this position.[136] In addition, representatives increased the size of the Standing Committee to nine.[137] Next, members raised the question of legitimization, discussing successes at various schools.[138] Finally, members attempted to compile a list of federation demands to present to the government as requisites for the students' return to classes. This, however, proved to be an extremely difficult task. As one participant states, "We discussed one sentence on the blackboard for hours—adding and subtracting words."[139] Finally, in exasperation, the group decided that each school would elect dialogue representatives to form a nominally separate Dialogue Delegation to deal specifically with such matters.[140]

Meanwhile, on April 30, Zhao Ziyang returned from North Korea. Upon hearing reports of the massive number of students and city folk who attended the demonstration of April 27, Zhao had renewed his hope that the student movement could demonstrate to party hard-liners the necessity for reform and the innocuous nature of the students' actions, thus buttressing his beleaguered position within the party. Moreover, as Black and Munro note:

> Zhao felt that his hand was strengthened by the coming anniversary of the May 4th Movement, which was certain to mark a new climax for the student movement. This year the date was important for another reason, too: Hundreds of international bankers would flock to the Great Hall of the People on that day to hear Zhao's keynote speech to the Asian Development Bank. He felt confident that the hard-liners would not risk a crackdown at such a time.[141]

Consequently, Zhao took action to encourage a more moderate approach to the movement. On April 28, Hu Qili, propaganda chief of the CCP and a key member of Zhao's faction, met with the editors of nine major newspapers, informing them that they would be given leeway to print objective reports on the student movement.[142] In addition, in Zhao's May fourth speech to the Asian Development Bank, he declared that the student movement did not present a serious threat to political stability, as student slogans had included "Support the Communist Party" and "Support Socialism." Consequently, Zhao argued that "the issue of student demonstrations should . . . be handled through legal and democratic means in an orderly and reasonable atmosphere, through extensive consultations and dialogues."[143] Nonetheless, Zhao remained out of favor with Deng, and only with Deng's agreement could Zhao's views be implemented.

On the afternoon of May 3, the BSAF held a special general meeting to discuss tactics for the May 4 demonstration. To guard against infiltration by party spies, and also to discourage official claims that the movement was being directed by a "small handful" of nonstudents, federation leaders insisted that participants' representative qualifications be strictly checked before they were allowed to enter.[144] At the meeting, members decided that demonstrators would hold hands while marching to the Square. Zhou Yongjun took responsibility for march organization and communication, and Wang Chaohua drafted a New May 4th Declaration, to be read after student marchers convened there.[145]

The May 4 demonstration brought large numbers of students to Tiananmen Square, but it lacked the same sense of triumph that the April 27 demonstration had engendered. Inasmuch as the demonstration marked the seventieth anniversary of the May 4, 1919 movement, it was meaningful to the students and the general populace. Yet the demonstration itself was rather uninspiring and disorganized. One participant notes, "just after noon the different schools began converging in the Square. We didn't know where to go or where to stand; many of the school groups had already scattered."[146] Amid this chaos, Wu'er Kaixi read aloud the New May 4th Declaration. But the declaration was rather long and dry, and did not succeed in capturing the attention of the students.[147] Moreover, many participants did not even hear it.[148] Shortly after the document was read, Zhou Yongjun abruptly announced that the class boycott would now end and that students should return to their classes. Again, Zhou did not consult any member of the BSAF before making this statement.

After the demonstration there was great chaos and confusion on Beijing campuses, and many students began to take a negative view of the federation. On May 5, the Beida Autonomous Union conducted a survey on student opinions regarding a continuation of the boycott, distributing survey forms to each dormitory room. In the final tally, 853 rooms agreed to a continued boycott, 301 rooms opposed it, and another 300 expressed no opinion.[149] The union thus decided to continue the boycott. In reality, however, many Beida students went back to classes. Similarly, on other campuses some students continued the boycott, whereas many others returned to classes. In consequence, those who continued the boycott received enormous pressure from school authorities.[150] Overall, one student leader notes, "the prestige of [the BSAF] decreased tremendously" due to its poor handling of this issue.[151]

Virtually all student leaders agree that the period following the May 4th demonstration was a "low ebb" (*dichao*) for the student movement.[152] The BSAF Standing Committee meeting of May 5 was filled with a sense of despair. First, members removed Zhou Yongjun from the Standing Committee because of his repeated refusal to abide by Federation decisions.[153] A People's University Standing Committee member also resigned. At least one other Standing Committee member declined to attend the meeting. In the end, one member states, "We didn't have enough people to hold a meeting."[154] Indeed, for the next week, federation members, as well as students in general, were struck with a kind of malaise.

The Dialogue Delegation

Student activity did not come to a complete standstill, however. As noted above, prior to the May 4th demonstration, the BSAF had decided to establish a Dialogue Delegation (Duihua Daibiaotuan) to focus on realizing a student–government dialogue. Despite an overall feeling of despair, the BSAF's Dialogue Delegation continued to work toward a student–government compromise. Originally, the federation felt that a smaller group would be able to work more effectively on specific matters related to a dialogue, such as the wording of student demands. Yet as federation efforts to hold a dialogue with the government continued to be thwarted, its leaders began to realize that the government was highly unlikely ever to talk with a self-proclaimed autonomous group. Consequently, by designating the Dialogue Delegation as a nominally separate group with no formal ties to the federation, BSAF members hoped that the government would find it easier to engage in a dialogue with the delegation, which made no formal claim of autonomy. In this way, students sought to adopt a practical strategy that would assuage official fears.

On May 3, about forty students, representing ten schools, convened in a classroom at Shida to discuss the establishment of the delegation. No concern was given to representative qualifications. Shortly after the meeting began, Xiang Xiaoji (a student at the University of Politics and Law) suggested that the group prepare three subjects for a dialogue with the government: (1) the nature of the student movement (to counter official claims that the movement was an instance of "counterrevolutionary turmoil"); (2) the implementation of political reform as a necessary complement to economic reform; and (3) the human rights articles in the Constitution (e.g., freedom of association, expression, religion, and travel). Xiang then proposed that in each dialogue with the government, the group could focus on one of these subjects. The group supported this proposal and elected Xiang to chair the delegation.[155]

On May 5, the group met again, this time at the University of Politics and Law. In the intervening day, Xiang contacted the president of the University of Politics and Law and received his support for the efforts of the delegation. Xiang also obtained the use of a large conference room, as well as an adjoining smaller room, on the top floor of the teaching building at the University of Politics and Law. In addition, the university had a telephone installed in the room for the group to use.[156] Around thirty students attended the meeting. Any student who had been democratically elected at his or her campus had the right to attend, but members requested that each school send only three to five representatives. Most of those who attended were law or social science students.[157] Xiang sat at the end of the table, recognizing people to speak.[158] The meeting was very orderly; as one participant explains, "We were determined to avoid the political fights that often went on in the federation leadership."[159] The delegation then divided into three groups, each to prepare one of the three subjects suggested by Xiang at the previous meeting.[160] The group decided to meet daily in its newly established headquarters.

On May 6, the group drafted a petition to the government. It read:

> Recently, university students from Beijing and the entire country have engaged in street marches, petitioning, etc. to express our demand for a dialogue with the government and party. Party and government leaders have also on many occasions expressed a willingness to dialogue with students. ... We have been democratically elected by Beijing students, so that the vast body of students may help the party and government improve their work, to push forward our country's reform, opening, and modernization process. We earnestly request ... an immediate dialogue to deal with issues of deepening political and economic reform and hastening the establishment of a democratic constitution. We wish representatives of the Central Committee, the NPC, and the State Council to immediately arrange a time and place, and discuss dialogue procedure, so as to ensure a smooth and effective dialogue. We request that on the basis of news freedom, news agencies be allowed to cover this dialogue and print a completely open and truthful report. (We expect to receive a reply by approximately 3:00 P.M. on May 8.)[161]

Thus, at least for the time being, the students distilled their various demands into one: an open dialogue that would be truthfully reported. Four members of the delegation took the petition to the public liaison offices of the Central Committee of the CCP, the NPC Standing Committee, and the State Council.[162] All three liaison officers had been contacted earlier and had agreed to meet the student representatives. When the students arrived, the liaison officers were already waiting to meet them.[163] However, this did not signify official quiescence in the face of student demands. As one delegation representative relates, this "was a most difficult step for the government. On the one hand, the government didn't agree to have a dialogue with the students, but it also didn't dare to refuse this kind of appeal."[164] Consequently, although the liaison officers accepted the petition, by May 8 no reply had been given. When delegation representatives returned to the liaison offices that evening, they were told: "We don't have a reply for you. But the government feels that dialogue is good, and we are working toward that."[165] As days passed, the government continued to stall on the issue.

Thus, by May 10, the student movement had come to a virtual standstill: the BSAF had lost much of its legitimacy and seemed unable to devise a new plan to recharge the movement's momentum. Further, the Dialogue Delegation, despite its focused efforts, was stymied in its attempts to bring about a genuine student–government dialogue. Wall posters continued to appear, and students continued to discuss political issues at public gatherings, but aside from these activities, one student leader states, "it seemed the movement was finishing."[166]

Summary

The events of April 15–May 10 demonstrate the profound influence of the political environment on student strategy and behavior. First, as noted by many scholars, the students' demands were reformist rather than revolutionary in nature. Indeed, none of the student leaders whom I interviewed said that they hoped for an end to Communist Party rule (at least prior to June 4). A number of studies attribute the reformist quality of the students' demands to the traditional role of Chinese intellectuals as censors of the government, charged with overseeing official morality yet nonetheless tied to the well-being of the regime. However, this argument cannot explain why it was not only students and intellectuals but also workers and common city folk who expressed these relatively mild criticisms of the government during the movement of 1989. A more persuasive explanation, I suggest, is that the previous forty years of CCP monopolization of all political structures rendered it impossible for any citizen to envision a practicable alternative to its rule. Thus, although popular discontent with the government was seemingly profound among all social ranks, none believed that it would be useful (or rational, given the party's history of repression) to call for an end to CCP rule. Consequently, the vast majority of demands voiced by all ranks of society during the movement of 1989 were reformist in nature.

Nonetheless, even though the protestors did not call for the overthrow of the CCP, the party still found some of their demands to be quite threatening. In particular, party elites felt that tolerance of unofficial newspapers and student groups would undermine the fundamental legitimacy of the party. Had the students narrowed their demands to include only those that did not threaten party legitimacy (such as a national discussion of education policy and fees), the students might indeed have achieved some success. However, as long as the students remained focused on the more threatening demands for autonomous association and media expression, their chances of succeeding were slim.

At the same time, students consciously chose some strategies that would lessen the likelihood of official slander and repression, and increase the chances of a favorable government response. For example, they established organizations to maintain order in the movement so as to deny the government an excuse to criticize or suppress the demonstrators. Further, students established the Dialogue Delegation in the hope that the party would be less threatened by a group not associated with the "illegal" federation.

Similarly, the students' concern with establishing a security line to separate students and nonstudents, as well as with maintaining order in general, derived from the reality of CCP domination of the political structure and the media. The students believed that orderly behavior would lessen the chances of official slander (and therefore also repression), and would also prove to the citizenry that the students were not disorderly or violent. Students did desire stronger ties with other social sectors yet felt that a separatist strategy was the only way to maintain order in their ranks and demonstrate the absence of ill-intentioned "outsiders," thereby decreasing the likelihood that their actions would be met with force. Moreover, as events at Xinhuamen and the critical official characterizations of the movement demonstrate, this student reasoning was quite well-founded.

The political environment also influenced interactions among student leaders. To begin with, party penetration of the campus made students hesitant to cooperate with others whom they did not fully know and trust. Further, knowledge of likely reprisals made student leaders hesitant to compromise with each other for fear that a bad decision could have dangerous repercussions. Consequently, student organizations were often plagued by an inability to make and implement decisions. Moreover, students were unable to truly unite in a powerful overarching federation.

Finally, this period demonstrates the persistence of government intransigence regarding student demands. For over three weeks, students had demonstrated, organized, and petitioned the government. Yet the official position remained unchanged. As summarized in the editorial of April 26, the government would not tolerate continued "disruptions" in the capital and would not recognize the legitimacy of any autonomous student organization. As the next chapter will show, these patterns did not change during the final three weeks of the movement. Indeed, these phenomena only increased in intensity as the final weeks of the movement unfolded.

Chapter 4

Student Mobilization and Organization in China, May 11– June 4, 1989

Initiated on May 14, the hunger strike pushed the movement to a new level of intensity and conflict. First, the locus of the movement shifted to Tiananmen Square. Previously, the students had engaged only in marches to the Square, holding brief sit-ins or rallies. Now the movement became fixed (*dingdiande*), with virtually all student organizations and activities focused on Tiananmen. Second, as students deprived their bodies of nutrition, the tenor of the movement rose to fever pitch. Students now actually were inflicting physical harm upon themselves in order to protest government policies, arousing strong emotions among both participants and observers. At the same time, the hunger strike encouraged a new wave of popular support for the movement. Third, spreading news of the hunger strike spurred thousands of students from outside Beijing to pour into the city. This not only increased the physical number of students inhabiting the Square, but also brought a greater diversity of opinions and ideas regarding the "correct" direction of the movement. Consequently, many more autonomous student organizations (as well as many nonstudent groups) formed to represent the new participants in the movement. Finally, during this period two of the most famous student leaders, Wu'er Kaixi and Wang Dan, became kind of "freelance" activists; the two sporadically consulted with (and were nominally affiliated with) numerous organizations yet also took many individual actions that greatly influenced the movement.

These changes intensified many of the organizational problems that had plagued the movement from its start. As vast numbers of new students now entered the movement—and many of them sought leadership positions—problems of trust multiplied exponentially. With the party clearly bent on ending the movement, the danger of infiltration became all the more real. Moreover, the hunger strike raised the stakes, injecting a clear element of physical risk. With the announcement of martial law on May 19, the threat of physical harm grew yet more pronounced. As a result, student leaders were even more hesitant to bow to majority decisions with which they disagreed or to trust student leaders with whom they were not well acquainted.

Perhaps most important, the hunger strike called into question the legitimacy of the preexisting student movement groups that did not officially sanction the strike. For, in this dangerous atmosphere, many believed that the hunger strikers' willingness to sacrifice their bodies for the movement endowed them with a charismatic moral legitimacy that could not be matched by any other claim of authority. These students felt that only those participating in the hunger strike had the right to lead the movement. This definition of legitimacy was ultimately anarchical: it implied that individuals with moral legitimacy (derived from their commitment to self-sacrifice) were under no obligation to obey the will of *any* organization or majority. In consequence, it became exceedingly difficult for any leadership to control the actions of the hunger-striking students. Indeed, even well-recognized hunger-strike leaders continuously stressed that they had no authority to make decisions on behalf of the hunger-striking students. As a result, it became nearly impossible to convince all of the students to withdraw from the square and end the movement.

This concept of legitimacy underscored a radicalizing trend in student behavior.[1] For, according to this notion, whoever risked the most became the most worthy of respect. Similarly, more radical and confrontational actions were seen as "proof" of one's sincerity. Conversely, moderate or concessionary actions were considered by many to be marks of cowardice in the face of danger, or collusion with the authorities. Thus, in this period, the efforts of groups such as the BSAF and the Dialogue Delegation to moderate their slogans and behavior in the hope of receiving a more favorable official response were increasingly condemned. Instead, slogans and actions became more confrontational. Of course, this change in behavior did little to encourage the party to alter its previous stance. Indeed, it only confirmed the worst fears of Deng, thus buttressing the strength of the conservatives and further undermining the power of Zhao.

The Hunger-Strike

By May 10 students were frustrated with the movement's loss of momentum and their inability to influence the government. Yet many remained highly agitated and were determined to restore vigor to the movement. Seeing more extreme action as the only way to ensure that the efforts of the movement would not be lost, some students insisted that a hunger strike was the only remaining option. These students were correct in anticipating that the hunger strike would bring new life to the movement. Yet the strike also exacerbated the organizational problems that had dogged the movement since its inception, for it was initiated spontaneously, without the formal sanction or involvement of any of the existing movement groups. Consequently, the hunger strike not only created more rifts in the student movement leadership but also raised the question of whether *any* organization would have the ability to control the actions of the student protestors. Indeed, many of the hunger strikers argued that they had taken the step as an individual and spontaneous decision, and thus no organization could have authority over them. As a result, it was increasingly difficult for student leaders to maintain order within the movement. And, without order, the movement would have little chance of receiving a favorable government response.

Various students had suggested a hunger strike prior to May 10, but none of these early proposals received widespread support.[2] During this "low point" in the movement in early May, however, some influential student leaders began seriously to advocate this strategy. The most enthusiastic proponents of the hunger strike were students from Beida and Shida. On the night of May 11, six student leaders from these two schools (Wu'er Kaixi, Wang Dan, Wang Wen, Cheng Zhen, Ma Shaofang, and Yang Zhaohui) met at a small restaurant to discuss the idea.[3] At a Beida Autonomous Union meeting the following morning, Wang Dan, Wang Wen, and Yang Zhaohui proposed that the union prepare to begin a hunger strike the following day. Wang Dan noted that this would be two days before Soviet President Mikhail Gorbachev's planned visit, and would thus give the government enough time to respond. Wang Dan also announced that he, Wang Wen, and Yang Zhaohui had already received the agreement of Shida students Wu'er Kaixi and Ma Shaofang.[4] The Beida Autonomous Union, however, did not unanimously agree to this proposal. Indeed, at a meeting a few days before, the group had discussed the possibility of a hunger strike but decided that it should be used only as a "last-ditch" strategy.[5] Thus, at the May 12 meeting the committee became divided over the issue. Finally, Wang Dan, Chai Ling (who had advocated a hunger strike in earlier meetings), and the others in favor of a hunger strike declared that they would begin a strike regardless of the decision of the union. Should the union not join their action, they stated that they would initiate a hunger strike in the name of the student masses.[6]

This action threatened to undermine completely the legitimacy of the BAU. For those advocating a hunger strike took the position that they had no need for the official sanction of the union—or, in fact, any organization. In the high-stakes atmosphere surrounding the movement, they argued that it was more important to proceed with the "correct" strategy than it was to bow to democratic procedures. Faced with this ultimatum, the union decided that its members could support the hunger strikers as individuals and would allow them to use the group's broadcast and communication equipment, but that the union would not officially sanction the strike. Nonetheless, those union leaders who opposed the strike still entertained the hope that the hunger strike never would be implemented. As one such leader states, "We absolutely did not want them [Chai Ling and Wang Dan] to succeed."[7]

After the meeting, those committed to the hunger strike drew up a poster with the hunger strikers' two basic demands: (1) that the government hold a dialogue with the students, and (2) that the government reassess its charge that the movement was creating chaos. Thus, although these students were embarking on a more radical method of protest, their demands were virtually identical to those of the Dialogue Delegation and other student groups.[8] The hunger-strike proponents displayed the poster at the Beida triangle; throughout the day thousands of students gathered to read it. Yet by nightfall only forty students had signed up to join the hunger strike.[9] Concerned by this lack of enthusiasm, Chai Ling made a rousing and emotional appeal to the students gathered at the triangle, emphasizing that they must have the courage and devotion to sacrifice their lives in order to see the "the true face of the government."[10] The speech deeply affected the students; they listened intently and broke into applause and excited speech when she finished. By the end of the night, two hundred students had pledged to join the hunger strike.[11]

The insistence of these few leaders on a hunger strike also caused conflict with the federation. On the night of May 11, the BSAF issued a decision stating that, at present, it opposed large-scale activities and would focus on small-scale actions. Yet at a BSAF meeting the following morning, hunger-strike proponent Yang Zhaohui entered and announced that students at Beida were planning a hunger strike to begin the following morning. Presenting the decision as a fait accompli, Yang told the group: "We want to hunger strike; the BSAF must support us! . . . We want to go to Tiananmen to hunger strike, and we demand that the BSAF send people to protect us."[12] Upon hearing this, some Standing Committee members erupted in anger, declaring that these students had no right to use BSAF resources to engage in such an unsanctioned action.[13] Yang Zhaohui returned to Beida with this news and brought Chai Ling back to the meeting. Upon arriving, Chai Ling defiantly told the group: "The hunger strike is a spontaneous movement of students; you do not have the ability to lead us. . . . No matter what you say, Beida has already agreed on a hunger strike, and we will do it."[14] This statement was profoundly anarchical, as it implied that no person or organization had the right to control the "pure" and "spontaneous" actions of the students. Similar statements would be repeated by the hunger strikers throughout the remainder of the movement, stymieing all attempts to organize or lead the hunger strikers.

After listening to Chai Ling's words, one Standing Committee member resignedly asked the other members: "How much popular trust does the BSAF have? Do you think that the BSAF's words can still control things?"[15] The Standing Committee members had begun to realize that the group risked a great loss of legitimacy should it criticize or censure the hunger strikers. As one Standing Committee member states, "We felt that the hunger strike was inevitable, so we had no choice but to write a statement of sympathy and support."[16] Finally, the group decided on a policy similar to that of the BAU: although the BSAF would not officially sanction the strike, it would support those who individually chose to engage in such action.[17] Once again, those students who believed that a hunger strike was the right policy felt that compromise would destroy the movement. As a result, they ignored the dictates of democratic rule.

At the same time, Liang Er (a Standing Committee member who fundamentally was opposed to the strike) made an agreement with Wu'er Kaixi and Wang Dan. Wu'er and Wang planned to participate in the hunger strike, yet Liang felt that they respected the BSAF and were basically reasonable and trustworthy. Thus, the three agreed that Wu'er and Wang should try to lead the hunger strike in such a way as to ensure that it would not undermine the authority of the BSAF.[18]

The following morning, the instigators of the hunger strike drew up a hunger-strike statement to be read upon arrival at Tiananmen Square. The statement was highly charged, focusing on themes of patriotism, sacrifice, devotion, purity, and altruism. Throughout the statement, death was presented as the ultimate proof of these honorable qualities. The hunger-strike leaders wrote:

We do not wish to die; we want to be able to study properly. Our homeland is so poor. It seems irresponsible of us to desert our homeland to die. Death is definitely not our pursuit. But if the death of a single person or a number of persons would enable a larger number of people to live better, or if death can make our homeland stronger and more prosperous, then we have no right to drag on an ignoble existence. . . . It is through death that we await a far-reaching and perpetual echo by others. . . . When a person is about to die, he speaks from his heart. . . . Farewell comrades, take care, the same loyalty and faith bind the living and the dead.[19]

Brief handbills also were printed, stating the conditions and demands of the hunger strike. The handbills read:

Hunger Strike Statement—Capital University Students Voluntary Hunger Strike. We hunger strike to: (1) protest against the government attitude toward the Beida class boycott; (2) protest the government's avoidance of dialogue; (3) protest the government's constant charge that the movement is "chaos." We demand: (1) dialogue; (2) a truthful assessment of the movement as patriotic and democratic.[20]

On the afternoon of May 13, the hunger strikers from Beida met at the May Fourth Monument on campus and set off for Tiananmen Square.[21] Hunger strikers from Shida soon joined them.[22] Upon arriving at the Square, the group—now numbering around eight hundred—gathered at the base of the Monument to the People's Heroes.[23] Once settled, Wang Dan and Wu'er Kaixi immediately volunteered to be leaders. A "security team" (*jiuchadui*) sent by the BAU then formed a circle around the hunger strikers.[24] Wang Dan read the hunger-strike statement and announced that the strike had officially begun.[25] Shortly thereafter, Wang Dan, Wu'er Kaixi, and Ma Shaofang went through the security line to attend a press conference.[26] As the day passed, and news of the hunger strike spread, contingents of hunger strikers from other smaller schools joined the students from Beida and Shida at the base of the monument.[27]

At this time, no definite leadership or organization was in control of the hunger strikers. Participants were not really concerned, though. As Chai Ling notes, "We had a basic recognition that the government would likely make its position known before May 15 [the date of Gorbachev's arrival]; we didn't think the hunger strike would continue for an unlimited period of time."[28] Thus, until May 15, the hunger strikers felt that little organization was necessary. In reality, however, it proved difficult to conduct a hunger strike smoothly for even two days without organization. As one BAU member laments: "They [the instigators of the hunger strike] were very rash. They thought they could just go to Tiananmen, sit, and wait for the government to respond. They didn't consider the cold [weather], water, bathrooms. . . . The night of May 13 was very cold, but many were in shorts and t-shirts."[29] Seeing these problems, the BAU collected money for supplies and organized the transportation of water, clothing, umbrellas, and other necessities to the Square.

Dialogue with Yan Mingfu and the Arrival of Gorbachev

Later that day, it appeared that the hunger strikers' expectations might be correct: the Party initiated a second dialogue with the students. With Soviet leader Mikhail Gorbachev due to arrive in less than two days, party elites hoped to pacify the students and convince them to withdraw from the Square. Further, as hundreds of international reporters would soon converge on the capital, party leaders wished to avoid any embarrassing foreign media coverage. In the end, however, these efforts failed—in part due to the party's duplicity, yet also as a result of the charged atmosphere that had developed following the initiation of the hunger strike.

Shortly after the hunger strike formally commenced, Secretary of the Central Committee Secretariat Yan Mingfu sent a liaison officer to invite representatives of the Dialogue Delegation, the BSAF, and the hunger strikers to meet with him at the party's United Front Department. Vans driven by other liaison officers picked up student leaders and prominent intellectuals from various campuses, bringing them to the conference.[30] In total, forty to fifty protestors attended the meeting, including students Xiang Xiaoji, Shen Tong, Wang Chaohua, Wu'er Kaixi, Wang Dan, and Chai Ling, and prominent intellectuals such as Wang Juntao, Liu Xiaobo, Dai Qing, and Chen Zeming.[31]

The intellectuals served as arbiters between the two sides, although they strongly urged the government to engage in a dialogue with the students.[32] The students had been caught relatively off guard when the vans suddenly appeared to pick them up and had no coherent plan of action.[33] Moreover, those in attendance included representatives of different student groups that had not previously agreed on common demands or strategies. In addition, hunger-strike leader Chai Ling left the meeting after only a short time, ostensibly due to exhaustion.[34] After much discussion, those present at the meeting agreed on two things: (1) the next day the government would hold a dialogue with the Dialogue Delegation, to be broadcast live on China's Central

Television Station (CCTV); and (2) the hunger strikers would withdraw from the Square for the duration of Gorbachev's visit.[35] As this was to be the first meeting of Soviet and Chinese leaders since the Sino-Soviet split, all agreed that if Gorbachev was unable to visit the Square, China would "lose face."[36] Moreover, Yan Mingfu intimated that there were splits in the party, and that the reformist faction within the party would be harmed if the students interfered with the proceedings surrounding the Gorbachev visit.[37] However, as no command structure had been established to control the hunger-striking students, no one could guarantee that all students actually would evacuate the Square before Gorbachev's arrival.

On the afternoon of the next day (May 14), student leaders and government officials again gathered at the United Front building. Representing the students were members of the Dialogue Delegation, thirteen of whom had been elected to speak for the group (including Xiang Xiaoji, the chair of the Dialogue Delegation). Wu'er Kaixi and Wang Dan attended as hunger-strike representatives, yet officially they were not to speak, as they were not members of the Dialogue Delegation. Zhou Yongjun also came to the building in the desire to attend the meeting, but was not allowed inside the conference room. Thus, it appears that the students' strategy of creating a group less threatening to the CCP did indeed facilitate the dialogue.

Those gathered again discussed the live broadcast of the meeting. Informed by government representatives that a soccer game was currently being broadcast on CCTV, the students were assured that the dialogue would be videotaped and broadcast immediately after the game. In addition, government officials guaranteed that the meeting would be audiotaped and broadcast over loudspeakers at Tiananmen Square within one hour after the dialogue began. The students agreed to this, and the dialogue formally commenced. Before long, however, the students became disorganized in presenting their views. Dialogue Delegation representative Shen Tong describes the meeting:

> The dialogue delegates presented the students' views to the officials, taking up in order the three areas of discussion we had been preparing since our first meeting. . . . While we were speaking, the student observers behind us sent endless notes and proposed more questions for us to raise, so we began deviating from what we had prepared. The meeting started to get out of hand. . . . The representatives of the hunger strikers raised their hands to speak, but before anyone could recognize them, and while others were still speaking, they turned on a tape recorder and played the text of their declaration. . . . Suddenly the atmosphere became very emotional.[38]

Moments later, representatives of the hunger strikers burst into the room, demanding that the negotiations halt: the dialogue had not been broadcast, and students in the Square were furious, feeling that they had been deceived by the government.[39] As students poured into the room, government officials fled to their offices. Although Xiang Xiaoji made numerous attempts to renew the dialogue, there was no turning back.[40] Both students and government officials left in confusion and frustration.

Back at the Square, chaos reigned as word of the failed dialogue spread. As one student leader notes, "Because originally we thought the hunger strike would end on May 15, when the May 14 dialogue failed, the movement suddenly became unclear."[41] Not having discussed a next step should the government continue to evade student demands, students argued over the proper course of action. In the predawn hours of May 14, sixty-four representatives convened under the direction of Chai Ling to discuss whether or not the students should clear the Square for Gorbachev's arrival.[42] Students made no attempt to check representative credentials, however, and many did not receive word of the meeting.[43] When a vote was taken, forty-six wished to remain at the Square, seven voted to withdraw, and the rest abstained.[44] Meanwhile, unaware of this meeting, the BSAF announced that students should move to the east side of the Square to clear a space for Gorbachev's arrival. Around 4:00 A.M., Wu'er Kaixi made a personal appeal to the students to evacuate to the east side, telling them, "This is a patriotic movement, and should not interfere with important matters of the state."[45] Most students did move to this new location, but some refused to do so. Most notably, the hunger-strike contingent from People's University and from the Chinese department at Shida refused to move, stating that "Everyone on hunger strike must make their own decision [regarding whether or not to move], because to hunger strike is a personal decision."[46] Moreover, even when students did move, others soon came to take their place.[47]

As dawn broke, thousands of students remained in the Square. The planned gala welcoming ceremony for Gorbachev had to be canceled. Instead, Gorbachev was welcomed quietly by a small group of Party officials at the Beijing airport, located miles from the city center in a sparsely populated region. After being greeted, Gorbachev was whisked to the city center in an official car that silently entered the back door of the Great Hall of the People.

Party leaders were tremendously embarrassed. Moreover, party conservatives pointed to Zhao as the person responsible for this debacle. After his return from North Korea, Zhao had counseled moderation. In so doing, he had encouraged the students to continue in their action. Thus, party conservatives argued, Zhao had caused the nation enormous humiliation. At this point, what remained of Zhao's political power completely deteriorated. At a meeting of Deng, Li, Zhao, and other top party cadres on May 17, Zhao again called for a moderate response to the students, but was voted down. Moreover, Deng announced that the army must now be used. That evening, as well as the following day, Li appeared on television, stating that the party would not budge with regard to the students' demands and indicating that the conservative faction had prevailed. As Timothy Cheek relates, Li "conveyed the impression of a man who needed to make no compromises."[48] On May 18, party leaders decided to declare martial law. To avoid consultation with the NPC, Li Peng applied the decree to only eight of Beijing's administrative districts.[49] Late in the night on May 19, Li and Yang Shangkun called a special meeting to announce the party's decision. Zhao did not attend, ostensibly because of poor health.[50] Shortly thereafter, Zhao was stripped of his post as vice-chair of the Central Military Commission and disappeared from public view. With that, the die was cast; the student movement would end without any party compromise. As long as Gorbachev remained in town, the party would not act. After his departure martial law would be imposed.

The Hunger-Strike Command

The failed dialogue with Yan Mingfu gave rise to greater confusion and frustration among the student protestors. Moreover, as Gorbachev's arrival passed without any party compromise, student leaders faced the prospect of a prolonged occupation of Tiananmen Square. Consequently, some of the hunger-strike participants began to realize the need to establish some sort of organization to attend to the needs of the hunger strikers. Nevertheless, due to the hunger strikers' belief that their participation in the movement was fundamentally an individual act, the organization that arose to "lead" them was exceedingly weak. Indeed, even those who became leaders of the new organization proclaimed that no individual hunger striker would be expected to abide by the decisions of the group or its leaders. Consequently, the hunger-strike organization did little to restore order to the Square or direction to the movement. Coupled with the increasingly negative attitude of the party toward the student protestors, an unfavorable end to the movement became highly likely.

One of the most instrumental founders of the new hunger-strike organization was a student named Li Lu. In late April, Li had departed from

Nanjing University in Jiangsu Province and traveled to Beijing to join the student movement. Upon arriving, he systematically sought out all of the autonomous student organizations and their leaders, hoping to aid them in their activities.[51] Li was not warmly received, however. Not only was he a stranger, but he did not have a student identification card.[52] Thus, from the start many suspected that he was an infiltrator and did not trust him. Nonetheless, within a week of his arrival, he was taken into the confidence of Chai Ling, who quickly came to regard him as both trustworthy and an able leader.[53]

When Li arrived at the Square early in the morning of May 15, he was distraught to see that student protestors seemed completely disorganized.[54] Fearing that the movement would soon end if things continued in this manner, and also fearing for the safety of the hunger-striking students, Li told Chai Ling that they must establish a command organization.[55] Li also suggested that, if the government did not respond to student demands before the lives of the hunger strikers became endangered, hunger-strike leaders should sacrifice their lives (through self-immolation) both to pressure the government and to save the lives of the students.[56] Upset yet moved by this suggestion, Chai Ling agreed. Subsequently, she gave a speech discussing the situation and asking for volunteers to help organize the hunger strike. Many were moved to tears, and over ten students came forward.[57] Around 8:00 A.M., Chai Ling gave a speech formally establishing the Hunger Strike Command (*jueshituan zhihuibu*). The group had no legitimacy or structure at this time, however; it simply had been declared to be in existence, and was comprised only of volunteers.

To address these problems, the group announced that each school's hunger-strike contingent should send representatives to discuss the basic workings of the group.[58] Approximately forty schools sent representatives, each of whom was required to show student identification prior to entry.[59] Once the representatives were assembled, Chai Ling opened the meeting and immediately introduced Li Lu, whom most students had not previously seen. She then suggested that Li chair the meeting. As chair, Li described the nature of the command group. He announced that the sole purpose of the group was to protect the lives of the hunger-striking students; the command would not have leadership status, and would have no authority to force decisions on hunger-striking students.[60] Moreover, Li declared that, although at the present time an election was not possible, all hunger-striking students had the right to participate in the Hunger Strike Command and to call a meeting to recall any Hunger Strike Command leader.[61] Explaining this stance, Li states, "as the students were risking their lives in hunger striking, we had no power to ask them to heed our views."[62]

Thus, in actuality the Hunger Strike Command had no authority. Rather, it argued that any spontaneous decision by an individual hunger striker must be respected, and that no dedicated hunger striker could be obligated to bow to a majority decision. Nonetheless, Li Lu and the others who had formally established the group did ask the students to abide by two general rules. First, they asked that no new students join the hunger strike. Second, they requested that the hunger strikers go to the hospital should they fall ill, and not resume a hunger strike after they returned. In this way, the command hoped that the hunger strike would have a "natural ending."[63] Yet, the command had no power to enforce such rules, and after only a few days it was apparent that they were being widely ignored.

The only real power of the Hunger Strike Command derived from its control of a broadcasting system that had been erected at the square. On May 14, Feng Congde arrived at the Square with a black "hunger-strike" banner and a tape of the hunger-strike declaration. Subsequently, he prepared to establish a broadcast station. A professor from Beida had given Feng $Y400 (approx. $US 50), and a Hong Kong reporter had donated $Y1,000 (approx. $US 120) to the BAU for this purpose. Feng and his helpers decided that the broadcast station would use a battery rather than normal electricity, so the government would be unable to cut the station's electrical current. Throughout the day, Feng traveled around collecting equipment. By the late afternoon, the station had been erected at the base of the Monument to the People's Heroes.[64]

With no other effective way to communicate with students at the square, control of the broadcast station became crucial to anyone wishing to influence or lead the students. As Feng relates, "I had the impression that in front of the [TV] cameras, it appeared that the broadcast station was in control. Holding the power to broadcast was an extremely important thing."[65] Yet Feng did not allow everyone to use the equipment; specifically, he froze out any persons associated with the BSAF. As he explains, "Because the previous week I had lost trust in the BSAF, I kept [the station] under strict control."[66]

As a result, even though the Hunger Strike Command held no real power, others soon contested its leadership. Indeed, on May 15, Wang Dan, Wu'er Kaixi, Ma Shaofang, Cheng Zhen, and Wang Wen declared that the command group was illegitimate, and must be rechosen. Chai Ling protested that this could not be done, as Li Lu was not currently at the Square.[67] Yet the others insisted on a reelection, calling a representative meeting to vote on a new leadership. In the final tally, Chai Ling and Cheng Zhen were elected as dual overall commanders; Chai Ling was responsible for the situation at the square, and Cheng Zhen was in charge of communication with the higher authorities.[68] Hunger-strike representatives also chose a standing committee consisting of Chai Ling, Cheng Zhen, Wang Dan, Zhang Boli, Feng Congde, Wang Wen, and Yang Zhaohui.[69] Shortly thereafter, Li Lu returned. Upon hearing the news of the reelection, he said, "If this is the case, I'll return to Nanjing, as Nanjing also needs me."[70] Panicky, Chai Ling began to cry, saying that Cheng Zhen and Wang Wen were really of little use and that she could not do everything on her own.[71] As a compromise, a tripartite position of vice-commander was created, with Li Lu, Zhang Boli, and Feng Congde filling these roles.[72] Hereafter, although others were nominally affiliated with the group, the actual core of the Hunger Strike Command would consist of four students: Chai Ling, Li Lu, Feng Congde, and Zhang Boli. Moreover, the broadcast station at the base of the Monument to the People's Heroes would remain firmly in their hands.

The group immediately set about their self-designated task of protecting the students. First, they established a security line around the four sides of the memorial, with volunteer student security marshals standing guard.[73] The hunger-strike group also created a security pass system to ensure that only students with proper credentials could enter the hunger-strike area. Next, students cleared an aisle (dubbed a "lifeline") leading from the monument to the outside of the Square, to ease the passage of ill students to the hospital. The Hunger Strike Command gave students no specific instructions regarding the establishment of the security line and the lifeline. As Li Lu explains, "This was all decided on spontaneously by the students; we suggested doing this, but they decided how."[74]

Medical workers also contacted students to help coordinate their activities regarding the health of the hunger strikers. Representatives from twenty-nine hospitals established a Capital Hospitals Epidemic Prevention Group (Shoudu Yiyuan Fangyi Lianhe Xiaozu), and a Red Cross Group also was created. However, many student hunger strikers did not welcome the efforts of these groups. Indeed, rumors spread that the Red Cross workers actually were plainclothes security who were kidnapping students rather than taking them to the hospital. Consequently, on numerous occasions students attempted to stop the medical workers from coming into contact with hunger-striking students.[75]

By May 17, Tiananmen Square was in crisis. As news of the hunger strike spread, thousands of students from outside Beijing poured into the Square, and hundreds of new students began to hunger strike. Some notified the Hunger Strike Command that they had joined the hunger strike, but others were unable to, due to the strict security around the Monument to the People's Heroes. Moreover, many schools undertook independent actions.

For example, on May 16, approximately three hundred students from Nankai University and the Beijing Film Institute began a water strike. In addition, students from the University of Politics and Law began a kneeling hunger strike in front of Xinhuamen, thus opening another "battlefront."[76] Moreover, the hot days and cold nights had taken their toll on the hunger strikers; by May 17, close to a thousand students had collapsed. The hunger-strike leaders were in a greatly weakened physical condition, too; many already had collapsed on at least one occasion.[77]

Further complicating the situation, on May 17 students received news of an impending rainstorm. Seeing no other obvious solution, Li Lu organized each school's contingent of hunger strikers to move to the south of the square, ten meters at a time, one group at a time. After three to four hours of moving the hunger strikers in this manner, eighty buses arrived to shelter the hunger strikers.[78] However, many hunger strikers were hesitant to board the buses; as they had been sent by the Red Cross, students feared that this was a ploy to lure the hunger strikers onto the buses and then simply drive away to an unknown destination. Only after the tires had been punctured and the drivers had vacated the buses would all of the hunger strikers finally agree to board.[79] One of the buses was reserved for the Hunger Strike Command. Hereafter, this bus, which was parked on the north side of the Monument to the People's Heroes, would be the locus of decision making at the square.

City folk and other nonstudents also became increasingly active during this period. Perhaps most important, the Beijing Workers' Autonomous Federation (Beijing Gongren Zizhi Lianhehui), which was established in late April with the help of former student leader Zhou Yongjun, announced that, on May 22, the group would sponsor an "all-city worker march, using the method of peaceful petitioning, to support the university student movement."[80] In addition, throughout this period tens of thousands of onlookers gathered around the square to support the students and observe the momentous gathering.

Some, however, grew restless. On one occasion, a mixed crowd of students and nonstudents moved toward the Great Hall of the People and began to push against the gate. Fearing the eruption of violence, as well as government slander of the movement, student leaders pushed their way to the front of the crowd, held hands, and begged the crowd to relent. As one student leader describes the event, "We felt like we were holding back the sea."[81] Later, a rumor spread that in the midst of the crowd were many ex-convicts.[82] After events such as these, student leaders became increasingly fearful of actions by nonstudents. Consequently, student leaders insisted on even stricter security measures.

Simultaneously, on May 16, Yan Mingfu came to the Square and spoke to the students. In his speech, he cried and asked students to evacuate the Square, saying, "You must give the reformist faction time." Wang Dan then took the microphone, announcing that he and Wu'er Kaixi agreed. Before he had uttered more than a few words, though, he collapsed.[83]

Given this crisis-ridden and confused situation, the Hunger Strike Command convened a meeting of school hunger-strike representatives to decide on the proper course of action. Approximately fifty students attended the meeting, yet hunger-strike leaders made no attempt to check representative credentials. In the meeting, debate was intense.[84] One of the meeting attendees, Zhou Yongjun, was particularly vociferous in advocating withdrawal from the Square. However, he later was ejected from the meeting when four students from the University of Politics and Law entered and said he was not a University of Politics and Law representative. Finally, a vote was taken: 70–80 percent opposed leaving the Square, arguing that the government had not adequately addressed student demands.[85]

The BSAF and The Voice of the Student Movement

With the start of the hunger strike, the BSAF suddenly became marginalized. The focus of the movement shifted to Tiananmen Square, where the BSAF did not have a clear presence.[86] As the BSAF officially had not sanctioned the hunger strike, its leadership was not sure how to respond to the new situation. Though the group eventually helped to establish supply stands and a broadcast station at the Square, in reality "the BSAF never made a clear decision to enter and set up at Tiananmen."[87] The Hunger Strike Command, in contrast, was visibly located in the Command Bus. Moreover, as students became dispersed at the Square, university campuses, and throughout Beijing, it became very difficult for the BSAF to hold representative meetings. As Wang Chaohua notes, "actually, the BSAF didn't hold any representative meetings at this time, because things were too chaotic."[88] The BSAF Standing Committee gathered for a few meetings, yet rarely could muster a majority of its members. Consequently, during this period Wang Chaohua and Liang Er became the two most consistently important actors within the BSAF Standing Committee, acting as accountants for the group, procuring supplies through officials at major universities, and setting up supply stations at the Square.[89] As Liang was also a major leader of the Shida Autonomous Union, at this point the BSAF and the SAU virtually became one. Although Wang and Liang undertook actions in the name of the BSAF, in essence the BSAF had ceased to function as an organized and stable federation. As Wang Chaohua states, "After [May 14], I began to just individually deal with matters as I ran into them."[90]

Perhaps more important, the hunger strikers were now seen as the most progressive and important force in the movement, and the hunger strike had become the focus of government concern. Thus the Hunger Strike Command became quite powerful: not only was it seen by many as the core of the most "pure" and "devoted" elements in the movement, but its nominal control over the hunger strikers also gave it great leverage with the government. Further, as the Hunger Strike Command held exclusive control over the broadcast station, the BSAF had no means of communicating with the students at the Square.

Concerned with this marginalization of the BSAF, as well as with the lack of attention given to those students who had joined the protest yet were not participating in the hunger strike, Wang and Liang worked to establish a second broadcast station at the Square. As Wang explains:

> I was unsatisfied with the hunger-strike broadcasts because the contents only dealt with hunger-striking students. I felt broadcasts should be directed toward every aspect. For example, no one had done anything to help the students working as security, and consequently they were often unable to get food. . . . I also felt that the hunger-strike school representative meetings really only included those students at each school who were on hunger strike, which was a minority of students at each school—so they couldn't say that they really represented all students, as the BSAF did.[91]

Searching for a solution, Wang and Liang looked to a small announcement station erected at the square on May 15 by some Qinghua University students. Although this station—called The Voice of Qinghua—had a very limited broadcasting range, Wang and Liang saw in it an opportunity to establish a broadcast station that could compete with that of the Hunger Strike Command. Consequently, Wang convinced the Qinghua students to link the station with the BSAF and raised funds to expand its broadcast power.[92] Thus, on May 17, The Voice of Qinghua was moved and expanded, and placed under the auspices of the BSAF. Led by a security team composed of Qinghua students, a group of the BSAF-sponsored students marched to the southeast side of the Monument to the People's Heroes. After arriving, the security team formed a circle, and the others began to set up the broadcast station and a materials station. Along with the manpower and materials provided by Qinghua students involved in The Voice of Qinghua, supplementary materials, broadcast equipment, and manpower were gathered by Shida students.[93] The students designated the new broadcast station

The Voice of the Student Movement (Xueyun Zhisheng). Its power was three to four times greater than that of the hunger-strike broadcast station.[94]

Relations between the two broadcast stations quickly soured. Aware of the stronger broadcast power of the new station, Feng Congde approached The Voice of the Student Movement to request that it broadcast the hunger-strike declaration. A student working at the station accepted the declaration but delayed in broadcasting it, explaining that he first had to check it over. After half an hour of waiting for the declaration to be broadcast, Feng left the station, feeling "hopeless, and a little mad."[95] When Feng returned later, the security around the station refused to let him enter. Finally, Wang Chaohua saw Feng outside and told the security to relent. Yet they were unable to reach any agreement about the relationship of the two broadcast stations.[96] Later attempts by representatives of the hunger strike to broadcast announcements from the new station similarly ended in failure.[97]

This inability to cooperate was not surprising; by this point, the BSAF and hunger-strike leaders had little trust in one another. First, due to Feng Congde's strict control of the hunger-strike broadcast station, the BSAF leaders did not believe that Feng sincerely wished to share power with the BSAF. Most believed that Feng simply craved access to their more powerful broadcast equipment. Second, many rumors circulated regarding the financial situation of each group. For example, reports spread that Wang Chaohua had taken $Y5,000 (approx. $US 600) from the hunger-strike group to finance the second broadcast station.[98] Thus, hunger-strike leaders were enraged when they were denied access to the station. Wang Chaohua, however, claims that she garnered the funds from the SAU.[99] Similarly, there was some confusion about the financial status of the BSAF. Hunger-strike leaders claim that the BSAF had over $Y1,000,000 ($US 120,000) in funds donated to support the hunger strike that had not been disbursed to the Hunger Strike Command.[100] The BSAF leaders, in contrast, claim that the BSAF actually had few funds at the time. Moreover, they point out that access to the BSAF funds required the signatures of at least five Standing Committee members. In the chaotic atmosphere of the time, it was exceedingly difficult to find enough Standing Committee members to perform this task.[101] Thus, whereas the BSAF leaders claim that Hunger Strike Command requests for the BSAF funds were often delayed by the difficult disbursement procedure, as well as by the lack of sufficient funds in the BSAF treasury, hunger-strike leaders believed that the BSAF was deliberately attempting to deny the Hunger Strike Command its rightful funds. As the stakes involved in the movement grew, the willingness of these various student leaders to negotiate and compromise only declined.

Tensions between the Hunger Strike Command and the BSAF were now manifest in the two opposing broadcast stations. As the two stations often aired vastly different opinions and directives, and as the sound from each station could be heard only by those in a particular location, this division caused great confusion among students at the Square. Such uncertainty gave birth to countless rumors, as broadcast announcements often were incorrectly heard, or were contradictory to other announcements that had been made. Consequently the students' anxiety level rose even higher.

Beida Autonomous Union Activities

Adding complexity to this situation, even before the hunger strike began, the BAU had begun to challenge the authority of the BSAF. As noted in the previous chapter, Beida and the BSAF had been in tension virtually from the start. To deal with this issue, shortly after the May 4 demonstration, the BAU held a "very formal" meeting to discuss the proper role of the BSAF.[102] During the meeting, the committee came to a consensus that the federation should not play an aggressive role in the movement; rather, it should simply serve as a forum where individual school representatives could share information, and where cooperative efforts could be coordinated among schools. No decision-making authority should be given to the federation; rather, each individual school should have the right to make independent decisions.[103]

Consequently, whereas the SAU became virtually indistinguishable from the BSAF after the start of the hunger strike, the BAU increasingly challenged the authority of the BSAF and undertook many separate actions to support the hunger strike. Indeed, immediately after the group of hunger-striking students from Beida set off to the Square on May 13, the BAU established a Beida Hunger Strike Support Department and began to procure clothing and water to send to the Square. The group subsequently established numerous stations at the Square, including a collection stand (to receive donations), a communication stand, a general supply stand, and a water stand. The BAU also constructed a small supply stand in front of the Beida hunger-strike group to cater specifically to its needs. Another supply stand disbursed food.[104] The Union devised a method of communication among the various stands, and set up a telephone as well. Finally, the BAU recruited students to serve as security, dispatching several hundred new security workers to the Square each day.[105] Thus, although the BAU originally took the same stance on the hunger strike as did the BSAF, it did not hesitate to establish a clear presence at the Square.

Leaders of the BAU insist that these actions do not imply that the group was attempting to establish an alternative power center at the Square. Rather, committee members maintain that upon realizing that no other group was taking responsibility for support, supplies, and communication at the Square, the BAU naturally stepped in to attend to these needs. In addition, campus officials at Beida were very supportive of the student movement. Thus, the BAU knew that it could easily obtain cars, telephones, and other supplies needed to carry out these tasks.[106] These were indeed invaluable services, as supply and communication mechanisms were desperately needed. However, the group claims that it did not wish to translate this importance into leadership authority. As one leader states, "I was proud of the Beida Autonomous Union. At the Square, we were the only really well-organized, hard-working group; and, we were not involved in power struggles."[107] Thus, although the BAU had taken an independent stand toward both the BSAF and the hunger strike, it was relatively uninvolved in the conflict over decision-making power between the BSAF and the Hunger Strike Command.

The Outside Students Autonomous Federation

At the same time, the rise of a new organization of students from outside Beijing further complicated the issue of movement leadership. Moreover, as students from outside Beijing began to take part in activities at the Square, fears of infiltration—and accusations thereof—rose. In addition, the process of information dispersion and communication became even more convoluted.

Since April, students from outside Beijing had been traveling to Tiananmen Square to take part in protest demonstrations and marches. Before the hunger strike, however, most of these students had stayed in Beijing for only a short time. After the hunger strike began and the movement became fixed at the Square, many outside students began to camp out there. As news of the hunger strike spread throughout the country, thousands of new students from outside Beijing poured into the capital. As one Lanzhou student relates: "Before [the hunger strike began] I had been involved in protest activities in my province, but only in a very limited way. May 13–14 was a dividing point in my life. When I heard of the hunger strike in Beijing, I became extremely fervent. Two days later, I traveled to Beijing, feeling very holy and pure."[108]

Upon arriving in Beijing, however, many "outside" (*waidi*) students found that conditions at the Square were not welcoming. First, existent organizations were strained beyond their capacity in simply tending to the needs of Beijing students and did not feel that it was their responsibility to care for the "outsiders."[109] As the same student from Lanzhou describes his arrival: "At Tiananmen, it was very moving, but also very tough. My first impression was not pleasant. We had donated money to the hunger-strike fund. Then we spent the night at the Square, and needed food, water, and warm clothes. But Beida didn't give us any warm clothes, just a few biscuits."[110] Indeed, one member of the BAU admits, "We treated people from outside Beijing a little differently."[111] Similarly, BSAF leader Wang Chaohua expresses irritation with the outside students, stating, "My feeling [towards these students] was, 'Why have you come to Beijing?' It was a great headache; there was no way to manage [the situation]."[112] Li Lu, representing the sentiment of the Hunger Strike Command, shows the same frustration, stating: "At that time, our ability was really limited. . . . Not only did we have to try to control all kinds of internal radical demands, but it was even more impossible to control the outside people."[113] In addition, simple logistical problems made it difficult for the outside students to gain access to supplies. As the Square was already filled with students from Beijing, the outside students were forced to camp on its outskirts. All of the supply stations, however, were located toward the center. Given the strict security system that had been established to regulate movement within the Square, outside students found it nearly impossible to reach the supply stations or to communicate with student leadership there. Thus the outside students felt both isolated from, and ignored by, the existing organizations at the Square.

To deal with these problems, on May 18 some students called a meeting in front of the Museum of History.[114] At the meeting, many student representatives from outside Beijing complained that they were excluded from the leadership at the Square. After great discussion, those present decided that the outside students would form their own organization to focus on their needs, but that the organization would cooperate with the BSAF.[115] Hence, on May 18, the Outside Secondary Schools Student Autonomous Federation (Waidi Gaoxiao Xuesheng Zizhi Lianhehui, OSAF) formed.

One of the first acts of the OSAF was to insist that students from outside Beijing be allowed to work in the Square security system, to ensure that outside students could maintain access to supplies and communicate with other organizations. Indeed, OSAF students quickly took control of the entire security system at the Square. Yet, although this helped to equalize the power of Beijing and non-Beijing students, it also created further confusion. As the outside students working as security often did not recognize student leaders from Beijing, many important leaders report that they had great difficulty moving around the Square and contacting other student leaders. Thus, although the OSAF did not contest the legitimacy of the BSAF or the Hunger

Strike Command, its presence added to the complexity of decision making and exacerbated problems of confusion and suspicion at the Square.

Prelude to Martial Law

Although by now there were hundreds of thousands of protesting students at Tiananmen Square (thousands of whom were on hunger strike), and despite an enormous demonstration on May 17, the government remained intransigent. Between May 18 and 19, students received some clear indications that it was not willing to accede to student demands, despite the hunger strike. On May 18, the party called student representatives in for a "dialogue," but in fact used the meeting only to reassert its previous charges that the movement was being controlled by "outside forces" and that it was creating disorder.

Students had been notified of the government's willingness to meet with them early in the morning on May 18, when two official messengers brought Wang Chaohua word that it would hold a dialogue at 11:00 A.M.[116] Wang immediately began to search out members of the Dialogue Delegation. However, on May 17, the Dialogue Delegation had decided to leave the Square and base itself at a Beijing art institute, wishing to meet in a more tranquil and stable atmosphere.[117] The art institute normally was one hour away, but immense crowds filled the Square and nearby streets and public transportation had come to a virtual halt. It would be impossible to reach the Dialogue Delegation before the meeting was to begin. In addition, Chai Ling and Wu'er Kaixi were in the hospital. Wang sent a representative to find Wu'er and bring him to the meeting, but encouraged the government messengers to ensure that Chai Ling would remain in the hospital during the dialogue.[118] As Wang relates, "[One of the government messengers] asked, 'What is your greatest difficulty?' I felt that I was most unable to persuade Chai Ling and Feng Congde . . . [so I said], 'If you can control [Chai and Feng], I think that things can be dealt with much better.' "[119] Thus, Chai Ling never received word of the meeting. A messenger sent by Wu'er Kaixi did inform Feng Congde of the dialogue, but Feng declined to attend, feeling that he was more needed at the Square.[120]

Of the eleven students who ultimately comprised the May 18 delegation, Wu'er Kaixi and Wang Dan enjoyed the highest prestige.[121] When the contingent gathered to go to the meeting, the two demanded that they alone speak during the dialogue; yet they had virtually no time to prepare for the meeting. Wang Chaohua hastily drafted a proposal for the government and gave it to Wu'er Kaixi, hoping to provide them with some guidelines for discussion. The proposal demanded that the government (1) provide a live and direct broadcast of the dialogue, and (2) reassess the movement. The statement then suggested that the government might fulfill the second demand by publishing an editorial or article to refute the editorial of April 26 or by having a high-ranking official make a speech on the subject.[122]

The dialogue was televised nationally, but it did not bring the two sides any closer to a compromise. Li Peng opened the dialogue by stating, "Today we will discuss only one topic: how to relieve the hunger-strike participants of their current predicament."[123] Then Li looked around at the students and added: "You are young, at most twenty-two or twenty-three years old; my youngest child is older than you. . . . You are all like our own children. . . ."[124] Before Li had finished this sentence, Wu'er Kaixi boldly interrupted, angrily telling Li, "We are short on time . . . the reality is not that you asked us to come talk to you, but that the great numbers of us at the Square asked you to talk with us . . . we should speak first."[125] Wu'er and Wang Dan then described the status of the hunger strikers at the square, pointing out that some two thousand had already collapsed. Next, they presented student demands for an open and equal dialogue (to be broadcast live), and for a reassessment of the movement. At this point, some of the other students interrupted with other comments regarding the status of the hunger strikers and the contents of student demands. Soon thereafter, government representatives began to speak of various cases of "unrest" and "disturbances" resulting from the movement, while students refuted these claims. After about an hour of this sort of discussion, Li Peng issued his final statement. In it, he made an attempt to appease the students, but ultimately he reverted to the same official rhetoric that had so incensed them, stating:

> Neither the government nor the party Central Committee has ever said that the broad masses of students are creating disorder. We have never said such a thing. We have unanimously affirmed the patriotic fervor of the students. . . . Nevertheless, things often develop independently of your good will. . . . There is complete chaos in Beijing. Moreover, chaos has spread throughout the country. . . . Much unrest has occurred in China. Many people did not want unrest to occur, but it occurred anyway.[126]

The official government position had not changed. Instead of signaling a desire to compromise with the students, party representatives continued to charge that the movement was creating instability and disorder.

Excerpts from the dialogue were broadcast nationally that evening, while students listened in despair. However, shortly before dawn of the next day, the government made another attempt to contact the students. Shortly before 5:00 A.M., Li Peng and Zhao Ziyang made a surprise appearance at the Square. Li uttered only a few words of greeting, but Zhao wept at the sight of the students, saying: "We have come too late. I am sorry, fellow students. You have the right to criticize us. It is proper for you to do so."[127] After this, there was no mistaking the fact that the party was indeed split. Yet, Zhao's words implied that the hard-liners had gained control within the party and that the movement's fate was sealed.

On the afternoon of May 19, the students received a clearer and more ominous signal: news arrived that the army was beginning to surround the city. Intellectuals who had established a base at the Workers' Cultural Palace were notified that martial law was to be declared at midnight. The intellectuals immediately sent for student leaders. Two representatives of the BSAF arrived and were told of the situation. However, the representatives professed that they could not make any decisions.[128] Simultaneously, Wu'er Kaixi and Liu Yan went to the United Front Department, demanding to speak with Yan Mingfu. After a long wait, Yan came out of his office and told the two that martial law would be announced that night. Yan also warned the students that they must allow the reform faction to strengthen its position, saying that if students continued to take the initiative, they would have to take responsibility for the consequences.[129] Meanwhile, around the square rumors of martial law and army advances spread.

In this ominous atmosphere, the Hunger Strike Command called a meeting to decide on the proper course of action. A security team surrounded the Command Bus, allowing entrance only to those approved by Chai Ling and Li Lu. Wu'er Kaixi, who had raced back from the United Front Building to report the statements made by Yan Mingfu, attempted to join the meeting, but the security team was instructed to block his entrance.[130] On the bus, the group discussed many options. In the end, the students agreed that the hunger strike should end.[131] After the vote, Wu'er Kaixi was finally allowed to enter the bus. Although Wu'er was angered by the group's refusal to allow him to participate in the vote, all were happy to discover that he agreed with their decision.[132] The group decided that the hunger strike would end that night but that the students would continue to occupy the Square. Then Li Lu, Chai Ling, and Guo Haifeng held a press conference to announce the decision.

Many hunger-striking students were outraged by the decision, however. As one student relates: "When the Hunger Strike Command broadcast a return to eating, everyone was extremely dissatisfied, because there had been no discussion or exchange of ideas, or explanation. Since the security wouldn't let anyone in, we had no way of knowing how decisions had been made."[133] In particular, Feng Congde, who had been in the hospital at the time of the meeting, charged that the decision had not been made democratically, and that those who had made it had "sold out" the movement.[134] Consequently, Feng called another meeting to reconsider the question. For one hour, representatives had their credentials examined. In the end, over eighty school representatives were allowed to attend. However, Feng admits that during the meeting "there was no time for the representatives to go back to their schools and collect opinions, so we had to have each guess how many students at their school supported the hunger strike, and then later check [the figures]."[135] In the final tally, 80 percent of the representatives reported that between 80 and 100 percent of the student hunger strikers from their schools wanted to continue the strike. Subsequently, Feng went to the hunger-strike broadcast station and announced the results. He also told the students that if anyone thought their representative had been incorrect in his or her estimation of student opinion, they should report to the broadcast station.[136]

Thus, by the night of May 19 confused messages had been sent out by members of the Hunger Strike Command. Officially, the original decision to resume eating remained in place; a press conference had been held to announce the decision, and the State Department had been informed of the strike's end.[137] Yet at the same time students within broadcast distance of the hunger-strike station had heard the opposing announcement of Feng Congde. In addition, The Voice of the Student Movement, under the direction of Wang Chaohua, simultaneously implored all of the hunger strikers to continue the hunger strike together, arguing that if some continued while others did not, those who continued the strike would be in danger.[138]

As had been foretold, at midnight Li Peng announced the imposition of martial law. In response, Feng Congde called for a two-hundred-thousand-person hunger strike to protest the government's use of force. Although moved by Feng's plea, most did not heed his directive.[139] Nevertheless, in a spontaneous movement, hundreds of thousands of citizens filled the streets of Beijing to block the entrance of the army. As morning broke, students and citizens looked around in jubilation; the efforts of the people had been successful, and army troops had not entered the city. A great question remained, however: What should be the next step for the movement, and who should lead it? For, despite this victory, student leadership continued to be deeply divided, while the Party remained determined to bring the movement to an end.

The Capital All Ranks Conference, the Temporary Command, and the Reorganization of the BSAF

As martial law progressed, leadership at the Square became even more confused. Concerned about this, some prominent dissident intellectuals worked to establish an overarching organization to unify the many separate groups now operating at the Square. As a culmination of these efforts, on May 23 the Capital All Ranks Joint Conference formally was established. However, the tense environment that had exacerbated organizational problems throughout the movement also led to great conflict within this organization. As martial law further heightened the students' perception of risk, they became even more hesitant to cede decision-making power to a body over which they did not have complete control. In addition, the lack of any organization possessing authority over the hunger strikers made it impossible to enforce any majority decisions on them.

By May 20, virtually all of the student movement organizations were in chaos. As Feng Congde had failed to convince the students to renew their hunger strike, the strike had formally ended. Consequently, the Hunger Strike Command no longer had a task, and disbanded.[140] Moreover, many Hunger Strike Command leaders went into hiding during the first few days of martial law, fearing that they would be arrested if the army entered the square.[141]

Meanwhile, members of the BSAF and the OSAF tried to reach an agreement to deal with the new situation. On the evening of May 20, BSAF and OSAF representatives met on the east side of the Monument to the People's Heroes. Wang Dan chaired the meeting even though he was not a formal member of either group. Those gathered did not reach any important conclusions. Rather, debate centered on who the overall commander should be. Wang Dan was the obvious choice, and was supported by most representatives, but many "outside" students insisted that a non-Beijing student act as commander. In the end, participants agreed that Wang Dan would share power with a student from Qingdao.[142] In actuality, however, Wang held the most power.[143] As the meeting closed, the representatives decided to survey student opinion and meet again on the following day, May 21.

This next meeting was far from successful. Before it began, Wang Chaohua strictly checked the identification of each person wishing to attend the meeting; only those whose names appeared on an official "black list" of verified BSAF representatives were allowed to enter. About forty persons passed the screening. In the course of the meeting, participants basically agreed to withdraw from the Square. Afterward, they returned to their school groups to survey opinions. This exercise did not produce a consensus, however. As Wang Chaohua's list contained names of only the BSAF representatives, no representatives of the OSAF or the previous Hunger Strike Command had been allowed to attend the meeting. Consequently, outside students and former hunger strikers expressed outrage at the proposal, asking, "Who gave the BSAF the right to discuss retreat?"[144] Ultimately no decision was made, and Square leadership remained in chaos.

Concurrently, some important intellectuals had been discussing the organizational problems of the movement. In particular, members of the nongovernmental Beijing Social Economics and Science Research Institute (Beijing Shehui Jingji Kexue Yanjiusuo, BSESRI) participated in these discussions. The BSESRI originally was formed in 1986 by intellectuals (such as Wang Juntao and Liu Gang) who had been active in the April 5 movement of 1976, the Democracy Wall movement of 1978–1979, and various other prodemocracy activities in the early 1980s.[145] The institute was the first privately owned and operated social science research establishment to be formed in Communist China.[146] According to one of the group's founding members, a guiding principle of the institute was to "support and nurture all democracy movement leaders."[147] Consequently, throughout the late 1980s, many important student leaders at Beida and the University of Politics and Law (and, to a lesser extent, at Qinghua University and Shida) received guidance from BSESRI members.[148] In addition, members of the institute had often lectured to student groups, such as the Democracy Salon at Beida. Thus, when the movement of the spring of 1989 began, many student leaders had sought advice from members of the institute. Indeed, one BSESRI member relates that during the movement "Wang Dan often called me from the street, asking what to do."[149]

Yet, until May 20, the members of the group did not attempt to become directly involved in the organization of the movement. Some intellectuals had formed a Federation of Intellectuals (Zhishijie Lianhehui) earlier in May, but the group held only a founding meeting and did not undertake any actions as an organization.[150] Rather, these intellectuals chose to serve as intermediaries between the students and the government or as advisers to the students. In addition, many drafted letters of support for the students.[151] Overall, these intellectuals were cautious in their support, in part because they believed that the government could be swayed only through moderate actions. Yet, perhaps more important, these intellectuals were not treated deferentially by all student leaders. Students such as Wang Dan and Wu'er Kaixi, as well as most members of the BSAF, often sought their advice, yet many hunger-strike leaders viewed the intellectuals with indifference, and even hostility. This attitude was largely due to the hunger-strike leaders' belief that the intellectuals' promotion of compromise with the government derived from the weakness of their devotion to the movement. In the view of the hunger strikers, only those who were willing to physically sacrifice their bodies for the movement deserved to lead. For example, on May 14, twelve noted scholars addressed the students at the square. Standing at their side, Chai Ling reports: "I thought, no matter what you say, you are also eating. We've all been fasting for so long, how can you intellectuals understand us?"[152]

Nonetheless, upon witnessing the disintegration of the movement after the announcement of martial law, some members of the BSESRI decided that an overarching organization was needed to coordinate the movement. On May 19–21, representatives of the various groups present at the square held some informal meetings to discuss this idea.[153] The first formal gathering met on the night of May 22, on the second level of the Monument to the People's Heroes. Over thirty persons attended the meeting, which was chaired by scholar Zhang Lun. Virtually all of the important intellectuals who had been involved with the movement were present. Most important BSAF and independent leaders also attended, such as Liang Er and Wang Dan. Some members of the Hong Kong Student Union were present as well. No members of the Hunger Strike Command attended, however. Chai Ling declined an invitation, and the others either were not present at the Square or were uninterested in attending.[154] At the meeting, the group discussed the organizational problems of the movement, but the atmosphere was very tense. In the end, the participants made no substantive decisions; they decided only to hold a formal meeting the following morning.[155]

At the next meeting (May 23), the group formally established a Capital All Ranks Joint Conference (Shoudu Gejie Lianxihui).[156] The group included representatives from every autonomous organization that had been established during the movement; not only were the various student organizations included, but worker, citizen, and intellectual groups as well. In addition, two students—Wu'er Kaixi and Wang Dan—were invited to join as individuals.[157] The group decided to meet at noon every day.[158]

The Joint Conference decided to form a Temporary Command to manage the square.[159] In the meantime, the BSAF was to retreat back to its headquarters and completely reorganize. As the former Hunger Strike Command remained the group with the most control over the students at the Square, those at the Joint Conference decided that the hunger-strike leadership core should serve as the basis of the Temporary Command.[160] Thus, Chai Ling became the general commander; Zhang Boli, Feng Congde, and Li Lu were made vice-general commanders; and Guo Haifeng was named general secretary. Yet, representatives of other groups were included as well; Wang Chaohua, Wang Dan, and Lian Shengde (a prominent leader of the OSAF) were chosen to sit on the Standing Committee of the group; Liu Gang was named chief of staff; and Zhang Lun was appointed chief of security.[161]

Great confusion existed concerning the proper authority of the Temporary Command, however. Once again, in this increasingly risk-laden environment, no leader felt that he or she could allow any major decisions to be made by others, as others might lack the sufficient "rationality" or "devotion" to make proper judgments. Moreover, as martial law progressed, many feared that a poor decision could bring physical harm to the student protestors.

In the minds of many intellectuals, the Capital All Ranks Joint Conference should have been the preeminent decision-making body of the movement. Although the intellectuals agreed that special deference should be given to student groups, as they had spearheaded and led the movement for most of its duration, the intellectuals nonetheless believed that the Temporary Command was only a subsidiary of the Joint Conference. As one scholar definitively states, "the Temporary Command was required to obey the decisions of the Joint Conference."[162] In this way, the intellectuals sought to gain some control over the movement, to ensure that their more moderate views could be implemented and disaster avoided.

Members of the BSAF, however, had a very different opinion of the Temporary Command and the Joint Conference. In their view, the movement had been led by Beijing students, not intellectuals or workers. Further, as the BSAF represented the entire federation of Beijing students, it was the only body that could truly represent and protect the interests of the broad masses of students. Consequently, no other organization should be allowed to lead the movement. Thus, leaders of the BSAF felt that, although the Joint Conference was a useful coordinating body, it should not dictate policy. In the words of Wang Chaohua:

> The Joint Conference never had leadership status. It was always secondary to the BSAF. Although the Joint Conference included peasants, city folk, workers, and intellectuals, they all had entered the situation looking for the students, desiring that the students do one thing or another. So we thought . . . they were more like army advisors . . . we didn't accept the necessity of their leadership.[163]

BSAF leaders expressed the same view toward the Temporary Command. As Wang Chaohua states, "My understanding was that during the period of the Temporary Command, the BSAF and the Command would have an employer–employee relationship, that the Command was kind of a subunit of the BSAF."[164] Similarly, Liang Er relates that "My impression . . . was that as soon as the BSAF returned [from its reorganization], the hunger-strike group would immediately transfer power."[165]

The four core members of the former Hunger Strike Command held yet a third view of the situation. Believing that they had the truest understanding of student interests, these students asserted that the Temporary Command was the preeminent authority at the Square. As Li Lu states: "In my impression, the Joint Conference was a coordinating body, to do support work and give [the Temporary Command] advice. It was not to lead or accompany us."[166] Similarly, former hunger-strike leaders felt that the Temporary Command was not subservient to the BSAF. Li Lu argues that the "Temporary Command was organized because the leadership of the BSAF was ineffective . . . when we had discussed [the issue of] the BSAF, we decided that it should go back and reorganize, and after forty-eight hours we would discuss the question of authority."[167]

For the next two days, May 24–25, these conflicting understandings of organizational hierarchy remained fairly latent, as all had agreed that during this period the Temporary Command would manage the Square, and the BSAF would reorganize. At the Square, the Temporary Command attempted to establish a basic order. Commanders Chai Ling, Li Lu, Zhang Boli, and Feng Congde first gathered a Campground Joint Conference (Yingdi Lianxi Huiyi) to act as a sort of parliamentary decision-making body for students at the Square. The commanders then declared that this body would decide upon all major actions undertaken by the Temporary Command. The Campground Conference was theoretically comprised of representatives from each school group at the Square. However, the Temporary Command leaders admit that it was impossible for them to judge which students were indeed legitimate representatives. As Li Lu relates: "One can definitely ponder the legitimacy [of the Campground Conference], but in this crisis situation, there was no other choice. . . . Its authority was supported by each school, but at the same time, we had no way of supervising [the group's] representative basis."[168] Nonetheless, in the minds of the four core leaders of the Temporary Command, this Campground Conference was now the highest decision-making body of the movement.

Concurrently, the BSAF retreated from the Square to reorganize.[169] First, the group established a new central office at Beida's building no. 41. Next to the meeting room, students set up an equipment room, so that BSAF decisions could be immediately xeroxed and prepared for distribution. Further, in an attempt to enhance its representative legitimacy, the federation directed each school's autonomous committee to hold new elections. Each school was to elect three representatives, to ensure that at least one would always be able to attend meetings. The BSAF also asked each school's committee to provide the federation with a chart of its organizational structure and a list of members from each department. On May 25, the BSAF held its first representative meeting following this reelection process. The meeting went smoothly, with representatives successfully creating a constitution and a new finance department. In the eyes of the BSAF leaders, the federation was now a stable, competent, and legitimate body, and was ready to regain control over the movement.

Prelude to June 4

Given these circumstances, further confusion inevitably erupted in late May, as these various groups and leaders attempted to make and implement decisions regarding the proper "next step" of the movement. Moreover, as martial law continued, fears rose among those involved in the movement. The stakes were now perceived to be extremely high: a bad decision could have devastating consequences for the movement. As Li Lu describes the atmosphere at this time:

> How can we continue the movement? What can be done about the government's hard-heartedness? What can be done about the army? In this period . . . we discussed these things intensely. This was the most emotional period, even more serious than during the hunger-strike period. Contradictions were completely white hot; this seemed to be the final battle. Everyone seemed to be making a final fight against death. We had lost hope, but at the same time our hope had increased.[170]

Indicative of the intensity of emotion at this time, numerous attempts were made to kidnap student leaders and to seize control of the movement through a "coup." As Zhang Lun reports:

> When I returned to the Square [after martial law had begun], someone told me that the security line and broadcast station had been seized by the OSAF.

Every time something like this happened, I would yell, "This won't do—no!" and they would retreat. There were two other relatively important [coup attempts]. On one occasion, some city folk came and seized the broadcast station. . . . On another occasion, a very organized contingent sat neatly at the base [of the broadcast station]. Finally, I told them to leave, and they did.[171]

Similarly, Li Lu relates that, "According to my knowledge, [one particular student] tried to seize power seven or eight times."[172] In addition, attempts were made to kidnap hunger-strike leaders Chai Ling, Li Lu, and Bai Meng.[173] As Bai Meng describes his experience,

On May 26, [OSAF leader] Lian Shengde kidnapped me. He brought a special security contingent and encircled the entire broadcast station, and then three people tied me up. I was extremely angry, but couldn't do anything about it. Lian told me to broadcast that Chai Ling, Li Lu, and Zhang Boli had been dismissed, and that the overall commander of Tiananmen is Lian Shengde.[174]

The movement remained in this confused and tense state through its end on June 4.

On May 27, the Joint Conference held an important meeting to attempt to ameliorate this turbulent situation. Representatives of all of the major factions and groups that had formed during the movement attended, including Wu'er Kaixi, Wang Dan, Liang Er, Feng Congde, Chai Ling, Lao Mu, Zhang Lun, Wang Juntao, Liu Gang, Chen Ziming, Liu Xiaobo, and many others. The meeting lasted from 11:00 A.M. to 5:00 P.M.; in the end, all agreed to withdraw from the Square on May 30.[175] Representatives chose this date because it was ten days after the start of martial law, and thus symbolically would show that the movement had "broken" martial law. Further, representatives agreed that it would be best to "self-end" the movement before the authorities arrived to crush it.[176] Thus, the group decided that, on May 29, Wang Dan, Wu'er Kaixi, and Chai Ling would act as representatives of the Joint Conference and announce the May 30 withdrawal.

However, in the interim, Chai Ling and the other leaders of the Temporary Command reconsidered this decision. Li Lu describes this change of position as follows:

On the May 27, Feng Congde and Chai Ling came back and told me of the proposal to withdraw on the 30th. I asked, "Where did this proposal originate?" [Feng] said, "At the Joint Conference." I asked, "How did the Joint

Conference make this decision? Did they discuss it with the students at the Square? What is the basis of legitimacy at the Square?" After I asked these things, Feng Congde and Chai Ling changed their minds. I asked, "How should we make this decision?" I said, "The highest authority here is the [Campground Conference]; if we make any decision without their opinion, it will be difficult to implement."[177]

Thus, that night the Temporary Command leaders called a meeting of the Campground Conference to discuss the proposal. After much discussion, students voted the proposal down. Instead, they agreed to remain at the Square until June 20.[178]

Unaware of this change of plan, on May 29, Wu'er Kaixi and Wang Dan arrived at the Square to announce the withdrawal. Chai Ling then informed them that she had changed her mind. In consequence, when Wu'er and Wang took the microphone, they "could only say that the Joint Conference 'suggests' that the students withdraw."[179] Immediately after this statement, Li Lu instructed Zhang Boli to announce that the Temporary Command had decided to stay at the Square.[180] With this, the Joint Conference lost much of its legitimacy, for no longer could it claim to represent the opinion of all major groups involved in the movement. Thus confusion over movement leadership continued. Moreover, many students remained at the Square.

On May 30, a prominent member of the Beijing Workers' Autonomous Federation, Shen Yinghan, was kidnapped by Beijing Public Security forces. Shen apparently had been riding his bike near the Beijing Hotel when two policemen emerged from a jeep and dragged him into their vehicle. In the scuffle, Shen dropped two notebooks on the ground. Witnesses later took the notebooks to the BSAF, where it was discovered that the notebooks were inscribed with Shen's name and contained records of the Beijing Workers' Autonomous Federation. The BSAF immediately notified the Workers' Federation and sent representatives to Shen's house. They were told that Shen had never returned home.[181] Upon inquiring about Shen's whereabouts at the Beijing Public Security Bureau, government representatives told the Workers' Federation that it was an illegal organization and that its activities opposed martial law. At the same time, the officials at the bureau claimed to be unaware of Shen's situation.[182]

On June 1, some noted intellectuals and artists made one final effort to influence the students at the Square. That morning, some prominent intellectuals and celebrities began a new hunger strike.[183] They did so because they felt that it was the only possible way to gain legitimacy in the eyes of the students at the Square. In addition, they hoped that their high profiles would pressure the government to refrain from using force to suppress the movement. Yet, at this point it was too late to convince all of the students to leave the Square. Indeed, the Temporary Command already had begun to centralize the remaining students, who were determined to stand together and face the army if and when it ultimately entered the Square. Students who were part of the Campground Conference moved to a group of tents, after which each tent chose a designated leader, so that orders could be quickly passed on to each person.[184]

In fact, at this point it was too late to alter the outcome of the movement: the repression already had begun. As Li Lu reports:

> On June 1, news came . . . that the army was already preparing to enter the city. Although we had no clear idea of what measures [the army] would take after entering, this report was clearly more serious than what we had heard before. [The report] included news that the army . . . had been cut off from connection with the outside world, and was now already coming out [from underground, where the soldiers had been hidden] and was waiting at the street [subway] entrances.[185]

By the morning of June 2, members of the Temporary Command began to receive reports that soldiers had been captured, and weapons confiscated, by students and citizens. The Temporary Command immediately sent representatives to persuade the captors to release the soldiers. The representatives also questioned each captured soldier about his orders. The meaning of these developments was clear. As Li Lu states: "I felt this was the first wave of a large operation . . . a preview. . . . The atmosphere became increasingly intense."[186]

Indeed, Li Lu was correct. Late in the day on June 3, the first reports of bloodshed reached the square. At 9:00 P.M., news arrived that people had been killed at Muxidi, just a few blocks west of Tiananmen. The Temporary Command called upon all remaining students to emerge from the tents and gather at the Monument to the People's Heroes. There, the remaining five thousand students stood shoulder-to-shoulder, holding hands in fear and confusion. As Li Lu expresses his thoughts at the time,

> All decisions were now unclear. We couldn't find the head of our intelligence department. No one knew where the army was, we had no news, we only knew that the army was approaching Tiananmen from three directions, and that the people the army ran into were being killed. We didn't know how long it would be until they arrived. We didn't know what to do. If we withdrew, which roads were deadly? Which were safe?[187]

Finally, those remaining held a voice vote to decide on whether or not to withdraw. Unfortunately, Feng Congde, recalls, "The 'yeas' and 'nays' were equally large."[188] Yet, Feng relates, "I believed there were more who wanted to leave. So we announced withdrawal."[189] With that, the group began to form an orderly line and, led by Feng, Chai, and Li, marched out of the Square. The group soon encountered a contingent of soldiers, who encouraged the group's peaceful retreat.

Thus the movement ended. Within days, authorities distributed a national "wanted" list including the names and photographs of twenty-one of the top students, intellectuals, and workers who had been involved in the movement. Many of these dissidents went into hiding and eventually fled the country. Others were not so lucky. Moreover, hundreds, if not thousands, had been killed during the army takeover. Perhaps most ominously, the official government assessment of the movement remained virtually unchanged from that expressed in the *People's Daily* editorial of April 26. On June 3, the first two pages of *People's Daily* read:

> The April 26 *People's Daily* Editorial . . . explicitly called for taking a clear-cut stance in opposing and halting turmoil. . . . Above all, we want to say that the party and the government have fully confirmed the patriotic passion of the large number of students all along and never said they were stirring up turmoil. . . . [Yet,] under the agitation of an extremely few people, some people have . . . without approval . . . organized marches, demonstrations, sit-ins, and hunger strikes at will, and have occupied Tiananmen Square for a long period of time. . . . Is it possible that all these acts still do not constitute a serious upheaval? Under such a highly chaotic situation . . . if [the government] did not take decisive measures . . . there would be even greater turmoil in the capital and pandemonium in the country.[190]

After the army crackdown, the official interpretation of the movement became even more severe: in reports by various high-ranking leaders after June 4, the movement was described as a "shocking counterrevolutionary rebellion,"[191] which had fomented a "struggle involving the life and death of the party and the state."[192] The movement had not succeeded in altering government policy. Indeed, in its wake, both political and economic reforms regressed while repression increased.

Conclusion

As in the period of April 15–May 10, student behavior from May 11 to June 4 was deeply influenced by the political environment within which the students acted. As it became clear that the CCP was ready to deal with the movement by force, the risks involved in participating in it rose even higher. Consequently, student leaders feared that even a small mistake could have devastating repercussions and became even more hesitant to compromise with or trust one another. This tension-ridden environment made it increasingly difficult for any student leader or organization to maintain order and unity within the student ranks.

The decision of some students to initiate a hunger strike without the sanction of any student movement group only exacerbated these problems. To begin with, this spontaneous act further undermined the authority of the existing student movement groups, particularly as the hunger strikers became the center of public attention. Yet, even more important, the arguments raised by the hunger strikers questioned the right of any organization or majority to enforce its decisions. As the hunger strikers claimed that devotion was the only proof of one's moral rectitude, they argued that those who were willing to sacrifice and risk the most deserved the most power. Moreover, they argued that such risk could be assumed only through an examination of one's individual conscience; an organization or group could never have the right to influence such a personal decision. Consequently, calls for moderation and compromise were branded suspect while more radical actions were viewed with respect.

The resulting organizational mayhem made it difficult for the students to clear the Square before Gorbachev arrived on May 15. When this caused the cancellation of the welcoming ceremony, Deng's fears about the movement were confirmed and the arguments of the conservative faction were buttressed. Zhao's fate, and the movement's fate, became sealed. Having no organizations to rival the party's power, the students' only hope of influencing government policy was through the support of a powerful party leader. Although students fervently argued that they did not wish to become involved in intraparty struggles, in reality they could not expect their action to have any positive result if they did not gain sympathy from within the highest ranks of the party. Moreover, despite their intentions, the students' action was quickly perceived by each party faction as an instrument to enhance its own power.

As a result, it was in the best interests of the students to choose strategies that would work in favor of Zhao's reformist faction. In this endeavor, the most useful were those that would demonstrate that the students were loyal, orderly, and pure in motive. In short, the students stood to gain the most by proving that they did not pose a threat to the party. During the first phase of the movement, students did attempt to employ such strategies. As the risk involved in participating in the movement grew, however, students became increasingly unable to maintain organization and unity. Consequently, their chances of seeing the movement through to a positive end were greatly diminished.

At the same time, the students' concern with remaining separate from nonstudent demonstrators appears to have been a conscious and well-reasoned strategy to lessen the movement's chances of official repression. In contrast to analyses that look to Chinese cultural and historical traditions or to student elitism to explain student exclusivity, virtually all of the interviewees consulted in this project stated that this policy was enforced for strategic reasons. As one influential movement participant explains,

> the security line [separating students and nonstudents] was employed mainly because the students feared government repression. During every democratic movement, the government said it was 'chaotic,' that the demonstrators were 'used' by others. The students had to be very careful, so the government couldn't say they were inducing violence or chaos, or that freedom leads to bad things.[193]

Similarly, another student leader relates:

> in order to control the movement and keep it nonviolent, we needed a security line. From the April 5th Movement [of 1976, when people gathered in Tiananmen Square to demonstrate in memory of the late Premier Zhou Enlai], we learned that the CCP may have plain-clothed agents who can burn a car or something else and later accuse the people in the demonstration. This happened many times in PRC history, and happened again in 1989.[194]

A third student notes that the students' separatism "was a strategic position, so as to not give the government the pretext to suppress the student movement."[195] In the same way, a fourth participant states: "The security line was especially important after martial law. We had to be well-organized in order to protect ourselves. Any small violence could have had huge repercussions."[196] In brief, student leaders in China were well aware that the CCP had searched for pretexts to suppress popular movements in the past and would likely do so again during this movement. To lessen this possibility, students insisted on strict measures to enforce order and student "purity." In other words, the students' strategy was primarily a logical response to the patterns of repression they had experienced in the past.

Certainly, the decision to separate students and nonstudents may also have derived in part from Chinese historical conceptions regarding the superiority of intellectuals. However, when asked to explain the reasoning behind the creation of the security line, none of the students whom I interviewed mentioned this.[197] Indeed, contrary to some claims, most student leaders expressed regret that the students could not unite more fully with other urban groups and stressed that, despite the construction of the security line, efforts were made to contact and work with sympathetic nonstudents.[198] For example, rather than expressing sentiments that workers were somehow unworthy of equal participation in the movement, one student leader states, "it is not true that the students looked down on the workers. To the contrary, all of the students knew that help from the workers was very important. [Our separation from other groups] was just a strategic method, so the government wouldn't repress or unfairly characterize the movement. . . . We had lots of informal connections with workers."[199] In fact, many student activists traveled to factories to mobilize workers. As one student leader relates, "Shida sent student organizers to factories to help organize autonomous worker organizations. We sent five propaganda teams to Capital Steel and some other major factories, and it worked out well."[200] Many documents produced by student groups during the movement also displayed a great concern with mobilizing and uniting with the nonstudent masses. For example, the student-produced *News Bulletin* (*Xinwen Kuaixun*) invited contributions from "Chinese people of all ranks, from all provinces."[201] Similarly, a great many student-produced flyers and pamphlets were addressed to "PRC citizens, fellow countrymen"[202] and closed with exhortations such as "Working brothers, be courageous, stand up. . . . The people must unite if we want peace and stability!"[203] In addition, after helping to investigate the detention of worker-activist Shen Yinghan, the student federation issued a proclamation calling on all students and urban residents to speak, march, and demonstrate: "Urban comrades, today at dawn the Students' Federation resolved that at sunset the Standing Committee will organize a large-scale demonstration of students, workers, citizens, and reporters to support the workers."[204] Moreover, many student leaders note that the BSAF gave funds to the Beijing Workers' Autonomous Federation.[205]

At the same time, student leaders readily admit that representatives of the worker group originally found it difficult to contact representatives of the BSAF due to the strict security lines and pass system at the Square. This, however, does not necessarily denote a bias against workers. Indeed, when students from outside Beijing flocked to the Square in mid-May, they voiced similar complaints. In addition, intellectuals expressed frustration with the students' hesitancy to work with them. Overall, students remained separate from all groups whose devotion or discipline they suspected. And, in the students' view, these "suspect" groups included not only workers but also other students and intellectuals.

The students' particular concern about allying with workers formally was that their lack of organization could bring disorder to the movement. As interviewees note, even the most organized worker group (the Beijing Workers' Autonomous Federation) contained very few individuals, having a core of only some one hundred and fifty activists, whereas tens of thousands of students formed hundreds of formal autonomous organizations.[206] Moreover, the Beijing Workers' Autonomous Federation did not publicly declare its existence until May 13, by which time students already had been organizing and engaging in large-scale marches and demonstrations for a full month.[207]

In addition, students were aware of the party's differential treatment of student and worker activists and feared that greater union with workers could subject students to harsher treatment. Indeed, as in the cases of previous protest activities in the post-Mao period, throughout the spring of 1989 the government made it clear that, although students would be allowed to engage in various sustained protest activities, even the slightest worker activism would be severely punished. No students were arrested from the beginning of the movement on April 15 through its forced end on June 4, despite the fact that they had engaged in a great many illegal activities. Moreover, beginning on May 13 and continuing through June 4, students had occupied Tiananmen Square, to the great embarrassment and annoyance of the Communist Party (particularly during the May 15 visit of Soviet leader Mikhail Gorbachev). Nonetheless, despite continual official threats, no students were arrested. Prior to June 4, the only persons to be arrested were workers. Overall, the government was willing to tolerate sustained, large-scale activities on the part of students, yet crushed even small-scale worker activism. Of course, the students' narrow mobilization strategy may have made it easier for party elites to ignore their demands. Yet, had the students united more fully with the working class, it is likely that the movement would have been repressed much sooner. Or, conversely, the movement might have resulted in revolution—an outcome that was almost equally undesirable in the minds of the reform-oriented students. Thus, the students' decision to create a security line to separate students and nonstudents represented a fundamentally strategic choice based on practical considerations. Moreover, rather than detracting from the movement's overall effectiveness, this strategy may have prolonged its life and increased its chances of eliciting a favorable government response.

Chapter 5

Student Mobilization and Organization in Taiwan, March 1990

During the Month of March movement in Taiwan, students behaved in much the same way as they had in mainland China. In both cases, students relied on peaceful methods of protest, occupied the central square in the capital, and petitioned the government for political reform. More important, students in both movements displayed a great concern with maintaining order. As an outgrowth of this, leaders strictly enforced a separation of student and nonstudent protesters, using a security line (*jiuchaxian*) to delineate different groups. In addition, student leadership and organization in both movements underwent numerous transformations and divisions. In both cases, a subgroup of students spontaneously initiated a hunger strike, circumventing the established student authority of the time and contributing to a radicalizing trend in student actions and proposals. At the same time, notions of charismatic legitimacy arose and came into conflict with representative organizations.

These similarities derived largely from commonalities in the political environment faced by students in both movements. First, at the national level, students were subject to single-party dominance over major policy decisions and the media. Consequently, student leaders consciously and carefully devised strategies to minimize the possibility of official slander. Second, in both China and Taiwan students experienced party penetration of the campus. As a result, student dissidents were aware that their actions were under surveillance and could incur serious punishment. In this atmosphere, student activists felt that trust in their fellow collaborators was crucial. More negatively, students constantly feared that their goals would be betrayed by incompetent or traitorous individuals. In this environment, when a student undertook a more radical action than his or her peers, it was seen as proof of that student's integrity and loyalty to the cause.

Within the framework of these basic similarities, however, there was a difference in the degree to which students in each movement displayed these behaviors. Although student organization underwent almost continual transformation and conflict during both movements, student animosity, fear, and distrust were much greater in China. Consequently, student behavior in Taiwan did not become as disorganized or radical as was the case on the mainland. In part, this difference may be explained by the fact that the movement in Taiwan was of much shorter duration. Had the Month of March movement continued much longer, it is quite likely that these behavioral characteristics would have intensified. At the same time, however, these differences in degree seem to have derived from the greater extent of party control and repression in mainland China.

Of equal interest, despite the basic similarities in student strategy, leadership, and organization, the movement in Taiwan was quite successful in achieving its goals, whereas the movement in China not only failed to fulfill its aims but actually sparked a backlash against political reform. What role did student behavior play in effecting this more favorable outcome in Taiwan? As in China, moderate and orderly student behavior strengthened the position of party reformers, while more disorganized and radical behavior buttressed the conservatives. In both movements, the students' exclusion of nonstudents from their protest ranks decreased the threat posed by the movement and thus aided party reformers. At the same time, in Taiwan, students were better able to maintain unity and order than were students in China. Overall, then, the student movement in Taiwan did more to benefit the more reform-oriented party faction, making a positive outcome more likely. At the same time, though, the students' separatist strategy also may have made it easier for the government to ignore their demands, as Lee Tenghui did until after he was reelected.

Student Organization before March 1990

The history of student protest activities in Taiwan before the spring of 1990 highlights the important ways in which Taiwan's political environment shaped the development of autonomous student organization there, a pattern that would continue throughout the Month of March movement.[1] The earliest instances of student-led protest in Taiwan focused on Kuomintang domination of the university student government and campus media. Yet, the presence of KMT-sponsored "advisors" on campus, as well as the reality of KMT suppression of student protest activity, created an environment of fear and uncertainty among student dissidents. Consequently, early student activists exercised great caution when they engaged in protest activities on campus.

The first major wave of dissident activity involving students in Taiwan was led and dominated by intellectuals and professors. Known as the Protect the Diaoyutai Islands (Bao Diao) movement, this series of events began as a KMT-supported nationalistic response to two international incidents that confronted KMT elites with a crisis of legitimacy. First, in spring 1971, the United States granted management of the disputed Diaoyutai islands to Japan.[2] Second, in October 1971, Taiwan lost its seat in the United Nations, leading to the severance of diplomatic contact with numerous countries. Angered and unsettled by these events, the KMT encouraged intellectuals and students to rise up in protest. Yet the ensuing movement quickly expanded into unanticipated calls for political and social reform. Unwilling to tolerate such dissent, dominant party elites abruptly closed this window of opportunity for protest from below. Upon those whom the KMT was unable or unwilling to co-opt, the party launched a vituperative attack. Activists were accused of causing instability during a time of national crisis, and several were "invited" by security agencies to "come in for a talk." Finally, during the academic break of early 1973, four participants (two students and two intellectuals) were detained by the Investigation Bureau (Diaochaju, the equivalent of the American FBI).[3] Thus, by mid-1973 KMT actions had brought this initial wave of intellectual and student activism to a halt. Moreover, alarmed by the arousal of student passions, the KMT made a concerted effort to absorb and control student activism by putting a renewed emphasis on KMT-sponsored groups on college campuses.[4]

It was not until the late 1970s that students again engaged in any overt form of dissent. Still, as in the early part of the decade, they acted only in support of actions already organized by dissident intellectuals and did not initiate any protest activities on their own. Off campus, around 1977 some independent (*dangwai*) groups began to publish journals and support candidates for political office. Afraid and unable to become active on campus, yet inspired by these dissident groups, some students joined these activities. Whenever authorities uncovered this student participation, however, those involved were quickly punished.[5]

As the 1980s began, student dissidents began to organize their own opposition groups, focusing on "the KMT's system of day-to-day campus domination" that had precluded student-initiated protest action in the 1970s.[6] In particular, early campus activities aimed at ending KMT control over the student government. Although the system differed at each campus, at no university did the student body directly choose the student government chair. Rather, school authorities and/or KMT-sponsored student groups largely monopolized the nomination and selection process. To protest this policy, in December of 1981 students at National Taiwan University (Guoli Taiwan Daxue, or Taida) established the first recorded autonomous student dissident group in Taiwan. Named the Five-Person Small Group (Wuren Xiaozu), the group was exceedingly small, and its members acted with only the greatest caution.[7] As one member of the group relates, "At the very start, we only dared to sneak into classrooms in the very early morning and write 'Popular Election' (*Pu Xuan*) on the blackboard; [also,] in the middle of the night [we would] distribute pamphlets on campus advocating 'Popular Election.' "[8] With the words "popular election," the group was demanding a direct and unqualified popular election of student government representatives.

Soon thereafter, student activists at Taida and other schools prepared various underground student newspapers and journals.[9] Like the Five-Person Small Group, students in these groups sought an expansion of campus democracy and freedom. Yet campus laws restricting public speech, along with the presence of military advisors on campus, made it very difficult for these groups to mobilize and organize the vast majority of the student population.[10] Thus these early student activists could only meet secretly and distribute their literature.

Through the early 1980s, these activities remained sufficiently small-scale and underground as to avoid official punishment. By the mid-1980s, however, student opposition activities began to assume a much more public profile. As with the protests of the early 1980s, many of these actions were concerned with furthering on-campus democracy and freedom. The first such action to achieve widespread recognition occurred in 1984, when a small group of students at Taida distributed copies of a blank newspaper with a small explanation stating that party censorship had blocked the article that had been prepared. Dubbed the White Paper Protest, this action was the first in a series of increasingly provocative student protest activities calling for campus reform.[11]

The next major student protest took place on May 11, 1985, when approximately ten Taida students donned T-shirts printed with the characters "Popular Election" and walked to Taida's main gate, shouting, "Long live popular election!" and "I love Taida!"[12] This public act of defiance entailed great risk for the participants; there could be no mistaking their identity or intent. Indeed, campus authorities swiftly punished them: four students received varying numbers of small and large demerits. Most important, his participation placed activist Lee Wen-chung on probation, as he had now accrued two large and two small demerits. Should he become involved in any future protest activities, Lee faced certain expulsion.[13]

Although Lee remained free of further demerits for the remainder of that academic year, in the spring of 1986 a "computer error" stalled Lee's registration for two months. As he negotiated with campus authorities, they demanded that Lee no longer participate in any "disturbances"; only then would the "error" disappear. After Lee protested this treatment, he received a notice from the army informing him that his obligatory two-year service would begin early; he was to report to duty in six days. Further angered by the military's involvement in the affair, Lee began a hunger strike. Yet the authorities remained intransigent. The day before Lee's scheduled departure, a crowd of students gathered on campus. Uniformed and plainclothes officers quickly arrived on the scene, ordering the students to disperse. When the students resisted, many were beaten, and several were injured. The next day, Lee left Taipei to join the army. Shortly thereafter, campus authorities placed six of Lee's student supporters on probation: one more infraction, and they too would face expulsion.[14]

Despite the awareness of recent repression, beginning in 1985 relatively organized and provocative underground student journals and groups calling for campus reform arose at many of the Taiwan's top universities.[15] Most notably, in the 1986–1987 institution year, students at Taida published a new periodical called *Love of Freedom*. In conjunction with this publication, the students held numerous on-campus speech meetings, ultimately collecting nearly two thousand signatures in support of campus reform. In March, these students formed an orderly procession to the Legislative Yuan, where representatives from the KMT and the newly formed opposition party, the Democratic Progressive Party (DPP), accepted their petition.[16] In the months that followed, KMT domination of the Taida campus relaxed dramatically: KMT party branch offices were withdrawn from campus and a "Love of Freedom" candidate was elected chair of the student government.[17] The new reformist student chair worked doggedly to realize a popular election of the next chair. Despite great pressure and evasiveness on the part of school authorities, he was successful, and in May 1988 Taida's first popular election was held. From this time through the Month of March movement, Taida's student government would be chaired by seasoned reform-oriented activists.

At most other schools, however, the KMT continued to penetrate and dominate student groups and activities.

In summer 1987, students engaged in their first cross-campus protest activity. At this time, students involved in underground journals at various schools gathered to discuss university law reform, ultimately forming the University Law Reform Association (Daxuefa Gaige Lianhehui).[18] The group later sponsored demonstrations at schools throughout Taipei, calling for freedom of speech and the free and direct election of student government officers.[19] None of the major leaders of Taida's Love of Freedom group participated in this new intercampus alliance, however. At Taida, the struggle for campus reform was largely complete; consequently, these former leaders now concentrated their efforts on student government work or social movement participation.[20]

Realizing that student activism had now spread throughout the island, the KMT moved to co-opt and defuse the growing demand for reform. In July, the party announced plans for university law reform, and the Department of Education announced that it would commence research on the issue. The University Law Reform Association took an active part in these debates, holding mass teach-ins and meetings, producing literature, and meeting with legislators.

Yet, once the KMT had taken the initiative, students were able to play only a passive role in the campus reform process. As a result, protest actions revolving around university law reform became increasingly unsatisfying. At the same time, powerful new issues and movements were arising off campus. Most notably, the farmers' movement became highly visible and mobilized. In addition, in June 1987 the DPP began a major push for a complete re-election of the National Assembly. In this context, the University Law Reform Association dissolved, and two new student movement organizations arose. In early 1988, students formed a new cross-campus group, the Democratic Student Alliance (Minzhu Xuesheng Lianmeng). Members were sympathetic to leftist social and economic critiques, and focused on causes such as environmental protection and the livelihood of Taiwan's farmers. At the same time, however, they continued to press for greater educational reform. Concurrently, student activists at Taida, who had been largely uninvolved with the University Law Reform Association and now had little connection with the Democratic Student Alliance, formed a separate cross-campus alliance: the Student Publication Editing Research Group (Xuesheng Kanwu Bianji Yanxihui). This group set reform of the National Assembly as its main goal. In the late spring of 1988, overt tensions between the two groups emerged. On May 4, the Democratic Student Alliance held a sit-in petition protest in front of the Department of Education, demanding more government funding for education.[21] Angered that the Democratic Student Alliance had planned this action without notifying the Student Publication Editing Research Group, the latter publicly stated that it would not participate in the demonstration and questioned the motives behind the Democratic Student Alliance's fund-raising actions.

This series of events helped to crystallize the development of two different student movement "lines": Taida, and "non-Taida" (*fei Taida*). Although some Taida students were associated with the Democratic Student Alliance, and some Democratic Student Alliance groups also participated in actions sponsored by Taida activists, a clear division between these two lines had now emerged. In addition, a third group of student dissidents actively worked with the DPP, focusing on the issue of Taiwan's independence.

Despite divisions among these groups, on September 28, 1989, students from all activist circles participated in the largest student demonstration to date. On this day, over two thousand students took to the streets of Taipei, marching to the Department of Education and the Legislative Yuan to "protest university law, and build a new university."[22] After this large demonstration march, campus authorities interrogated many participants. At Taiwan Normal University, two student leaders received one large demerit each.[23]

Although students were punished for these activities, and despite the fact that many student groups and journals were forced to disband, the government did loosen campus restrictions somewhat.[24] For the most part, this loosening followed President and Party Premier Chiang Ching-kuo's decision in 1987 to terminate martial law, a decree that had been in effect since 1949. With this change in national policy, students generally began to enjoy increased freedom of expression and assembly on campus.[25] By the late 1980s, the student government at several schools had fallen under the control of non-KMT, pro-reform students. Most prominently, non-KMT students gained a majority in the student assembly at Taida and Cheng-chih University. Further, in both the 1988–1989 and the 1989–1990 academic years, non-KMT student activists won the chairmanship of Taida's student government.[26] Under this reformist student leadership, the student government at Taida and several other schools pressed for further campus reform. These non-KMT student government officers also developed close ties with reformist professors.[27] As was the case in mainland China, early student activists often sought the advice of these professors, frequently inviting them to give lectures and lead discussions sponsored by the organization.[28] Still, at most other institutions the student government remained firmly in the hands of the KMT, and the campus environment was little changed. Thus, as the movement of 1990 began, student contingents from different schools were emerging from very dissimilar experiences and backgrounds.

These divisions and differences inhibited sustained cooperation among reform-oriented students. Perhaps most important is the fact that these distinctions hindered communication among student activists of different groups, as students in one group typically did not develop close personal relationships with students of other groups. As in mainland China, this lack of familiarity bred a lack of trust among students belonging to different groups. Furthermore, in an environment of continued KMT and military presence on most campuses, student activists were hesitant to cooperate with students with whom they were not well acquainted. Although KMT suppression of student protest activities had become much less extreme by the late 1980s, students remained fearful and uncertain of the consequences of their actions and leery of party infiltration. Also, the different foci of these various student groups inhibited sustained cooperation among them. As the Month of March movement progressed in the spring of 1990, these realities would cause great tension and instability in both organization and leadership.

The Month of March Movement

The Month of March movement formally began on March 16, 1990, but was preceded by a one-day student sit-in in front of KMT headquarters on March 14. Existing student movement divisions clearly influenced the process leading up to this one-day protest as well as events during the protest itself. Most interestingly, the student organizers of the March 14 event were experienced activists with ties to the reform-oriented student government at Taida and established social movement groups, while the initiators of the March 16 demonstrations at the Chiang Kai-shek Memorial were mostly first- and second-year students with little or no experience of activism. When the Taida-based organizers of the March 14 demonstration joined the later protest at the Memorial, conflict emerged. As student activists from other circles also entered the movement, organizational difficulties only increased. In addition, the violence that occurred during the March 14 protest impressed upon the students the risk involved in their action and added to their uncertainty regarding the likely government response to their activities.

As noted in Chapters 1 and 2, the protests of March 1990 arose as a response to the coming National Assembly election of a new president. As the March 21 selection date approached, many citizens were angered and alarmed by the factional struggle between more traditional KMT elites and the reformist Taiwanese Lee Teng-hui. On the one hand, many feared renewed KMT domination by conservative and military party elites (particularly Lee Huan and Hao Po-ts'un). On the other, the coming National Assembly's power to choose the president stood out as concrete evidence that, despite recent political reforms, the KMT still reigned supreme.

Concerned with these issues, on March 8, Taida's reformist student government chair, a seasoned female activist named Fan Yun, invited representatives of some social movement groups to meet at a teahouse to discuss possible protest actions.[29] As the existing method of choosing the president did not directly reflect the opinions of the people of Taiwan, students argued that the group should work to stop the current election and demand that it be held only after the convocation of a meeting on constitutional reform. Accordingly, some students proposed that a one-day demonstration be held on March 14 in front of KMT headquarters. This date fell on a Wednesday, the day scheduled for a meeting of the party's Central Committee.[30] When the nonstudent groups did not agree to this proposal, the students declared that they would hold the demonstration anyway.

Despite this disagreement, the meeting participants concurred on a slogan to express their unanimous opinion regarding the current political system: "Return Political Rights to the People, Rebuild Constitutional Politics" ("Huanzheng Yumin, Chongjian Xianzheng").[31] Through this slogan, these groups wished to stress that their opposition to the election should not be construed as merely an expression of support for Lee Teng-hui in his battle against the conservative faction; rather, they wanted to display their dissatisfaction with the current undemocratic system of presidential selection.[32] Before the meeting closed, the attendees agreed that, although only students would participate in and organize the March 14 demonstration, representatives of all the groups would hold a press conference to announce the agreed-upon slogan.

Soon thereafter, the political atmosphere changed. Under the coordination of Lee Huan and Hao Po-ts'un, on March 9 nonmainstream presidential candidate Lin Yang-kang withdrew his candidacy. The next morning, alternative vice-presidential candidate Chiang Wei-kuo also announced his withdrawal.[33] With this, the KMT factional conflict over the presidency appeared to have been resolved. Many members of the populace breathed a sigh of relief, content that reform-minded Lee Teng-hui would remain president.[34] In this new atmosphere, on the night of March 9 Taida professor and Taiwan Professors' Association member Chang Ch'ung-tung sent an emergency message to Taida's student government representatives, asking the students to cancel the planned demonstration.[35]

On the afternoon of March 10, members of virtually every student activist group in Taipei, as well as the various social movement groups that had attended the March 8 teahouse meeting, assembled to discuss the new situation.[36] They agreed that, despite the apparent "victory" of Lee Teng-hui, the constitutional system remained problematic. In particular, they pointed to the provision stipulating that a complete reelection of the entire National Assembly would occur only after China's reunification. Yet, despite this basic agreement, the various groups could not reach a consensus on a course of action.[37] Many moderate students and social movement groups worried that a large-scale action might upset the delicate victory Lee Teng-hui had won over KMT conservatives. At the same time, members of the Democratic Student Alliance argued that a concerted student action to oppose the constitution would require prior grass-roots education and mobilization.[38]

The following day, March 11, Taipei student activists of all circles met again. Although virtually all of the groups reaffirmed that they would not participate in the planned March 14 sit-in, a handful of students (mostly affiliated with Taida's student government) declared their determination to go ahead with the demonstration. Despite this disagreement, all reaffirmed their support of the previously chosen slogan.[39] They also agreed on Four Big Demands: (1) reelect the National Assembly; (2) abolish the old constitution; (3) present a schedule for political reform; and (4) convene a National Affairs Conference to discuss political reform.[40] Following the meeting, the group held a press conference at the Legislative Yuan to announce the slogan and demands.[41] Later, those who remained determined to stage the March 14 demonstration formed a temporary Taida Student Democratic Activities Alliance (Taida Xuesheng Minzhu Xingdong Lianmeng). On March 13, these students gathered in front of Taida's main gate. There, participants who were also members of the KMT burned their party cards.[42]

On the morning of March 14, approximately one hundred students gathered near the KMT central offices.[43] As the students approached the entrance to the headquarters, however, were blocked by police. Between 8:00 A.M. and 11:30 A.M., the demonstrators clashed with police four times. Finally, at 11:50 A.M., the students broke through the blockade, promptly posting banners inscribed with the designated slogan and the Four Big Demands.[44] At this point, police stopped confronting the students. As the day wore on, approximately three hundred joined the protest, which remained peaceful. Leaders of various social movement groups also visited and expressed support. Buoyed by the high spirits of the demonstrators, the original protestors considered remaining in front of the offices or moving to the Chiang Kai-shek Memorial for a long-term sit-in. Ultimately, however, they

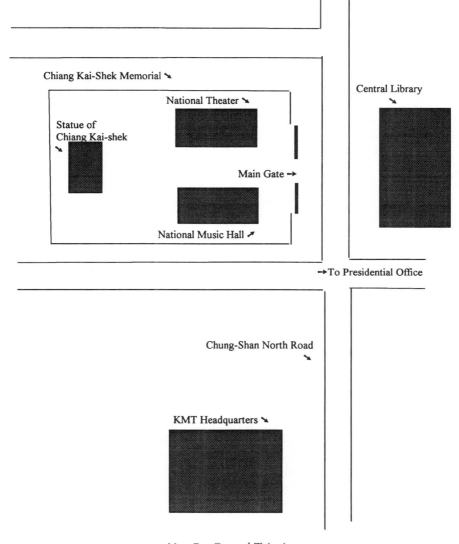

Map 3   Central Taipei

decided that they were not prepared to begin a more sustained action. Thus, at 5 P.M. the demonstration leaders instructed the crowd to disperse.[45]

The general public reacted to the demonstration quite favorably. Although the protest was not covered on television or in the country's largest newspapers—*China Times* (*Zhongguo Shibao*) and *United Daily News* (*Lian-*

hebao)—several smaller newspapers did present fairly objective accounts of the action. Indeed, news of the demonstration appeared on the front page of *Liberty Times (Ziyou Shibao)*. Reflecting the paper's positive description of the demonstration, the caption under a large photo of student demonstrators read, "To protest the illegitimacy of the National Assembly and the presidential election system, nearly one hundred Taida students held a peaceful sit-in at KMT headquarters yesterday."[46] The *Independence Evening News (Zili Wanbao)* and the *China Daily News (Zhonghua Ribao)* also ran relatively unbiased articles on the demonstration.[47]

Perhaps the most important explanation of this positive response is that, during the day of March 14, KMT factional conflict reemerged, and Lee Teng-hui's appointment to the presidency again appeared uncertain.[48] At the same time, news leaked of a new National Assembly proposal to give the elderly representatives a substantial pay raise. This combination of a successful demonstration and an atmosphere of renewed tension regarding the presidential election and the National Assembly prompted concerned students to engage in further protest. At the same time, however, the police presence at the March 14 demonstration impressed upon the students the risk involved in their action. In this atmosphere, the Month of March movement was permeated by conflict among students of different backgrounds and persuasions.

March 16–18

The Month of March movement did not begin as a result of the organized efforts of the March 14 demonstrators, or any preexisting student activist group. Rather, on March 16, three first- and second-year Taida students with little activist experience started the demonstrations spontaneously. Indeed, most reform-oriented student groups did not formally join the action until March 19. Yet the events of the first three days set the mood of the rest of the movement. To begin with, at least three instances of real or threatened police suppression occurred, spurring the student protestors to establish an organizational structure. At the same time, the atmosphere of fear and uncertainty engendered tensions within this structure, leading to various organizational alterations. In addition, this anxiety led students to establish boundaries between students and nonstudents in an effort to maintain order and avoid government repression.

After the March 14 sit-in at the KMT offices, a second-year Taida student named Chou Ke-jen shared a drink with two friends, at which time they decided to embark upon an open-ended protest beginning March 16.[49] Subsequently, they called eight or nine other close friends, mostly from Taida and the Taipei Technical Institute (Taibei Gongji Xueyuan), asking them to join the action. Like Chou, these students were mostly beginning university students and held no important positions in any activist organizations.[50] Later, Chou met with Taida student government chair Fan Yun, telling her that a protest action must be initiated as soon as possible, and that he and some others were determined to see it through. Leery of such an unorganized action, and concerned that no experienced student activist seemed to know Chou very well, Fan Yun entreated him to wait until a meeting could be held where all interested groups could discuss and plan such an action. Chou, however, refused to wait.[51]

That night (March 15) Taida student government leaders and social movement group representatives again met to discuss possible plans to follow the March 14 demonstration. At the meeting, Fan Yun announced Chou's planned action, whereupon the group engaged in a lengthy debate. Finally, the Taida student government decided that it would not immediately join or formally sanction Chou's planned sit-in. Rather, the group would plan an united school action to begin on the nineteenth, which would give it sufficient time to mobilize and organize participants. At the same time, attendees agreed that under the principle of "camaraderie," Taida's student government would support those who chose to act before the nineteenth.[52] Thus, similarly to the decision of the All-Beijing Secondary Schools Autonomous Federation, the Beida Autonomous Union, and the Shida Autonomous Union to support the hunger strike despite their disagreement over the timeliness of the strategy, the existing student groups in Taiwan were forced to support the actions of the more radical student activists. In both cases, student organizations realized that a failure to voice support for the actions taken by these more "courageous" and "dedicated" students could result in a great loss of organizational legitimacy.

Consequently, at 5:00 P.M. on March 16, Chou and a handful of his friends sat down in front of the main gate of the Chiang Kai-shek Memorial in Taipei. Each wore a headband bearing a slogan such as "Dissolve the National Assembly" ("Jiesan Guoda"), "If the Old Thieves Do Not Fall, Democracy Will Not Come" ("Laozei Budao Minzhu Bulai"), and "Abolish the Temporary Provisions" ("Fachu Linshi Tiaokuan"). They also posted a long cloth banner, reading "Compatriots, how can we continue to bear the oppression of 700 Emperors?"[53] Although the demonstration had not been organized or sanctioned by any group, the demonstrators shouted the Four Big Demands that had been agreed upon at the meeting of March 11.[54]

As the evening wore on, more students arrived to join the demonstration, and hundreds of city folk came to observe and make donations. At the same time, more seasoned student activists (mostly from Taida) traveled to the Memorial, asking Chou and his friends to explain their plans. As these older and more experienced students were not acquainted with Chou and the others, they were somewhat suspicious of the younger students' motives and competence. The older students eventually left, but informed the demonstrating students that a meeting would be held the following day to discuss Taida's planned action for the nineteenth.[55]

At dusk, various social movement group leaders and six DPP representatives visited the square to voice their support of the students. A handful of reporters also appeared.[56] As it grew increasingly late, the protestors prepared to spend the night at the entrance of the Memorial.[57] This would mark the first overnight demonstration to occur in Taiwan. Yet the television stations made no mention of the demonstration in their evening news reports.[58]

As the night passed, an atmosphere of fear and uncertainty surrounded the demonstrators. Shortly before midnight, a student organizer suddenly arose, announcing a rumor that the police would come to clear out the demonstrators at midnight. Upon hearing this news, a handful of students and citizens ran to the square security office to investigate. As midnight neared, the atmosphere became increasingly tense.

Midnight passed, and there was no sign of any security forces.[59] Relieved but still frightened, the inexperienced students began to discuss the need for organization. As the demonstration had started and grown spontaneously, the movement had no clear plan of action. To resolve this problem, Chou and the other initiators announced that each school group should select representatives to attend an organizational meeting. In the middle of the night, a total of thirty-five student representatives met, forming what was later called the Inter-Campus Conference (Xiaoji Huiyi). After a long discussion regarding the goals, strategies, and organization of the movement, the students decided to establish a Five-Person Working Group to meet every five hours to assess the situation.[60]

As dawn came to the square on March 17, the atmosphere continued to be charged, as students again were reminded of the potential risks involved in their action. Early in the morning, military police emerged near the Presidential Office. After arranging in formation, the troops proceeded to the gate of the Memorial, where they noisily awakened the sleeping students and city folk. Although the troops used no force against the students, the demonstrators were frightened.[61]

In this tense atmosphere, on the afternoon of the seventeenth, Chou left the Memorial to attend the meeting of preexisting student movement groups, asking them to come to the square to help. Though these more experienced student leaders remained adamant that a large-scale action should not be taken until the nineteenth, they agreed to move their meeting to the Memorial. There, a new session of the Inter-Campus Conference was convened. As the more seasoned student activists were well known among those at the square, they naturally were chosen to serve as their schools' representatives in the conference. As the meeting began, members of the Five-Person Working Group, apparently frightened by the rumor of the previous night and the military action earlier that morning, complained that they were unable to handle all of the tasks involved in controlling and protecting the demonstrators. As a solution, attendees decided to create a new Policy Group to be responsible for planning all activities at the square. The membership of this new leading group included both inexperienced and experienced student activists. Further, among the latter, persons from both Taida and non-Taida dissident circles were present.[62] As its first order of business, the Policy Group established a Command Center to oversee organization and policy implementation, and six "departments": the Conference Group, the General Affairs Group, the Propaganda Group, the Security Team, the Mobilization Group, and the Finance Group.[63]

Almost immediately, however, prior student divisions became apparent. Most notably, students from Ch'ing-hua University who previously had been associated with the Democratic Student Alliance insisted that student demands include a call for economic as well as political reform. Consequently a heated debate broke out concerning the demand for a "democratic reform timetable." Ultimately, the Ch'ing-hua students succeeded in persuading the others to change the fourth Big Demand to read: "Propose a timetable for political and *economic* reform" (italics added).[64] Nonetheless, the movement's leadership remained divided on the issue.

That afternoon and evening, the movement received a shot of energy. During the afternoon, Taida president Sun Chen visited the square with a number of school officials, affirming the students' behavior and assuring them that they would not be punished for their actions. As Sun had previously worked to suppress student movement activities, the students were emboldened by his words.[65] At the same time, however, the rumored and actual military action of the previous night and morning continued to worry them. The students remained uncertain of the repercussions of their actions.

That evening, Policy Group member Liao Su-chen announced that the students and city folk should prepare to spend the night. At the same time, Liao expressed the hope that the students and masses would sleep in separate areas, explaining that "It is very important to us to establish student autonomy."[66] Thus the group established a "Supporting Friends Sit-In Area" to receive nonstudent participants.[67] From this point on, a strict separation of student and nonstudent protestors would be maintained, just as in the movement of 1989 in China.

At dusk, Lee Teng-hui made a televised speech, urging all ranks of society to face the coming election with a calm and rational attitude.[68] Although this message served as something of a warning to the demonstrators, a later TV broadcast injected them with new hope. The 7:30 P.M. TV evening news included a report on the sit-in—the first televised report on the student movement to appear in Taiwan. Even more inspiring, the report was quite positive, noting the "social power of the collective movement at the square."[69] The report invigorated the demonstraters, drawing many more participants and onlookers. By 10:00 P.M., over two hundred students had joined the sit-in, and close to a thousand city folk surrounded them. Citizen donations also grew; by the end of the night, students had collected over NT$63,000 (approximately US$2,500). In addition, the demonstrators enjoyed a visit by singing star Ch'en Ming-chang and received regards from numerous elected officials affiliated with the DPP.[70] Approximately one hundred students spent the night at the square.

Back at the campuses, students and professors worked to support and expand the movement. At Taida, Ch'ing-hua University, Ch'eng-kung University, and other schools throughout Taiwan, professors met to promote an all-school united action on March 19, calling for sit-ins and a class boycott.[71] Professors involved in Taida's branch of the Taiwan Professors' Association proposed a one-week class boycott. The week would be called Democracy Education Week and would feature lectures and discussion at the Memorial.[72] As word of these plans spread, students at Taida, Wen-hua University, Fu-jen University, Taiwan Normal University, and Yang-ming University, as well as other institutions, gathered to plan a large-scale mobilization effort to accompany the professors' proposed action.[73] Simultaneously, the DPP began to mobilize its supporters for a mass meeting to be held on March 18 at the square.

Early in the morning on the eighteenth, the movement organization changed again. As DPP officials informed student leaders of their planned mass meeting that day, and as the number of student participants grew, the Inter-Campus Conference discussed how to maintain safety and order. In particular, the Policy Group feared that students would be dispersed, or might be vulnerable to danger during the DPP mass meeting. Finally, the students agreed that during the potentially chaotic day of the eighteenth it would be best to establish a single leader, so as to avoid confusion. Feeling, however, that it would be too exhausting for a single person to hold this position for an entire twenty-four-hour period, the group chose three over-all commanders, each to act as the movement's leader during a portion of the day. Accordingly, Liao Su-chen became the morning commander (3:00 A.M.–12:00 P.M.); Fan Yun the afternoon commander (12:00–8:00 P.M.); and Lu Ming-chou the night commander (8:00 P.M.–3:00 A.M.). The group also decided that movement initiator Chou Ke-jen would remain the move-ment's external spokesperson.[74]

After the meeting, Propaganda Group member He Tung-hong announced the agreed-upon policy regarding the DPP meeting, stating: "As the DPP has planned a large-scale activity this afternoon, the Command Center has de-cided to remain separate from DPP activities and remain in separate areas; students will be an autonomous movement, and will not enter mass actions. Most media reports on the student movement have been affirmative; we ask the masses behind the security line to please sit; you do not have to come only to look at the excitement."[75] Morning commander Liao Su-chen then continued to explain the group's policy, stating, "Last night, there were con-stant rumors of dispersal, and that the protest would be ineffective, dampen-ing the spirits of the students; to dispel these rumors, we must maintain four principles: self-determination, separation, peace, and order."[76]

Also on March 18, the Propaganda Group distributed a "Square Bul-letin" ("Guangchang Tongxun") around the square. The bulletin included a chart of the new movement organization and provided the names and shifts of the three designated overall commanders. In addition, it outlined two "rules of action": (1) donations should cease, as the main need of the move-ment was now to increase the number of student and citizen participants; and (2) students should maintain a peaceful and idealistic attitude, and act in close coordination with the Command Center.[77]

At 12:30 P.M., Fan Yun assumed command. Around that time, the DPP mass meeting began. A crowd of over ten thousand DPP supporters gathered in front of the National Music Hall, where DPP organizers had erected a sound system. Just outside the main gate of the Memorial, the student pro-testers remained seated.[78] Throughout the afternoon, student representatives came to the front of the student sit-in area to speak. Inside the square, various DPP personages spoke to the crowd gathered in front of the Music Hall. As DPP leaders spoke, the crowd often became quite boisterous. However, the two gatherings did not compete with one another, and the integrity of the student sit-in area was respected. Indeed, whenever a student began to address the student protesters, DPP speakers remained silent until the student speaker had finished.[79] In addition, two DPP members came to the student area with a donation of NT$20,000 (approximately US$800), which had been collected from the crowd at the mass meeting. Student leaders at first refused the offer, but upon the insistence of the DPP visitors ultimately accepted. Around 5:30 P.M., most of the DPP meeting attendees formed a long procession, marching out of the square and along Chung-shan North Road.[80] As the DPP contingent marched, a number of violent clashes erupted when security forces confronted the protestors.[81]

Rather than being overrun by the great number of people attending the DPP mass meeting, the students succeeded in maintaining a separate presence at the Memorial. Moreover, this separation made it possible for them to avoid any connection with the violence that broke out during the DPP march. Importantly, this strategy helped to convince KMT party elites that the students should not be dealt with harshly. As reported in the *China Times* on May 20, the Taipei municipal police department announced that it would not interfere with the student protest, as it had been given the following instructions by Lee Teng-hui: "(1) Student safety must be protected. (2) Violence must not erupt. (3) Student and DPP protestors must remain separate."[82]

At the same time, the DPP's support and deference toward the students further bolstered their morale, attracting greater numbers to join the sit-in. To deal with this increase in participants, at 5:00 P.M. square commander Fan Yun announced that each school should select a representative to report news to the Command Center, so that the Command Center could provide movement updates every half-hour. At 9:00 P.M., Lu Ming-chou assumed command.[83]

Yet, although it appeared that the movement organization was becoming stabilized and strengthened, this was not the case, for student leaders were growing increasingly distrustful of one another.[84] That night, further conflict arose in the organization. Shortly after 9:00 P.M., students convened another Inter-Campus Conference meeting. At the gathering, school representatives demanded a larger role in policy-making, expressing dissatisfaction with the autonomous decision-making power held by the Policy Group. Many members of the Policy Group, however, lacked confidence in the competence and loyalty of the larger assembly. As one Policy Group member states, "[the Inter-Campus Conference] had students from anywhere; we didn't know who they were, or if we could trust them."[85] After an exhaustively long discussion, students finally agreed that the Inter-Campus Conference would act as the highest policy-making body of the movement.[86] The Policy Group hereafter would act only to execute decisions made by the conference.[87]

Adding to the conflict at the meeting, a second intense debate arose after one delegate proposed the initiation of a hunger strike as a method of increasing pressure on the government and hastening an official response. After a long and heated debate, representatives voted. The result was a stalemate. The motion did not pass, and the group remained divided on this important issue.[88]

Shortly after the meeting, the atmosphere at the Memorial again became tense. At 10:00 P.M., Huang Chen-t'ai, head of the Department of Higher Education, came to the square, suggesting to commander Lu Ming-chou that, regardless of whether or not the demonstrators were driven from the Memorial, students should maintain a distance from the nonstudent masses. Interpreting Huang's statement as a warning, Lu directed students to prepare for a possible government effort to disperse the demonstrators. Soon thereafter, a police contingent appeared on Chung-shan North Road, near one of the walls of the Memorial. A second contingent of troops moved toward the main gate of the Memorial. The Command Center announced that students should draw close together. The students remained silent for a time, then sang a song. Finally, the police retreated. Later, the Command Center sent some students to the city police station, where they received assurance that the police would not again approach the student demonstrators.[89] To help reduce miscommunication, student and police representatives agreed to meet once every hour.[90]

That night Lee Teng-hui held a meeting at his private residence, where he instructed Huang Chen-t'ai to visit the square again the following morning. There, he would read an appeal on behalf of Lee, asking the students to end the movement.[91] At midnight, rain began to fall. Soon thereafter, students temporarily moved to the covered area outside the National Theater to seek shelter for the night.

Late that night, the Inter-Campus Conference gathered again. Although the group now held the highest authority within the movement, its representatives did not trust one another. Perhaps most important, many pro-KMT students and professors had now entered the square. Indeed, student contingents from Yang-ming University, T'an-ch'uan University, Tung-hai University, and Ch'ing-hua University were dominated by student officials in still KMT-dominated student governments. Moreover, student leaders discovered that within the Ch'ing-hua contingent were two professors who served as KMT representatives on campus.[92] The motives of all of these pro-KMT participants is not clear; however, at least one such student admitted to me, "I was a member of the KMT and participated in the movement simply to hinder its ability to oppose the KMT."[93] Thus, leaders had valid reasons to suspect infiltration by KMT supporters hoping to undermine the movement.

This fear made it difficult for the movement organization to reach decisions. For example, at the start of this meeting of the Inter-Campus Conference, the chair (Taiwan Normal University student Ch'ai Ching-chih) announced that formal rules of conduct would be used. Many students in the conference, however, had not previously attended meetings of the student government or other student groups and were unfamiliar with these rules. Consequently, some of these students suspected that Ch'ai Ching-chih's intimate knowledge of, and preference for, these rules demonstrated that she was a KMT plant.[94] In this atmosphere, students reached few substantive decisions. First, the conference reasserted its status as the highest decision-making body. Second, the group discussed a proposal to set up a table to collect student votes regarding a possible hunger strike. After a long discussion, the proposal was shelved. Third, the group discussed the Four Big Demands and the appropriate length of the protest yet reached no consensus. Finally, the group granted the Policy Group the power to deal with mundane decision-making matters, as it had become clear that the Inter-Campus Conference was unable to reach timely decisions.[95]

Hunger Strike and "Democracy Education Week"

The next phase of the movement began on March 19. On this day, preexisting student movement groups formally joined the movement, and professors entered the square in force, formally beginning "Democracy Education Week." In addition, ten students spontaneously initiated a hunger strike. With the confluence of these events, the number of students, professors, and city folk at the square rose dramatically. Consequently, tensions within the movement organization increased. As it was enlarged to accommodate the new participants, the Inter-Campus Conference became increasingly paralyzed because students were hesitant to trust representatives with whom they were not acquainted. As it was now known for a fact that many pro-KMT students and professors were at the square, the movement leadership became increasingly fearful of infiltration. In addition, the spontaneous start of the hunger strike sapped the legitimacy of the movement organization.

On the morning of March 19, the students received their first official government response. At 10:00 A.M., Huang Chen-t'ai arrived at the square to read Lee's plea to the students. The statement read: "We know what you are concerned with, and I pledge to all that the government will hasten the pace of reform, and that we definitely will give everyone a clear explanation, soon. The days are very cold, please take care of your health, return home, and return to school soon."[96] The Policy Group discussed Lee's statement and decided that it was not sufficiently clear or concrete. Later, the group held a press conference to announce formally that the students were not satisfied with Lee's response.[97]

Meanwhile, outside the organizational structure of the movement, a handful of students undertook an independent protest action. Despite the fact that the Inter-Campus Conference had failed to reach a consensus on the idea of a hunger strike, Tung-hai University student Fang Lee-ting, joined by nine others who were not a part of the movement leadership, initiated a hunger strike. On the afternoon of March 19, the hunger-striking students announced their "Hunger Strike Statement," which read:

> The student sit-in at the square is already entering its fourth day . . . the students' Four Demands . . . have still received no clear response. In order to avoid inaction and the neglect of public opinion by the rulers, who will forcefully choose the president on the 21st, we have decided to begin a hunger strike. . . . We demand that Mr. Lee Teng-hui and Mr. Lee Huan publicly announce a government reform plan and reform timetable before the 21st. . . . Our hunger strike will end after the government accedes to our demands. If the government violates public opinion and forcefully chooses the president, we will continue to hunger strike until the last student leaves the square.[98]

Thus, like the case of 1989 in mainland China, a hunger strike began without the formal sanction of the organization purportedly in control of the movement. In both cases, the hunger-striking students felt that the future of the movement was so important that majority decisions could not be allowed to block the implementation of "correct" strategies. Moreover, as in the movement of 1989, this action undermined the legitimacy of the existing organization, as both official and popular attention suddenly became riveted on the hunger-striking students who had decided to make the "ultimate sacrifice" for the movement.[99] Consequently, just as the Beida Autonomous Union, the Shida Autonomous Union, and the All-Beijing Secondary Schools Autonomous Federation were belatedly forced to announce their support of the hunger strikers in 1989, so the Inter-Campus Conference soon announced that, despite its decision not to formally sanction the action, it would support the efforts of the hunger strikers. Otherwise, the organization risked a complete loss of authority over the direction of the movement. Indeed, from this point on, the Inter-Campus Conference could not claim authority over all of the students at the square. As in the movement of 1989 in China, leaders of the intercampus organization were forced to include hunger-strike representatives in all communications with government officials.[100]

Yet, at the same time, the hunger strike did not lead to a power struggle between the hunger strikers and the existing intercampus organization, as occurred in 1989 in China. In Taiwan, the hunger strikers did engage in autonomous activities, such as drafting statements, and did make separate decisions regarding when to leave the square. However, unlike the movement of 1989 in China, the hunger strikers in Taiwan did not overtly challenge or compete with the existing organizational structure for control of the overall movement. Perhaps the most important reason for this difference is that, in the Taiwanese case, none of the preexisting student leaders joined the hunger strike. Indeed, even those members of the Inter-Campus Conference who originally voted in favor of a hunger strike did not participate in the action after it spontaneously began. Further, the students who joined the hunger strike displayed little interest in competing with the Inter-Campus Conference. Rather, the hunger strikers seemed content to use their status simply to increase the pressure upon the government to respond to the students' demands. Thus, although great tension and conflict existed within the Inter-Campus Conference during the Month of March movement, and although the initiation of the hunger strike threatened the legitimacy of the organization, these conflicts never transformed into an actual split in leadership, or to the creation of competing organizations, as was the case in 1989.[101]

Nonetheless, for the duration of the movement, the hunger strikers would be seen as the "moral leadership" of the movement.[102] As one member of the Inter-Campus Conference describes the situation: "We supported the hunger strikers, but . . . we worried about them, because we feared that they could complicate the movement. . . . The hunger strikers easily could have led the movement in the direction that they wanted, because they had the moral high ground . . . when a government representative would come to the square, he had to go to the hunger strikers first."[103] As word of the hunger strike traveled across the country, new students and onlookers flocked to the Memorial. Shortly after noon, the number of students suddenly shot past a thousand. By dusk, over three thousand students had joined the sit-in.[104]

Meanwhile on March 19, the Inter-Campus Conference and activist students still stationed on the campuses began to implement Democracy Education Week. Early in the morning, all school groups at the square sent representatives back to their campuses to promote a class boycott and to recruit students to come to the square to attend substitute "classes."[105] In the afternoon, approximately twenty professors arrived at the gate of the Memorial, where they formally began to lecture and lead discussions on democracy and reform. Shortly thereafter, rain began to fall, and members of the Policy Group decided to relocate permanently inside the square. But first, student leaders sought out DPP representatives at the Memorial. (Although the DPP was no longer holding its mass meeting, many DPP leaders and supporters remained at the square to discuss and protest the election.) Representatives of the two groups agreed to a policy of mutual noninterference while they shared the interior of the Memorial. At 3:00 P.M., students began to move to the sheltered area beneath the National Theater.[106] Shortly thereafter, the Working Group erected a lighting and sound system in front of the theater.[107]

As dusk fell, the weather cleared. Subsequently, the student protestors reorganized, trying to maintain order despite the swelling number of students and city folk. Student leaders remained on the platform at the top of the stairs to the theater and asked the ordinary student demonstrators to relocate to the open area at the base of the stairs. Leaders also created two "security lines:" one to separate the student-leader area from the common-student area, and the other to separate the student sit-in area from nonstudent onlookers and demonstrators. Members of the Security Team enforced the lines. To enter either the student or student-leader area, one had to present credentials to prove one's status.[108] Through these methods, student leaders hoped to ensure that the demonstration would remain orderly, peaceful, and free of infiltration, thus thwarting potential government charges to the contrary.

During the evening and night of the nineteenth, student representatives spoke to the crowd from the "stage" that had been erected in front of the National Theater. Shortly after 6:00 P.M., some well-known singers arrived at the square, leading the demonstrators in songs.[109] With this performance student spirits rose to a new peak.[110] Yet the evening was not completely without tension. At 10:30 P.M., protestors heard an explosion outside the student sit-in area. The students became agitated and disorderly, but the security contingent quickly calmed them.[111]

In this atmosphere, late in the night on the nineteenth, the movement organization changed once again. Expressing their exhaustion, the Policy Group retired. The Inter-Campus Conference chose seven new members to replace them.[112] In addition, the Inter-Campus Conference formally established a Graduate Student Consulting Small Group and a Professor Consulting Group to regularize consultation with these two sectors.[113]

Throughout the next day, March 20, tension and uncertainty permeated the square. At dawn, a rumor spread that Lee Huan was coming. The Policy Group sent students to inquire about the rumor, yet could not substantiate it.[114] Rumors also traveled that the conservative faction was planning a coup against Lee Teng-hui. Moreover, talk of dissent and conflict among student leaders circulated. To begin, many were leery of the fluidity of the movement organization. The initiation of the hunger strike only further undermined its authority. Further, as news of KMT infiltration traveled, distrust spread among school groups and among students of different prior student and social movement groups. In this atmosphere, "proving" one's loyalty became increasingly important. Consequently, one Policy Group member states, the atmosphere became a "balance of terror. . . . [For, all recognized] the rule: more radical equals more powerful."[115]

As the number of students at the square increased, conflict also emerged over the meaning and aim of the movement. Perhaps most noticeably, during the afternoon of the twentieth, a Fu-jen University student came to the stage, demanding that the national flag be raised to show the patriotism of the demonstrators. This suggestion provoked great outrage among many of the students, and the square became chaotic as students disparaged the student speaker, trying to pull him from the stage. The security marshals quickly calmed the students, calling for restraint and tolerance. The student was invited to take the stage again, but he declined the offer.[116]

In this tense and increasingly chaotic atmosphere, the movement organization again attempted to bring about a student–government dialogue. At 7:00 A.M. on the twentieth, the Policy Group formally changed hands. A few hours later, the new Policy Group held a press conference, announcing that the students were sending a petition to the president and would expect a public response. At 2:30 P.M., the new Policy Group walked to the Presidential Office to deliver the petition. Presidential Vice-Secretary Ch'iu Chin-yi met them, but informed the group that Lee was not there. The contingent then returned to the square to reassess the situation. About an hour later, the group again traveled to the Presidential Office. Once more greeted by Vice-Secretary Ch'iu, the students presented three demands: (1) the president should immediately meet with the students; (2) the president should come to the square at 5:00 P.M.; and (3) the president should prepare for a televised dialogue, to be held at 7:00 P.M. Ch'iu gave no clear response.

The contingent returned to the Memorial to report the latest developments. Shortly thereafter, the Inter-Campus Conference announced that March 21, the date of the presidential "election" by the National Assembly, would be declared Democracy Shame Day. The conference also announced the beginning of an all-country, all-school class boycott on the twenty-first, to encourage all students to join the protest. In addition, the group invited students to skip two meals that day.[117]

Later that night, various entertainers took the stage. The most lively performance was a puppet show, presented by some theater arts students and featuring large caricatures of the "Old Thieves" (*Laozei*) in the National Assembly. The play began with National Assembly member "Dying for Money" (*Si Yao Qian*) entering the stage, introducing himself, and then suddenly leaving, explaining, "Sorry, my urine bag is full; I must go get a new one." The play continued as other fictitious national assemblymen, such as "Dying for Power" (*Si Yao Quan*) and "Shameless" (*Bu Yao Lian*), boasted of their power and manipulated Lee Teng-hui to promise his loyalty should he receive their vote for president.[118] The performance raised the spirits of the students, yet the government remained inattentive to their demands.

Meanwhile, within the ranks of the KMT elite, the mainstream and non-mainstream factions were beginning to resolve their struggle. Most important, in the days prior to the election, Lee Teng-hui made some important concessions to appease the nonmainstream faction. Significantly, Lee reportedly agreed to allow Lee Huan to assume the position of party chair while retaining his current post as party premier. In addition, Lee Teng-hui promised that Hao Po-ts'un would retain his post as defense minister. Further, Lee apparently consented to giving Chiang Wei-kuo a position in the postelection administration. Finally, Lee promised that he would not run for a second full term.[119] Consequently, Lee assured his election and his continued prominence within the party.

Dialogue and Withdrawal

The final phase of the movement began on March 21, the date of the presidential election. On this day, Lee Teng-hui finally consented to meet with the student protestors. Moreover, during the dialogue, Lee promised to attend to at least two of the students' demands. Yet, at the same time, the students did not feel that they had achieved a true victory, for it was not clear that their efforts had effected any real change in official policy. Thus, although the students eventually decided to withdraw from the square, no one was completely satisfied with the government's response.

In the predawn hours of the twenty-first, the students changed their organizational structure once again. First, the new Policy Group decided to add five more members, in order to raise the representativeness of the group and to ease the strain of the exhausted seven members.[120] With the results of the presidential election scheduled to be announced that afternoon, all felt that this would be a crucial day for the movement. Immediately after the meeting began, some Policy Group members proposed that the student demonstrators rush the Presidential Office, or at least move the sit-in to that location, in order to exert greater pressure on the unresponsive authorities. Yet the majority voted the suggestion down, fearing that such a move would be unduly provocative, as the law expressly forbade demonstrating near the Presidential Office. Moreover, many members of the Policy Group were exhausted and hardly had the energy to stay awake during the meeting, much less embark on a new and more strenuous protest action.[121] As this proposed action, unlike a hunger strike, would not be effective without the participation of large numbers of students, those who proposed the new strategy accepted the group's decision.

Instead, members of the Policy Group decided to renew their efforts to gain a dialogue with Lee Teng-hui. Since earlier student efforts toward this end had met with failure, they agreed to try sending a contingent of professors to the Presidential Office as intermediaries. The group also drafted a three-point statement to present to Lee, which read:

> (1) Lee Teng-hui must specifically affirm this student movement; (2) The National Affairs Conference must impartially and equitably include persons from all walks of life to discuss the affairs of the nation, and an effective program must be put forth regarding the students' Four Demands; (3) When Lee Teng-hui clearly recognizes these two demands, all of the students at the square will end the sit-in movement. Otherwise, the students will persist in their protest until the end.[122]

Immediately after this decision, Professor Consulting Group members He Te-fen and Ch'u Hai-yuen traveled to the Presidential Office. Upon their return, the two reported to the Policy Group that Lee had agreed to meet with student representatives at the Presidential Office at 7:00 P.M.[123]

Later that morning, news of Lee Teng-hui's nearly unanimous election reached the square.[124] The power struggle within the KMT appeared to have been resolved; Lee and the reformers had maintained their dominance. Now Lee could speak with the students from a position of strength.

Shortly thereafter, the Inter-Campus Conference convened. Immediately after the meeting began, He Te-fen announced the morning's events. Yet rather than welcoming the progress made by the professors, many student representatives were indignant that the Policy Group and professors had undertaken such an important action without first consulting the Inter-Campus Conference. These students charged that the professors were "taking over" the movement and compromising student autonomy. When Professor Ch'u subsequently broadcast the morning's events to the general assemblage of protesting students, the sit-in area became chaotic, as students cried out against the "secret" and "nondemocratic" decision-making process. Amid this outrage, the Command Center announced that each school representative would be given a copy of the three-point statement, so that each school group could discuss and vote on the matter. Subsequently, each school representative would be invited to take the stage and announce his or her school's decision.[125]

In the middle of this process, members of the Policy Group made a special announcement to the general body of students, apologizing for their irresponsible behavior and tendering their group resignation.[126] Around 2:30 P.M., the Inter-Campus Conference finally convened to formally discuss and vote on the three-point statement. After great bickering, the group decided to revise the wording of the original three points slightly, and to add a fourth, which read: "(4) In order to ensure that the above propositions are carried out, we have established an Inter-Campus Conference, which will continue to supervise the National Affairs Conference and will continue to organize until democratic reform has been completed."[127] Although student representatives agreed on the revision, He Te-fen pressed them to allow the general body of students first to vote on the original three-point proposal. For, she argued, the students had already studied the original three-point proposal, and it would waste time unduly to have them review and discuss a new proposal. The meeting with Lee Teng-hui was scheduled for 7:00 P.M., and evening already was approaching. He Te-fen also announced that if the majority of the students did not agree with the three-point proposal, then the Professor Consulting Group would resign. Finally, the Inter-Campus Conference agreed to vote first on the original proposal.[128] In the end, twenty-two schools supported the three-point proposal, seven opposed, and six abstained.

By the time the vote was counted, students had only forty minutes before the scheduled dialogue with Lee Teng-hui. With little time to agree upon the delegation to attend the dialogue, they hastily decided that each of the thirty-five schools represented at the square would send one representative, and that in addition all the members of the Policy Group, the Command Center, and the Working Group, two hunger-strike representatives, and professors Ch'u Hai-yuen and He Te-fen would attend. Thus, a total of fifty-three movement representatives went to the Presidential Office for the dialogue.[129]

Upon arriving at the Presidential Office, Fan Yun requested that a videotape be made to give to the student delegation, so that the students at the square could view the dialogue firsthand. After the government representatives agreed, Fan Yun read aloud the Four Big Demands. Next, one of the hunger-strike representatives requested that Lee display his desire for reform by speaking in Taiwanese rather than Mandarin during the meeting. Lee refused, explaining, "Others won't understand me." In a quiet voice, the same student then spoke of the current hunger-strike situation. The other hunger-strike representative warned that the hunger strike would continue until Lee gave a clear response to student demands. Before he had finished, another student interrupted, stating: "Mr. President, I don't ask for anything else; I have only one simple demand. We're very worried about the students at the square . . . we hope that afterwards we won't receive any pressure at home, school, or anywhere."[130] Before meeting delegates got very far on the subject, another student interrupted and directed the discussion back toward the Four Demands. At this point Lee acknowledged the righteousness of the students yet at the same time cautioned them to remain clear-headed, stating:

> First, I say to every student that I affirm each student's patriotism and concern for the country. This is my absolute affirmation.[131] In our current country, where materialism is the prevalent trend, if our youth don't have ideals, our country will have no future. Though we want to realize our ideals, in order to realize them, we must think about the method we choose. . . . We must use methods that everyone affirms; this is the only way we can win.[132]

Next, Lee argued that he had no authority to dissolve the National Assembly, explaining, "You . . . want me to dissolve the National Assembly, but in reality the presidency is not a dictatorship, or a military regime, or revolutionary government. . . . Dismissing the National Assembly is associated with constitutional change. So, after the constitution is changed, we can discuss this. Without changing the constitution, this is impossible."[133] Then Lee spoke of the National Affairs Conference, stating that, not only would he try to convoke the conference within one month of his inauguration, but that, "In reality, I had this idea early on; the only question was when it would be held. On this question, the administration has already begun preparations."[134] Finally, a student asked Lee why he had not come to the square. Lee replied that he had wanted to visit the square from the start but was unable to, as his security could not be assured. Shortly thereafter the dialogue concluded. In closing, Lee stated: "We want everyone to understand that we want reform, too, but we must work within certain restraints. You should all take care of your health, and return home and to school soon. Thank you."[135]

Although this dialogue was less antagonistic than the mainland Chinese students' meeting with Li Peng on May 18, 1989, the content of the dialogue and the stance of the authorities were quite similar. In both cases, although the students had demanded the dialogue, government representatives directed and dominated the discussion. In addition, in each instance the student delegates were somewhat disorganized, voicing various demands and presenting a somewhat confused image of what the students ultimately wanted. Of equal interest, however, leading government officials in each case stressed that they agreed with the students' aims and affirmed their patriotic nature. Also, during both dialogues the officials emphasized that they, too, favored continued reform. Yet at the same time government representatives in each instance voiced concern with the methods chosen by the students and instructed the students to end the movement.

The student delegation returned to the Memorial with somewhat ambivalent feelings about the dialogue. They had won no tangible concessions, yet at the same time Lee had promised to attend to two of their demands and had clearly implied that the other demands would be dealt with promptly once the conference had been convened. Concurrently, media reports took a negative turn. Indeed, while the student dialogue was in progress, all of the 8:00 P.M. TV news reports presented unfavorable pieces on the movement, claiming that it had "gone bad," or had "become excessive."[136] Thus, even though students felt satisfied that they had engaged in a dialogue with Lee and obtained a promise to respond to some of their demands, it was hard for them to feel that they truly had "won."

When the student delegation arrived back at the square, the student protestors clamored for a report. Consequently, Fan Yun took the stage, announcing that: (1) Lee had affirmed the students' patriotism; (2) Lee had attached importance to the students' Four Demands; (3) a National Affairs Conference would be announced within a month after Lee assumed the presidency; and (4) Lee would announce a timetable for reform either at his inaugural speech or at the National Affairs Conference.[137] Following this announcement, Fan Yun suggested that the students discuss and vote on whether or not to leave the square. Later, the videotape of the dialogue arrived at the Memorial. After gathering to watch, the students returned to their school groups to continue their discussion.[138]

Meanwhile, the thirty-seven hunger-striking students held a separate meeting to discuss a possible end to the hunger strike and withdrawal from the square. Late that night, the hunger strikers voted to end the strike and announced that they planned to withdraw the following day.[139] By 2:00 A.M., many students had begun to leave the square.[140]

At 2:30 A.M., the Inter-Campus Conference (now comprised of twenty-two schools) voted on whether to withdraw. A little over half of the school groups presented unanimous statements favoring withdrawal. At the same time, however, most of the groups were dissatisfied with Lee's response and stressed that the students should continue to oversee his efforts after the movement's formal end.[141] Many also called for the establishment of an intercampus organization to continue the movement's work.[142] In addition, some demanded that the media recant its negative coverage of the movement.[143] Finally, some schools criticized the leadership of the movement. For example, students from Yang-min Medical School Statement wrote:

> We are unhappy with a few things about this protest. . . . (a) We protest the Command Center's use of the microphone today, which was nondemocratic; all of the students at the square should be able to express their opinions. (b) We feel that the chair's voice was too prominent in the discussion of important issues. . . . This rally was not comprised of blind followers."[144]

Also, the China Medical Institute's statement expressed dissatisfaction with the three-point statement drafted by the Policy Group and the Professors' Consulting Group.[145] Nonetheless, in the final vote, twenty-one schools favored withdrawal, and only one opposed.[146] After the proposal passed, students drafted a withdrawal statement, which read:

> Having gone through 150 hours of peaceful protest, countless student words and democratic voices, sympathetic voices throughout the country have surged up before this empty space. All the country's compatriots—male and female, old and young, those of different party factions, and from different districts, noble and lowly, rich and poor—have all contributed to this history-changing democratic movement. . . . On March 21, President Lee finally gave a public response to our appeal and made a partial promise to address our demands. . . . Nonetheless, President Lee is obviously personally limited by the existent ruling structure . . . we also can't be careless. . . . From this day, we have decided to establish an all-school, all-country student alliance; we announce to every social circle . . . if we do not achieve our goals, we absolutely will not stop![147]

After the meeting ended, the Command Center requested that students prepare to spend their final night in the square.[148] Throughout the night, the vast majority of students retreated; only about a hundred students stayed through the morning.[149] At 6:00 A.M., student representatives awoke the remaining students, asking them to gather up their belongings. About an hour later, Fan Yun read the withdrawal statement and announced the establishment of an island-wide student government "to maintain a high interest in national affairs."[150] In addition, she announced that a "cleanup" group would deal with tasks immediately after the students' withdrawal. Student leaders also designated a special group to supervise the donations that had accumulated during the movement.[151]

Not all students were prepared to leave the square, however. Indeed, before Fan Yun had finished speaking, a Ch'ing-hua University student rushed the stage, yelling, "How can we leave after the TV news misrepresented the students?" A professor then took the stage, answering the student, "This protest was about the Four Demands; if you want to protest the TV, you will have to start a new protest." With this, the Ch'ing-hua student became further enraged, crying, "Why are professors being allowed to take part in a student discussion?" Below the stage, some voiced agreement, yelling "Protest!"[152] Nonetheless, the vast majority of the students who remained at the square agreed with the decision to retreat. Faced with the prospect of having only a few fellow demonstrators, the Ch'ing-hua student quieted down.

At 9:30 A.M., the students began their formal withdrawal. A group of about forty Ch'ing-hua students remained until 11:30 A.M., however, shouting, "Democratic reform—we will return!" as they retreated. At this point, only a few hunger strikers remained. At 4:00 P.M. the last hunger striker read the hunger strike withdrawal statement, and noted that he had stayed until the last student had left the square. Shortly after 5:00 P.M., Lee Tenghui's car made a circle around the Memorial, and returned to the Presidential Office.

Conclusion

What lessons can we draw from this progression of events? As with the movement of 1989 in China, student behavior during the Month of March movement in Taiwan fundamentally derived from a political environment of single-party domination of the media, the political system, and the campus. As in China, in Taiwan tensions in leadership arose among students who did not know one another. Experienced student activists such as Fan Yun were suspicious of the competence and motives of those who had not previously engaged in dissent, while inexperienced participants chafed at what they perceived to be the condescension of the older activists. Since the Policy Group held more experienced activists while the Inter-Campus Conference included many first-time protestors, these groups often conflicted. Further, seasoned student dissidents from different student movement circles (such as Taida's student government and the Democratic Student Alliance) clashed over strategy and goals. In an atmosphere of uncertain and potentially severe consequences, students were hesitant to compromise with those whom they did not fully know and trust. The risk-laden atmosphere also led to a radicalizing trend in student behavior. As students distrusted the motives of some of their fellow protestors (and rightly so, as attested by the presence of many one pro-KMT students and professors at the square), they proposed more radical actions (such as moving to the front of the Presidential Office or engaging in a hunger strike) to prove their dedication and increase pressure on the government. Similarly, students in both Taiwan and China were hesitant to work with older intellectuals, whom they considered too tied to the establishment and unduly moderate in their aims.

Similarly, as in China, student concerns with maintaining autonomy from other social groups arose from justified fears of slander and repression. Most important, the student leaders of the Month of March movement stress that separation was necessary to maintain order and assure student safety. As one leader states: "Our biggest question was how to avoid being slandered, being accused of being used . . . or being infiltrated by bad people. With the security line, everyone could see that we were all students."[153] Similarly, student leaders feared that the KMT would use any appearance of disorder as a pretext to crack down on the movement. In the words of another leader: "We feared that if the masses mixed in with the students, the KMT might use more forceful measures to control the movement. . . . We wanted support from [the masses], but also didn't want to act with them because we feared KMT suppression. It was a contradiction . . . we did not really want the security line, but we needed it to ensure our safety."[154] As one leader states, "outside of the [security] line, it was not organized; if we got rid of the line, there was no telling what would happen."[155] Further, student leaders felt that separation would ease the fears of the many demonstrating students who had little prior protest experience.[156] In all, virtually every student leader whom I interviewed explained that the students' insistence on maintaining "autonomy" and "purity" was a practical response to their political environment.

Interestingly, the students were particularly concerned to remain distinct from the DPP and its activities. Although student and DPP demands were almost identical, and despite the fact that many of the student protestors were DPP members, they feared that association with the party would raise the risk of official slander and violence. Historically, members of the DPP had been harshly repressed, and also were associated with more confrontational (and sometimes violent) protest tactics. Perhaps most notably, founders of the DPP had been involved in the Chung-li incident of 1977 and Kao-hsiung incident of 1979.[157] More recently, in August 1988, police attempting to arrest DPP legislator Hung Chi-chang (for his alleged involvement in violent demonstrations in May and June) had been met by approximately eighty protestors wielding clubs. In the three-hour confrontation that followed, three officers sustained head injuries and were hospitalized.[158] Similarly, in October 1989 a riot erupted as DPP members protested the arrest of DPP leader Hsu Hsin-liang. Fifteen officers and at least ten demonstrators were injured; fifteen protestors were detained.[159] Further, in January 1990 seven DPP members were charged with instigating a riot following a disputed election, and in February a DPP rally turned into a fifteen-hour street battle, resulting in the destruction of nineteen cars, the injury of over one hundred persons, and the arrest of five.[160] Finally, DPP members had instigated numerous fist-fights within the Legislative Yuan.

For these reasons, the students felt that, despite their agreement with the DPP's stand on constitutional reform, it would be unwise to join forces with the group. Rather than evidence of a condescending attitude toward the DPP, this strategy was seen as a necessary way to maintain order and avoid official repression. As one student leader explains, "Why did we fear [union with] the DPP? . . . [because] the media has historically given the DPP a bad name." Consequently, he continues, "Student leaders, even if they were DPP supporters, could not admit it."[161] Similarly to student leaders in China, students in Taiwan feared that the KMT would use any appearance of disorder as a pretext to crack down on the movement. Thus, although students in both Taiwan and China claimed to prefer a more inclusive mobilization strategy, in both cases they feared that it would have dangerous results.

What effect did this separation from nonstudent groups have on the movement's outcome? As in mainland China, this strategy appears to have had a restraining effect on officials dealing with the student protestors. In the spring of 1990, the student demonstrations remained peaceful and unmarred by any severe conflict with the authorities; at many DPP-sponsored activities, in contrast, violent confrontations occurred on many occasions. For example, on March 15 a violent conflict broke out when eleven members of the DPP attempting to enter the meeting place of the National Assembly were repelled by security forces.[162] The following day, security forces hauled off DPP chair Huang Hsin-chieh after he attempted to enter the Presidential Office a few blocks from the Chiang Kai-shek Memorial.[163] And during the course of the large-scale DPP demonstration in and around the Chiang Kai-shek Memorial on March 18, violence erupted between protestors and police a number of times.[164] Student demonstrators, in contrast, were treated mildly.

In fact, as noted earlier, media reports stated that the police department had been instructed by President Lee not to interfere with the student protest, stressing that "student and DPP protestors must remain separate." At the same time, the students' hesitance to unite fully with other social groups may have decreased Lee's perceived need to compromise. Indeed, although Lee did agree to two of the students' demands, this did not amount to a real change in policy. As Lee himself stated, plans for a National Affairs Conference were already in the works. Overall, then, even though the Month of March movement was far more successful than its counterpart on the mainland, it is doubtful that the student demonstrations in Taiwan actually brought about a meaningful policy change.

Finally, as in China, organizational difficulties threatened to derail the movement in Taiwan, especially when the time came to discuss withdrawal. In both cases, the official representative movement organization had no control over the hunger-striking students. Moreover, not all students agreed that the movement's goals had been satisfactorily achieved. Yet a crucial difference existed in the manner of the government's response to the demonstrators. In Taiwan the partial government concession to the students' demands defused the tense and dangerous atmosphere; consequently, students no longer felt compelled to engage in extreme actions. In fact, in this relaxed atmosphere such behavior appeared almost ridiculous rather than courageous. In addition, the generally more open environment in Taiwan helped make organizational difficulties less extreme. For example, though the hunger-strike group did detract somewhat from the legitimacy and power of the Inter-Campus Conference, this division never developed into an open rift, as was the case in China. Similarly, although the Inter-Campus Conference was ridden with dissent and distrust, students did not opt to "exit" the organization and form new groups of their own. As a result, unlike in China, all students departed the square at virtually the same time, and the movement ended peacefully.

Chapter 6

Conclusion

The findings of the preceding chapters shed new light on the process and outcome of the student movement of 1989 in Beijing. Overall, although cultural and historical traditions as well as idiosyncratic personality traits certainly shaped student behavior, it was the state that exerted the most profound influence on their strategies and actions. Specifically, the fear and distrust engendered by sustained single-party monopolization of state institutions, party–state domination of the media, party penetration of social organizations, and a high propensity for harsh state repression combined to create great organizational difficulties and impelled students to choose non-inclusive mobilization strategies. Looking comparatively at the movement of 1990 in Taiwan, a similar pattern appeared. Throughout each movement, students were presented with various choices in strategy and behavior. However, the political environment at the time rendered certain options risky or unwise. Thus, although student behavior during both movements might appear to have been irrational or flawed, in reality the actions of the students were largely a natural response to the political realities they faced.

Implications for Theories of Contentious Politics

The notion that the state has a great influence over protest behavior and outcomes is not new; prominent theorists of contentious politics have argued the point for at least two decades. In *The Contentious French*, for example, Charles Tilly contends that French protest behavior shifted over time as a reaction to changes in the state.[1] Similarly, in *Political Process and the Development of Black Insurgency*, Doug McAdam stresses that movement processes and outcomes are greatly influenced by the "structure of political opportunities" in which a protest group acts.[2] More recently, Sidney Tarrow has traced variations in protest behavior due to the rise and subsequent demise of the nation–state as the primary locus of political power.[3]

These and other studies have provided path-breaking analyses of public protest, and their basic insights remain at the forefront of social movement theory. Yet these conclusions came from case studies found almost entirely in the liberal West. As a result, many have wondered whether or not current approaches provide an adequate understanding of the influence of the state in more illiberal and overtly repressive systems. With this question in mind, a growing number of scholars have begun to focus on protest in explicitly nondemocratic settings.[4]

This book extends this new wave of inquiry. It finds that certain protest traits are intensified in more illiberal and repressive environments. Specifically, as one moves across the spectrum toward more oppressive regimes, intervening variables of fear and distrust become exponentially more pronounced, such that the crucial collective action resources of organization and mobilization are stymied. In severely risk-laden settings, organization is hindered by the need for preexisting bonds of friendship to overcome distrust and fear, and a heightened tendency toward protest radicalization. When movement infiltration and repression are extremely likely, networks based on anything less than the most trustworthy connections tend to be characterized by internal suspicion, leading to organizational instability and ineffectiveness. In such a risky atmosphere, successful organization may be possible only when it is based on personal friendship networks (and thus the highest level of trust).

Reflecting the assumption that all networks generally aid organizational development and strength, many scholars of 1989 portray the preexisting "democracy salons" at Beijing University as the building blocks of student organization during the movement.[5] Yet the findings uncovered here indicate precisely the opposite: the preexistent groups at Beijing University fostered conflict and division within the student movement organization. Moreover, the first cross-campus organization was born, not at Beijing University, where many autonomous student groups had been functioning for a number of years, but at Beijing Normal University, where students had virtually no prior experience of autonomous organization. Similarly, in Taiwan the student movement groups that formed prior to the spring of 1990 did not serve to strengthen organization during the Month of March movement. Indeed, these previously existing groups often complicated the organizational process, creating conflict, division, and distrust.

This finding seems counterintuitive. However, given the environment of fear that existed in both China and Taiwan, it becomes understandable. As noted earlier, this negative atmosphere caused student leaders to trust only those with whom they were well acquainted prior to the movement. With regard to preexistent organization, this had two detrimental effects. First, although the autonomous groups founded prior to each movement did foster trust *within* particular groups, they did not foster trust *among* groups. Second, when each movement began, members of each of the preexistent autonomous groups felt that their prior activity made them worthy of leadership. Consequently, during both movements student organization was characterized by almost continual conflict and change. In the end, only networks based on bonds of friendship provided the trust necessary for effective organization.

A severely fear-laden and distrustful environment also leads to protest radicalization, as more confrontational behavior is seen as proof of one's loyalty to the cause, and moderation is viewed with suspicion. Further, if the ruling party remains intransigent in the face of more conciliatory protest behavior, disagreement is likely to arise as to whether or not more radical measures are needed to force a response. In a high-stakes atmosphere, those calling for more radical activities may be unwilling to abide by democratic decisions; indeed, in the two cases studied here such individuals typically chose to abandon existing organizations rather than abide by a decision that they felt was too timid.

Finally, an extremely dangerous political environment may place great limitations on protest mobilization. To protect themselves from the very real threat of official slander and repression, protestors in illiberal regimes may feel pressed to demonstrate the "purity" of their ranks from outside infiltrators. Due to their need for absolute certainty regarding the motivations and behavior of those within their ranks, protestors may be unwilling to unite with groups whose proclivities or membership are uncertain. To further guard against repression, protestors may avoid overt connections with groups that have been the target of official repression in the past. These necessities place great constraints on a movement's ability and willingness to mobilize across different social groups.

Many prominent analyses of the student movement of 1989 argue that this unwillingness to unite with workers inhibited the success of the movement by making it easier for the government to ignore or repress it.[6] The findings of this study agree in part: the students' separation from nonstudent groups may well have encouraged official stonewalling. Yet, at the same time, this strategy was the students' only rational choice if they wished to avoid a crackdown. Students in China and Taiwan were well aware of this conundrum. In interviews, student leaders from both movements stated that, although they might have preferred to unite with nonstudent demonstrators, the illiberal political environment forced them to be constantly on guard to avoid official slander and punishment. Both the CCP and the KMT had slurred past protest movements with accusations of infiltration by persons of malicious intent, and both had a history of repressing certain social groups over others. Thus, the students had every reason to be concerned.

Indeed, in both cases the government soon made it clear that, whereas students would be allowed to engage in various protest activities, nonstudents would be treated differently. In China in spring 1989, authorities treated student protestors with relative moderation but severely repressed even the most small-scale worker activism. Consequently, students had good reason to believe that a strong student–worker alliance would have quickly fomented a severe response by the authorities. Similarly, in spring 1990 in Taiwan, police treated student demonstrators with great restraint, while during many of the DPP-sponsored activities police confrontations erupted in violence. Indeed, major newspapers openly acknowledged that Lee Teng-hui had instructed the police department to assume different attitudes toward student and nonstudent protestors. Seen in this light, the students' decision to remain separate from nonstudents appears to have been their only logical option.

Wider Comparisons

Although these conclusions strictly apply only to the movements in Beijing and Taipei, evidence from demonstrations in other locations and historical periods in China lends some tentative support to these findings. Accounts from Chongqing and Shanghai in spring 1989, for example, also stress the CCP's differential treatment of student and worker activists.[7] Concurrently, protest activities in these areas, as in Beijing, evidenced a conscious separation of students and workers. Perhaps more important, a detailed account of events in Hunan Province in spring 1989 indicates that there may be some connection between the level of perceived danger and the degree of student exclusivity. In *Anthems of Defeat*, Changsha student leader Tang Boquiao notes that the political atmosphere in Hunan was relatively relaxed; indeed, Tang argues that "this was one important feature of the Hunan pro-democracy movement which differentiated it quite sharply from that in Beijing."[8] At the same time, Tang relates that although students and workers in Hunan formed separate organizations, student and worker activities were much more closely linked in Hunan than in Beijing.[9] In addition, student organizations in Hunan seem to have been more stable. Though further examination is needed, it appears that the lower level of risk in Hunan may have had a positive effect on student organization and mobilization.

Some tentative comparisons with student protest movements in the Nationalist era also may be useful. In some ways, the political atmosphere in mainland China at this time was similar to that in the 1980s. For example, accounts of student demonstrations in this era indicate that the KMT, like the CCP in the 1980s, tended to avoid using force against students, while responding to worker activism with relative speed and severity.[10] Further, the Nationalist regime continually alleged that the student movement was incited and manipulated by nonstudents (in the later part of this era, Communists) with unsavory motives.[11] In addition, as a quasi-Leninist organization, the KMT, like the later CCP, had a network of informers on the most active university campuses and worked to dominate all student groups, including the student government.[12]

Yet the political environment of this era displayed some important differences from that of the 1980s. To begin with, during this period the KMT did not hold a monopoly on the media or have the ability to censor all media communication. Further, the KMT had little power to determine a student's future job placement and was unable to infiltrate and control all student groups and campus governments. More generally, the Nationalist regime never enjoyed a truly stable position of power and by the late 1930s faced an increasingly organized and popular opposition party, the CCP. The Nationalist regime also was in an increasingly weakened position internationally, as it battled large-scale Japanese invasions.

Consequently, KMT control of the campuses, and society in general, was fairly precarious. Thus, although student activists of this period acted in a dangerous environment, overall the risks faced by student protestors in this era were relatively lower than those faced by students in the late 1980s. Given this, my conclusions would suggest that student protestors in this period should have been able to organize more effectively and easily than student activists in 1989. In addition, it seems likely that students in this earlier period would have been less fearful of encouraging worker involvement in their protests. A survey of student behavior in this period indicates that this was indeed the case, though more directed study of these issues is needed.[13]

Beyond China

A look at political protest in other nondemocratic states indicates that many of the protest limitations and protestor concerns that appeared in China and Taiwan also characterize dissent in other illiberal contexts. To begin, many scholars of Latin American, Eastern European, and African politics remark that a "culture of fear" has characterized social relations in the non-democratic regimes of these regions.[14] As Corradi, Weiss Fagen, and Garreton note, "Free societies . . . do not know fear as the permanent and muffled under-tone of public life."[15] Most likely, they add, this is because in democratic societies

> the decentralization of power, the exercise of self-governance in local communities, the existence of myriad voluntary associations, the separation of state and religion, the plurality of sects and creeds within religions, the possibility of rapid social and geographical mobility, and, above all, the functioning of representative institutions are among the factors . . . that have relegated fear to being either an intimate or a transcendent experience.[16]

In nondemocratic societies, in contrast, "fear is a paramount feature of social action."[17]

Moreover, many find that the fear resulting from these illiberal features is accompanied by the same lack of trust that undercut the student protest movements in China and Taiwan. For example, Norbert Lechner relates that the repressive atmosphere of authoritarian societies "is manifested in the mistrust that pervades social relations."[18] Similarly, Patricia Weiss Fagen finds that "restrictions on social gatherings, on elections in social and sports clubs, and censorship of the press, television, and popular songs all conspire to draw people away from public life and into private spheres. Fears about talking freely in front of neighbors and colleagues, suspicions about people in unaccustomed places, and a reluctance to pursue friendships with new acquaintances follow."[19] In addition, Maria Helena Moreira Alves finds that, in Brazil, the aim of the authoritarian regime was "to make individual citizens feel uninformed, separate, fragmented, and powerless . . . uncertainty was also encouraged."[20]

Organization under such circumstances is exceedingly difficult. As a result, it appears that in a variety of nondemocratic, repressive political environments, networks based on friendship may be virtually the *only* sound basis of organization building. When involvement in movement leadership entails a real risk of lifelong unemployment or brutal imprisonment, individuals must have absolute trust in the competence and loyalty of their fellow leaders. Of course the trust provided by bonds of friendship aids organizational commitment and strength in democratic societies as well.[21] Yet, as the risks involved in protest in nondemocratic societies are inherently and demonstrably higher than those in democratic societies, personal ties in the former are vastly more important. As Karl-Dieter Opp and Christiane Gern conclude in their study of the East German protests of 1989, "in authoritarian regimes trust is mainly placed on friends"; as a result, these personal networks form the basic building blocks of organization.[22] Yet at the same time this very safety of the protestors seriously constrains their ability to form wider movement connections. As further demonstrated in the East German case, Lynn Kamenitsa notes that great suspicion arose among movement activists of different backgrounds, thus undermining the opposition's ability to create alliances and achieve compromise.[23]

Further, as was discovered in the cases of 1989 in China and 1990 in Taiwan, studies of other nondemocratic regimes have found that a fear-laden political environment encourages heroism and radicalized behavior among political activists, thus destabilizing organization. Certainly, many have noted that even protest movements in democratic settings tend toward escalation and radicalization.[24] Nonetheless, it appears that illiberal environments exacerbate these tendencies. As Juan E. Corradi notes, "the sacrifice an individual has to make to serve the common purpose of the group is much higher in a despotic than in an open regime."[25] In a study of political protest in Chile, Javier Martinez adds that, as a result, expressions of protest in authoritarian contexts "follow the unequal distribution of courage among individuals."[26] Consequently, Martinez finds that, "in this situation, the majority of the population plays the role of the dominated public, and an individual or small group plays the hero; heroism can be followed only by acts on a similar scale."[27] Student protest in predemocratic South Korea also showed this tendency. As Wonmo Dong relates, many have noted a "tendency among the Korean student activists that, 'the more radical and extreme, the greater the moral superiority of the activist leaders.' "[28] Echoing these conclusions in a comparative study of student protest in Thailand, Burma, Malaysia, and Singapore, Josef Silverstein found that, in each case, "when the battle [was] joined and compromises [were] offered . . . those who accept[ed] appear[ed] to be 'selling out.' "[29] This phenomenon is perhaps best encapsulated in the words of a prominent Uruguayan dissident, who notes, "I rather think that all the radicalization of the youth was . . . generated by the authoritarian framework itself."[30]

As seen in the case of China in 1989, such radicalization can have dire consequences for organizational stability. When more radical protestors refuse to work with those counseling moderation, an inclusive protest organization will be unable to reach decisions and may ultimately split apart. As increased radicalization transpires, further organizational splintering will result. In the end, then, the radicalism fueled by repressive nondemocratic regimes is yet one more factor that works to undermine attempts to forge strong and cohesive movement organizations.

A final factor operating in this direction also appears in the comparative literature. Studies of political protest in other nondemocratic contexts support the hypothesis that narrow mobilization strategies may be seen as necessary to counter official charges of movement infiltration by undesirable elements. As Charles Brockett argues in his study of peasant mobilization in Central America, "challengers not only respond to current regime actions, but also must anticipate future actions, calculations that in turn are based on memories and stories of past elite behavior."[31] Lynn Kamenitsa continues this argument, stating that, "in political terms, experiences in the previous opportunity structure may affect activists' willingness to cooperate with particular groups."[32] In China and Taiwan, the students' knowledge of previous slander and repression of worker and DPP activities, respectively, made them hesitant to unite with these social groups.

Due to the same concerns, separatist strategies are the conscious choice of protestors in many nondemocratic contexts. For example, Prizzia and Sinsawasdi find that in the Thai student demonstrations of the early 1970s, the students' "strategy for the organized protest allowed for each university and school having students in the demonstration to assemble in a particular area so that leaders could detect any 'third hands.' "[33] Moreover, the Thai students' exclusive behavior appears to have been well reasoned, for "throughout the violent confrontation the government used the media to broadcast distorted news reports claiming that the demonstrators were not students but communist agents, and that the student leaders [had been] forced to join a plot to overthrow the government."[34] Similarly, Silverstein notes that during student protests in Malaysia in the fall of 1974, the "government took the line that the students had been manipulated by sinister forces."[35] In the wake of student demonstrations in Singapore the same year, "the Foreign Minister and others spoke about outside forces seeking to weaken the nation and bring it down through the use of students. He was quoted as saying, 'By themselves, the students are manageable. . . . It is a different matter when outside forces intervene.' "[36]

These factors, all growing out of fear and lack of trust, combine to structure demonstrations in nondemocratic environments in ways that frustrate the formation of strong links across varied social groups and may prove self-defeating for the movements. These outcomes vary with the level of oppressiveness, as measured by sustained single-party monopolization of state institutions, party–state domination of the media, party penetration of social organizations, and a high propensity for harsh state repression. In the more democratic West, outright government repression may lead to electoral punishment, media exposure, lawsuits, and public outrage; in this context, broad-based mobilization may be more successful in propelling meaningful reform. The problem for protestors in more oppressive and exclusive regimes is that the narrow mobilization that is the ultimate outcome of state repression may be insufficient to propel real change, yet mobilization that includes groups the regime finds threatening is likely to provoke a crackdown.

Summary

Of course, political protest is risky in any political setting, and social movements in even the most democratic countries have often met with government slander and biased repression. However, in states where there are no strong alternative political parties or media sources, and no autonomous judicial system, the risks involved in protest are heightened immensely. This is evident in an extreme form in more totalitarian countries such as mainland China, where political detainees receive no fair trial and can expect excruciating torture and years of imprisonment, with virtually no domestic public knowledge of their fate. The risks faced by political activists in liberal democracies pale in comparison.

Thus, to facilitate the comparative study of political protest movements, it may be useful to envision political context as a spectrum ranging from the most repressive, closed, and politically penetrated environments to the least. Although organization and mobilization are difficult in even the least dangerous and restrictive situations, unique constraints on these resources of collective action appear in explicitly illiberal regimes. Moreover, these limitations become more severe as one moves across the continuum toward regimes that are more oppressive. Without a doubt, the individual personalities of particular influential activists have an impact on the strategy and behavior seen in any protest movement. Cultural and historical traditions, too, help to shape the manifestation and process of political protest. Yet, as the findings of this book suggest, the political environment may have the most basic and profound impact on the character of a social movement. Looking back to the student movement of 1989, then, it is important to acknowledge that the "blame" for the movement's failure may lie not so much in the individual or cultural shortcomings of the protestors, but rather in a political environment that rendered effective reform-oriented political protest close to impossible.

APPENDIXES

Appendix A

Autonomous Student Organizations in Beijing, Spring 1989

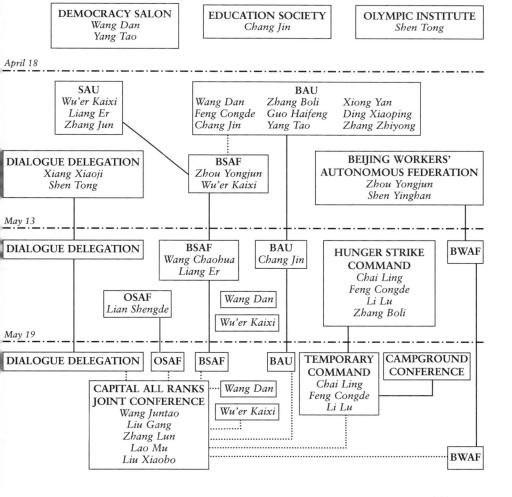

141

"Letter to All University Students"

(Text of Class Boycott Proposal)

Yaobang died with regret! All of the country's people mourn! During Hu's memorial, 100,000 Beijing University students, in compliance with the people's will, presented a seven-point petition to the Central Committee of the CCP, the NPC, and the State Council, demanding a public reassessment of Yaobang's great successes, the realization of our constitutional democratic rights, the hastening of China's democratic process . . . and reform.

But, the people have lost hope, as:

From April 15, the petitioning march of every university has grown, but the government has ignored the students' constructive demands, and moreover has used propaganda to put out false news and create lies about the student movement and sent police officers to restrain the students' just actions.

At 4:00 A.M. on the 20th, 1,000 cops at Xinhuamen, Changan, used belts, fists, and shoes to beat unarmed students. Many students were harmed. This became known as the "Xinhuamen Incident." After the incident, the government inhumanly called the harmed students a "small group of conspirators." This cannot but remind us of the Tiananmen Incident thirteen years ago: is history moving forward, or backward?

The people have already awakened, the feudal era is already past! On April 21, 100,000 students held a large-scale protest march to oppose violence, protest bloody repression, struggle for democratic freedom, and oppose dictatorship. Along the road, the masses everywhere expressed support.

At dawn on April 22, 100,000 students staged an organized sit-in at Tiananmen. After the memorial, the students waited to get a last look at Hu, but the car slipped out of the West Gate. The people lost hope, felt sad and tragic. Under this situation, three student representatives presented the "Seven-Point" petition, knelt for 45 minutes, yet still no one came out! The people are so disheartened, they can't believe it. A question arises in everyone: Do we have our own government?

The Chinese race has reached its most critical time. We must use our intuitive knowledge, ideals, flesh, and blood to write a new history. Taking on the responsibility of our nation, the young students suggest that we: (1) Establish an all-China "United Students Alliance" preparatory committee, to ensure that this movement has organization, order, and reason, so it can continue; (2) Call on all Chinese university students to undertake an unlimited class boycott. We will not stop until we reach our goal!

Beijing University Preparatory Committee
April 24, 1989

(Source: Robin Munro Collection, Document II.34.)

Autonomous Student Organizations in Taipei, Spring 1990

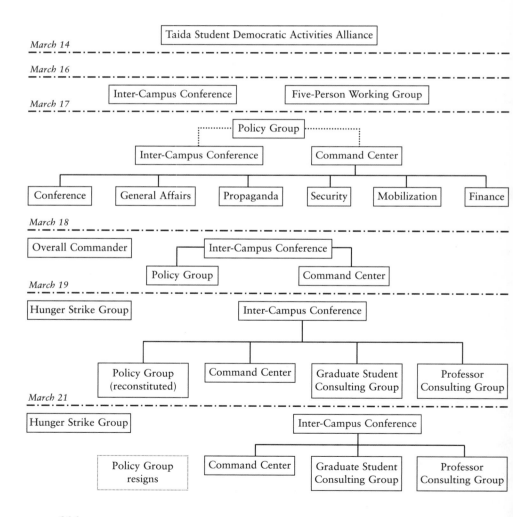

Notes

When the first interviews were conducted for this project, I was a graduate student at the University of California, Berkeley. Before completing the interviews, I had to receive approval from the university's human subjects committee. At that time, the committee required that I not reveal the identities of the interviewees, as it felt this might place them in some political danger. Respecting the concerns of this committee, I have maintained the confidentiality of those interviewees as well as those individuals whom I interviewed in 1998. The interviews have been numbered chronologically; numbers 1–20 denote mainland Chinese activists interviewed in 1994–1995; numbers 21–40 refer to Taiwanese activists interviewed in 1993–1994; and numbers 41–60 signify Taiwanese activists interviewed in 1998.

Chapter 1

1. Hu lost his position as party General Secretary in 1987 due to his tolerance of student protests calling for intellectual freedom and political reform. Many believed that his death was hastened by his ill-treatment by harder-line party elites. In addition, in early 1989 economic reforms had stalled, inflation was in the double digits, and there was a widespread belief that pervasive corruption in the Communist Party was to blame. See Corrina-Barbara Francis, "The Progress of Protest in China," *Asian Survey* 29, no. 9 (September 1989): 898–915; Jonathan Unger, "Introduction," in Jonathan Unger, ed., *The Pro-Democracy Protests in China: Reports from the Provinces* (Armonk, NY: M. E. Sharpe, 1991); Lee Feigon, *China Rising: The Meaning of Tiananmen* (Chicago: Ivan R. Dee, 1990); and Kathleen Hartford, "The Political Economy behind the Beijing Spring," in Tony Saich, ed., *Perspectives on the Chinese People's Movement: Spring 1989* (Armonk, NY: M. E. Sharpe, 1990).

2. Most prominently, thousands have been harassed and jailed for their participation in demonstrations and activities associated with the Falungong, a group primarily oriented toward health and spirituality, and only tangentially political. Similarly, virtually all major leaders of the China Democracy Party have been imprisoned since the group attempted to register local branches in the summer of 1998. Many of these persons face sentences of a decade or more.

3. See, for example, Geremie Barme, "Traveling Heavy: The Intellectual Baggage of the Chinese Diaspora," *Problems of Communism,* January–April 1991, 94–112;

Craig Calhoun, *Neither Gods Nor Emperors* (Berkeley: University of California Press, 1994); Andrew Walder and Gong Xiaoxia, "Workers in the Tiananmen Protests: The Politics of the Beijing Workers' Autonomous Federation," *The Australian Journal of Chinese Affairs,* January 1993, 1–29; Han Minzhu, ed., *Cries for Democracy* (Princeton, NJ: Princeton University Press, 1990); Joseph Esherick and Jeffrey Wasserstrom, "Acting Out Democracy: Political Theater in Modern China," Elizabeth Perry, "Casting a Chinese 'Democracy' Movement: The Roles of Students, Workers, and Entrepreneurs," and Liu Xiaobo, "That Holy Word, 'Revolution,' " in Elizabeth Perry and Jeffrey Wasserstrom, eds., *Popular Protest and Political Culture in Modern China: Learning from 1989,* 2d ed. (Boulder, CO: Westview Press, 1994). Similar themes emerge in the 1995 Long Bow Group film, *The Gate of Heavenly Peace.*

4. All interviewees, seventeen in total, were living in the United States at the time. Interviews were conducted in person, and typically spanned two to four hours.

5. Transcripts of this meeting are recorded in *Huigu yu Fansi* (Review and reflect) (Essen, Germany: German Rhine Writers' Association 1989 Student Research Group, 1993). Seventeen individuals participated in the meeting, including Bai Meng, Cai Chongguo, Chai Ling, Chang Jin, Feng Congde, Lao Mu, Li Lanju, Li Lu, Liang Er, Liu Wei, Liu Yan, Shen Tong, Wang Chaohua, Xin Ku, Yang Tao (from Hangzhou University, not Beijing University), Zhang Boli, and Zhang Lun.

6. Of the seventeen individuals I interviewed, four also participated in the meeting recorded in *Huigu yu Fansi*. Taken together, therefore, the interviews and meeting transcripts represent the views of thirty individual movement leaders.

7. Most of the major documents produced by student participants in the movement (in their original form) are gathered in the Robin Munro Collection, copies of which are located in many university archives, including UC Berkeley's Center for Chinese Studies Library. The "Tiananmen Archive" at Columbia University also includes other documents not found in this collection. Another useful compilation of movement documents may be found in *Bajiu Zhongguo Minyun Ziliao* (Data from the Chinese People's Movement of 1989) (Hong Kong: Chinese University of Hong Kong Student Union, 1991).

8. This movement also is known as the Wild White Lily (*Yebaihe*) movement, referring to the icon that came to symbolize the demonstrations. Information on this movement was derived from approximately thirty interviews with prominent student leaders, as well as all available primary and secondary written sources. Interviews were conducted in Taiwan in the fall of 1994 and summer of 1998. The most comprehensive compilation of primary documents may be found in Lin Meina, ed., *Fennu de Yebaihe* (Indignant white lily) (Taipei: Jianwang Chubanshe, 1990). The most useful secondary sources are: Fan Yun, ed., *Xin Sheng Dai de Ziwo Zhuixun* (Self-Reflections on the new era) (Taipei, 1991); He Jinshan, Guan Hongzhi, Zhuang Lijia, and Guo Chengqi, *Taipei Xueyun* (Taipei Student Movement) (Taipei: Zhongguo Shibao Chubanshe, 1990); and Deng Piyun, *Bashi Niandai* (The eighties) (Taipei: Taiwan Yanjiu Jijinhui, 1990).

9. This book generally will use the *pinyin* romanization system. Exceptions will be made for proper names that are widely recognized in the Wade-Giles style (as is the case for most prominent political figures in Taiwan).

10. Yen Chia-kan briefly served as president prior to the younger Chiang's ascension.

11. Moreover, despite the historical importance of the Month of March movement in Taiwan, virtually no English-language literature exists on the subject.

12. See, for example, Calhoun, *Neither Gods Nor Emperors;* Walder and Gong, "Workers in the Tiananmen Protests"; and Perry, "Casting a Chinese 'Democracy' Movement."

13. See Liu, "That Holy Word, 'Revolution.' "

14. See Calhoun, *Neither Gods Nor Emperors,* p. 19. Timothy Brook reaches a similar conclusion regarding government behavior during the movement; Timothy Brook, *Quelling the People* (New York: Oxford University Press, 1992).

15. It also is likely that the movement of 1989 in China influenced student protest strategy in Taiwan. Certainly all residents of Taiwan closely followed the events of the spring of 1989 in China and were distraught by the brutal end of the movement. Indeed, many prominent student leaders in Taiwan stressed that they consciously sought to avoid making the same mistakes as the protestors at Tiananmen. However, given this, it is all the more interesting that students in Taiwan ultimately engaged in behavior that was remarkably similar to that of their mainland counterparts.

16. See, for example, Calhoun, *Neither Gods Nor Emperors;* Walder and Gong, "Workers in the Tiananmen Protests"; Perry, "Casting a Chinese 'Democracy' Movement"; and Esherick and Wasserstrom, "Acting Out Democracy."

17. Though Black and Munro do not explicitly draw the same conclusion, they acknowledge that the students' separatism helped them to rebut official charges that the movement had been infiltrated by "bad elements." Francis also notes that the students were highly aware that association with potentially "disorderly" elements could precipitate a government crackdown. Schell recognizes these student fears as well. See George Black and Robin Munro, *Black Hands of Beijing* (New York: John Wiley and Sons, 1993), pp. 159–160; Francis, "The Progress of Protest in China," p. 913; and Orville Schell, *Mandate of Heaven* (New York: Simon and Schuster, 1994), p. 185.

18. On political institutions and the opposition, see Charles Brockett, "The Structure of Political Opportunities and Peasant Mobilization in Central America," *Comparative Politics* (1991), pp. 253–274; Hanspeter Kriesi et al., "New Social Movements and Political Opportunities in Western Europe," *European Journal of Political Research* 22 (1992): 219–244; Dieter Rucht, "The Impact of National Contexts on Social Movement Structures: A Cross-Movement and Cross-National Comparison," in Doug McAdam, John McCarthy, and Mayer Zald, eds., *Comparative Perspectives on Social Movements* (Cambridge: Cambridge University Press, 1996); and Sidney Tarrow, *Power in Movement* (Cambridge: Cambridge University Press, 1994). On repression, see especially Donatella della Porta, *Social Movements,*

Political Violence and the State (Cambridge: Cambridge University Press, 1995); Donatella della Porta, "Social Movements and the State: Thoughts on the Policing of Protest," in McAdam, McCarthy, and Zald, eds., *Comparative Perspectives on Social Movements;* and Brockett, "The Structure of Political Opportunities." On the media, see William Gamson and David Meyer, "Framing Political Opportunity," in McAdam, McCarthy, and Zald.

Chapter 2

1. For a taxonomy of scholarly definitions of democracy, see David Collier and Steven Levitsky, "Democracy with Adjectives: Conceptual Innovation in Comparative Research," *World Politics,* April 1997, pp. 430–451.

2. For a path-breaking analysis of nondemocratic regime types, see Juan J. Linz, "An Authoritarian Regime: Spain," in Erik Allart and Stein Rokkan, eds., *Mass Politics: Studies in Political Sociology* (New York: Free Press, 1970). A more recent and nuanced understanding of regime types is found in Juan Linz and Alfred Stepan, *Problems of Democratic Transition and Consolidation: Southern Europe, South America, and Post-Communist Europe* (Baltimore: Johns Hopkins University Press, 1996), pp. 41–48.

3. For an excellent study of media control and liberalization in Taiwan, see Chin-chuan Lee, "Sparking a Fire: The Press and the Ferment of Democratic Change in Taiwan," *Journalism Monographs* (April 1993).

4. In the PRC, in 1985 the Ministry of Education was transformed into a state commission and put under the leadership of then Vice-Premier Li Peng. See Ruth Hayhoe, *China's Universities and the Open Door* (New York: M. E. Sharpe, 1989), p. 43.

5. See Hayhoe, *China's Universities and the Open Door,* p. 31; Erwin H. Epstein and Wei-fan Kuo, "Higher Education," in Douglas C. Smith, ed., *The Confucian Continuum: Educational Modernization in Taiwan* (New York: Praeger, 1991), p. 182; and Deng Piyun, *Bashi Niandai* (Taipei: Taiwan Yanjiu Jijinhui, 1990), p. 4.

6. In the PRC, these studies amounted to 10–15% of curricular time for all students—a lower percentage than was typical of the Maoist period, but still a substantial amount of time (Hayhoe, *China's Universities and the Open Door,* p. 30). See also Ronald Price, "Moral-Political Education and Modernization," in Ruth Hayhoe, ed., *Education and Modernization: The Chinese Experience* (New York: Pergamon Press, 1992), p. 219; and Epstein and Kuo, "Higher Education," p. 190.

7. Although in Taiwan it technically was illegal to expel a student for such activities, campus authorities had been able to skirt this rule. According to regulations, a student could be expelled only if he or she received three large demerits (three small demerits amounted to one large). In 1985, National Taiwan University student activist Lee Wen-chung was given two large demerits and two small demerits for participating in a campus protest demonstration. Shortly thereafter, Lee was

accused of violating a registration technicality and punished with a third small demerit. He subsequently was expelled.

8. Epstein and Kuo, "Higher Education," p. 200.

9. Jurgen Henze, "The Formal Education System and Modernization: An Analysis of Developments since 1978," in Hayhoe, ed., *Education and Modernization*, p. 115.

10. Epstein and Kuo, "Higher Education," pp. 198, 200.

11. In the PRC, the field of politics and law was seen as a springboard to plum bureaucratic positions and thus was the most competitive of any subject; see Hayhoe, *China's Universities and the Open Door*, pp. 30, 41. Similarly, in the ROC competition for admission to the arts and humanities was higher than for any other fields (Epstein and Kuo, "Higher Education," p. 190).

12. Epstein and Kuo, "Higher Education," pp. 190–193.

13. For example, one student who was active in the mid-1980s reported to me that upon his graduation he was assigned to military service in one of the least desirable posts—the bleak and isolated island of Chinmen (Quemoy), located just miles from the mainland, on the front line of a potential battlefront with CCP forces. Not only that, but this student later discovered that, even though he had failed the eyesight exam to enter the army, the doctor's findings had been overridden by a higher military official so that the student was forced to serve anyway. Interview 52, July 23, 1998.

14. Orville Schell, *Mandate of Heaven* (New York: Simon and Schuster, 1994), pp. 186–227; Hongda Harry Wu, *Laogai: The Chinese Gulag* (Boulder, CO: Westview Press, 1992), pp. 1–53. See also Hongda Harry Wu and Carolyn Wakeman, *Bitter Winds: A Memoir of My Years in China's Gulag* (New York: J. Wiley, 1994).

15. Most notably, in 1979 opposition activists associated with the dissident journal *Formosa* were given lengthy prison terms, and some were physically assaulted and killed by forces associated with the ruling regime; see John Kaplan, *The Court Martial of the Kaohsiung Defendants* (Berkeley: Institute of East Asian Studies, 1981). In the early 1980s, a number of prominent dissidents also were assassinated by groups associated with the KMT: in 1981 Professor Chen Bun-seng was found dead on the National Taiwan University campus; and in 1984 dissident authors Chiang Nan and Henry Liu were murdered in the United States.

16. I draw here from Max Weber's ideal-typical model of charismatic, rational-legal, and traditional forms of legitimacy. According to Weber, charismatic legitimacy is defined as "devotion to the specific and exceptional sanctity, heroism or exemplary character of an individual person, and of the normative patterns or order revealed or ordained by him," whereas rational-legal legitimacy rests "on a belief in the 'legality' of patterns of normative rules and the right of those elevated to authority under such rules to issue commands." Max Weber, *The Theory of Social and Economic Organization* (New York: The Free Press, 1947), p. 328.

17. Yu Yu-lin, "Change and Continuity in the CCP's Power Structure since Its

13th National Congress," in Ramon Myers, ed., *Two Societies in Opposition: The Republic of China and the People's Republic of China after Forty Years* (Stanford, CA: Hoover Institution Press, 1991), pp. 62–63.

18. Kenneth Lieberthal, *Governing China* (New York: W. W. Norton and Co., 1995), pp. 221–222.

19. Yu, "Change and Continuity in the CCP's Power Structure," p. 70.

20. Ibid., p. 71.

21. See "Summary of Deng Xiaoping's March 1979 Speech at a Discussion of Theoretical Issues," *Guang Jiao Jing* (Hong Kong) 85 (November 16, 1979): 4–10. Cited in Lowell Dittmer, *China's Continuous Revolution: The Post-Liberation Epoch, 1949–1981* (Berkeley: University of California Press, 1987), p. 234 n. 59.

22. Zhao Ziyang, "Advance along the Road of Socialism with Chinese Characteristics," *People's Daily,* November 4, 1987, pp. 1–4. Cited in Edward I-hsin Chen, "Current Debates over Marxist Theory in the PRC," in Ramon Myers, ed., *Two Societies in Opposition,* p. 271.

23. Chen, "Current Debates over Marxist Theory in the PRC," p. 277.

24. Wu Jiaxiang, *Shijie Jingji Daobao,* no. 426; cited in Chen, "Current Debates over Marxist Theory in the PRC," p. 282.

25. Xiao Gongxin, "No Easy Choice: The New Authoritarianism," *Wenhui Bao* (Hong Kong), January 17, 1989; cited in Chen, "Current Debates over Marxist Theory in the PRC," p. 283.

26. Chen, "Current Debates over Marxist Theory in the PRC," p. 283.

27. Ibid., pp. 65–67.

28. Ibid., pp. 68–69.

29. Ho Yan-cheng, "Chen Yun on Counterattacks in the Ideological Sphere," *Jingbao* (1989), p. 29; cited in Yu, "Change and Continuity in the CCP's Power Structure," pp. 71–72.

30. Paraphrased description of "Li Peng's Government Work Report at the 2nd Session of the 7th NPC," *Dagong Bao,* March 21, 1989; cited in Yu, "Change and Continuity in the CCP's Power Structure," pp. 72–73.

31. Indeed, when the party deliberated over Lee Teng-hui's appointment to the presidency in 1988, Lee Huan twice intervened to thwart conservative mainlander attempts (led by Madame Chiang Kai-shek) to block Lee Teng-hui's appointment. See Peter Moody, Jr., *Political Change on Taiwan: A Study of Ruling Party Adaptability* (New York: Praeger Publishers, 1992), p. 158; and C. L. Chiou, *Democratizing Oriental Despotism: China from 4 May 1919 to 4 June 1989 and Taiwan from 28 February 1947 to 28 June 1990* (New York: St. Martin's Press, 1995), p. 106.

32. Moody, *Political Change on Taiwan,* pp. 156–157. Indeed, in the Central Committee election at the 13th Party Congress in July of 1988, Li Huan received more votes than any other delegate. See Jurgen Domes, "The 13th Party Congress of the Kuomintang: Towards Political Competition?" *China Quarterly* (June 1989), p. 348.

33. Moody, *Political Change on Taiwan,* p. 173; Linda Chao and Ramon

Myers, "The First Chinese Democracy," *Asian Survey* (March 1994), p. 223; and Shao-chuan Leng and Cheng-yi Lin, "Political Change on Taiwan: Transition to Democracy?" *China Quarterly* (December 1993), pp. 810, 813.

34. *Zhongyang Ribao*, February 3, 1990; and *Jiushi Niandai* (April 1990), p. 36. Cited in Moody, *Political Change on Taiwan*, p. 171.

35. *Zhongyang Ribao*, February 28, 1990; cited in Moody, *Political Change on Taiwan*, p. 172.

36. *Jiushi Niandai* (April 1990), p. 37; *Zhongyang Ribao*, March 5, 1990. Cited in Moody, *Political Change on Taiwan*, p. 173.

37. Ibid. There were 752 members of the National Assembly in total.

Chapter 3

1. See, for example, Andrew Walder and Gong Xiaoxia, "Workers in the Tiananmen Protests: The Politics of the Beijing Workers' Autonomous Federation," *The Australian Journal of Chinese Affairs* (January 1993), pp. 1–29; Craig Calhoun, *Neither Gods Nor Emperors* (Berkeley: University of California Press, 1994); Joseph Esherick and Jeffrey Wasserstrom, "Acting Out Democracy: Political Theater in Modern China," in Elizabeth Perry and Jeffrey Wasserstrom, eds., *Popular Protest and Political Culture in Modern China: Learning from 1989,* 2d ed. (Boulder, CO: Westview Press, 1994); and Elizabeth Perry, "Casting a Chinese 'Democracy' Movement: The Roles of Students, Workers, and Entrepreneurs," in Perry and Wasserstrom, eds., *Popular Protest and Political Culture in Modern China.*

2. See, for example, Calhoun, *Neither Gods Nor Emperors,* p. 163.

3. See, for example, Esherick and Wasserstrom, "Acting Out Democracy"; Vera Schwarcz, "Memory and Commemoration: The Chinese Search for a Livable Past," in Perry and Wasserstrom, eds., *Popular Protest and Political Culture in Modern China;* and Timothy Cheek, "From Priests to Professionals: Intellectuals and the State under the CCP," in Perry and Wasserstrom, eds., *Popular Protest and Political Culture in Modern China.*

4. Liu Xiaobo, "That Holy Word, 'Revolution,' " in Perry and Wasserstrom, eds., *Popular Protest and Political Culture in Modern China.*

5. Many analyses mention these ideas in passing. For example, Black and Munro, as well as Schell, note that the students' exclusion of workers was designed to guard against official slander, infiltration, and repression. Similarly, Francis remarks that students consciously enforced discipline in order to reduce the threat of violence. Perry and Lee also mention that the students' moderate behavior was a reflection of their lack of power vis-à-vis the state. Nevertheless, these scholars do not focus on the repressive and nondemocratic political opportunity structure as their basic explanatory variable. See George Black and Robin Munro, *Black Hands of Beijing: Lives of Defiance in China's Democracy Movement* (New York: John Wiley and Sons, 1993), pp.159–160, 221–222; Orville Schell, *Mandate of Heaven* (New York: Simon and Schuster, 1994), p. 185; Corrina-Barbara Francis, "The Prog-

ress of Protest in China," *Asian Survey* 29, no. 9 (September 1989): 913; Perry, "Casting a Chinese 'Democracy' Movement," p. 150; and Lee Feigon, *China Rising: The Meaning of Tiananmen* (Chicago: Ivan R. Dee, 1990), p. 130.

6. Walder and Gong, "Workers in the Tiananmen Protests," p. 28. See also Calhoun, *Neither Gods Nor Emperors;* Esherick and Wasserstrom, "Acting Out Democracy"; and Perry, "Casting a Chinese 'Democracy' Movement."

7. Andrew Nathan, *Chinese Democracy* (Berkeley: University of California Press, 1985), pp. 40–41.

8. Wei was released in November 1997 to the United States. He is forbidden to return to China.

9. Nathan, *Chinese Democracy,* p. 41.

10. Pepper, *China's Education Reform in the 1980's,* pp. 173–174.

11. Hayhoe, *China's Universities and the Open Door,* p. 47.

12. Lee, *China Rising,* p. 65.

13. Ibid., p. 66.

14. Feng Congde, in *Huigu yu Fansi* (Essen, Germany: German Rhine Writers' Association 1989 Student Research Group, 1993), p. 20. Feng Congde, later a key figure in the 1989 movement, was one of the students who was arrested.

15. Ibid.

16. Shen Tong, *Almost a Revolution* (Boston: Houghton-Mifflin, 1990), p. 135.

17. Feng Congde attended the first meeting of the "Committee for Action" but subsequently withdrew, as he felt that the group was unduly secretive (Feng Congde, in *Huigu yu Fansi,* p. 20).

18. Shen Tong, *Almost a Revolution,* p. 136.

19. Ibid., p. 139; Interview 12, March 4, 1995.

20. Shen Tong, *Almost a Revolution,* pp. 148–160. The May Fourth Movement of 1919 was led by students, faculty members, and administrators at Beida, who called for "science and democracy" to replace feudal practices and beliefs. Many of the movement's leaders later became active in forming the Chinese Communist Party.

21. Interview 12, March 4, 1995.

22. See, for example, Woei Lien Chong, "Petitioners, Popperians, and Hunger Strikers: The Uncoordinated Efforts of the 1989 Chinese Democratic Movement," in Tony Saich, ed., *The Chinese People's Movement: Perspectives on Spring 1989* (Armonk, NY: M. E. Sharpe, 1990); Josephine M. T. Khu, "Student Organization in the Movement," in Roger Des Forges, Luo Ning, and Wu Yenbo, eds., *Chinese Democracy and the Crisis of 1989* (Albany: State University of New York Press, 1993); and Lee Feigon, *China Rising: The Meaning of Tiananmen,* pp. 134–136. A unique counterassessment of this salon-centered approach can be found in Jeffrey Wasserstrom and Liu Xingyun, "Student Associations and Mass Movements," in Deborah Davis, Richard Kraus, Barry Naughton, and Elizabeth Perry, eds., *Urban Spaces in Contemporary China* (New York: Woodrow Wilson Center Press and Cambridge University Press, 1995).

23. Some Shida students had tried to form a kind of salon in 1986, but the

group was quickly disbanded by the authorities, and its leader expelled from school. Following this, few dared to try to organize on this campus (Interview 7, February 9, 1995).

24. Hu had continued on as a voting member of the Politburo even after he was forced to step down from the position of General Secretary (Lee, *China Rising,* pp. 124–125).

25. Ibid., p. 135.

26. Interview 12, March 4, 1995.

27. Zhang Boli, in *Huigu yu Fansi,* p. 50.

28. A chart of organizational development during the spring of 1989 is provided in Appendix B.

29. Feng Congde, in *Huigu yu Fansi,* p. 20.

30. Chai Ling, in ibid., p. 3.

31. Interview 12, March 4, 1995.

32. Shen Tong, *Almost a Revolution,* pp. 174–175.

33. Chang Jin, in *Huigu yu Fansi,* p. 4.

34. Feng Congde, in ibid., p. 21.

35. Ibid., p. 22.

36. Interview 12, March 4, 1995.

37. Feng Congde, in *Huigu yu Fansi,* p. 21.

38. Michel Oksenberg, Lawrence R. Sullivan, and Marc Lambert, *Beijing Spring, 1989; Confrontation and Conflict; The Basic Documents* (Armonk, NY: M. E. Sharpe, 1990), p. 22.

39. Wang Guobao, "Beijing Xueyun Qinghua Jianwen," *Tansuo* (Exploration) 66 (June 1989): 61.

40. Feng Congde, in *Huigu yu Fansi,* p. 22.

41. Chai Ling, in ibid., p. 4.

42. Feng Congde, in ibid., p. 22.

43. Shen Tong, in ibid., p. 57.

44. Shen Tong, *Almost a Revolution,* pp. 175–176.

45. Ibid., p. 178.

46. Ibid.

47. Zhang Boli, in *Huigu yu Fansi,* p. 6.

48. Chang Jin, in ibid., p. 5.

49. Zhang Boli, in ibid., p. 7.

50. Ibid.

51. Chai Ling, in *Huigu yu Fansi,* p. 28.

52. Interview 12, March 4, 1995. For a concurring opinion, see Feng Congde, in *Huigu yu Fansi,* p. 22. Interview 16, March 15, 1995, also confirms this assertion.

53. Chai Ling, in *Huigu yu Fansi,* p. 28. For the text of the poster, see Appendix B.

54. Shen Tong, *Almost a Revolution,* p. 186.

55. Interview 10, February 23, 1995.

56. Interview 7, February 9, 1995.

57. Ibid.

58. Interview 10, February 23, 1995.

59. Liang Er, in *Huigu yu Fansi*, p. 31.

60. Interview 7, February 9, 1995.

61. In the end, Wu'er simply yelled out a sentence, and those surrounding him repeated it. Those who heard the sentence then repeated it for those surrounding them, and so on (Interview 7, February 9, 1995).

62. Ibid.

63. Ibid.

64. Interview 10, February 23, 1995.

65. Interview 7, February 9, 1995.

66. Wu Moren, Ni Peihua, Wang Qingjia, Yan Jiaqi, Wu'er Kaixi, Bao Minghui, and Ni Peimin, eds., *Bajiu Zhongguo Minyun Jishi* (New York, 1989), p. 28.

67. Wang Chaohua, in *Huigu yu Fansi*, p. 35; Interview 7, February 9, 1995.

68. Feng Congde, in *Huigu yu Fansi*, p. 24.

69. Interview 7, February 9, 1995.

70. Wang Chaohua, in *Huigu yu Fansi*, p. 35.

71. "Petition," Beida Preparatory Committee, May 21, 1989, Tiananmen Archive, Columbia University, Document H-16.

72. Oksenberg et al., *Beijing Spring, 1989*, p. 27.

73. Wang Chaohua, in *Huigu yu Fansi*, p. 35.

74. Ibid.

75. *Bajiu Zongguo Minyun Jishi*, p. 29. The government later denied making this promise. In actuality, it is somewhat unclear whether or not it did make this statement, or if it was simply a rumor; see Feng Congde, Wang Chaohua, and Chang Jin, in *Huigu yu Fansi*, p. 36.

76. Chai Ling, in *Huigu yu Fansi*, p. 29.

77. Shen Tong, *Almost a Revolution*, pp. 187–189.

78. Feng Congde, in *Huigu yu Fansi*, p. 25.

79. Liang Er, in ibid., p. 33.

80. Interview 10, February 23, 1995.

81. Ibid.

82. Chai Ling, in *Huigu yu Fansi*, p. 30.

83. Shen Tong, *Almost a Revolution*, p. 190; Interview 12, March 4, 1995.

84. Interview 12, March 4, 1995; and Shen Tong, *Almost a Revolution*, p. 191.

85. Shen Tong, *Almost a Revolution*, p. 191.

86. Feng Congde, in *Huigu yu Fansi*, p. 26.

87. Ibid.

88. Chang Jin, in *Huigu yu Fansi*, p. 9.

89. Shen Tong, *Almost a Revolution*, p. 193.

90. Interview 12, March 4, 1995.

91. Ibid. See also Shen Tong, *Almost a Revolution*, pp. 213–216.

92. Interview 12, March 4, 1995.

93. Ibid.

94. Liang Er, in *Huigu yu Fansi*, p. 31.

95. Wang Chaohua, in ibid., p. 44.

96. Liang Er, in ibid., p. 31.

97. See Feng Congde, in ibid., p. 25; and Wang Chaohua, in ibid., p. 37.

98. See Wang Chaohua, in ibid., p. 33; and Shen Tong, in ibid., p. 63.

99. Interview 12, March 4, 1995.

100. Wang Dan did attend this first meeting, but at the time his connection with the BAU was tenuous. Shortly after Wang's election to the BAU on April 25, he was forced to resign, as other members felt that he was spending an undue amount of time attending press conferences (Interview 12, March 4, 1995).

101. Interview 7, February 9, 1995.

102. Ibid.

103. Interview 7, March 4, and Interview 11, March 3, 1995.

104. Ibid.

105. Apparently, students from the University of Politics and Law had promised to provide the group with food, so the group changed its meeting location (though the food never actually appeared) (Interview 7, February 9, 1995).

106. "It Is Necessary to Take a Clear-Cut Stand against Turmoil," *Renmin Ribao,* April 26, 1989; reprinted in Oksenberg et al., *Beijing Spring, 1989,* pp. 207–208.

107. Black and Munro, *Black Hands of Beijing,* pp. 147–148; Timothy Brook, *Quelling the People* (New York: Oxford University Press, 1992), p. 32.

108. Ibid.

109. *South China Morning Post* (Hong Kong), May 31, 1989, 12; FBIS, May 31, pp. 35–36. Cited in Oksenberg et al., *Beijing Spring, 1989*, pp. 203–206.

110. Scott Simmie and Bob Nixon, *Tiananmen Square* (Seattle: University of Washington Press, 1989), p. 37.

111. FBIS-CHI-89-079, p. 15; cited in Brook, *Quelling the People,* p. 30.

112. After the first broadcast, both meetings were postponed for one hour so that all members could listen to a repeated broadcast at 5:30 P.M.

113. Wang Chaohua, in *Huigu yu Fansi,* p. 39.

114. Interview 7, February 9, 1995.

115. Interview 10, February 23, 1995.

116. Interview 7, February 9, 1995.

117. Feng Congde, in *Huigu yu Fansi,* p. 27.

118. Shen Tong, *Almost a Revolution,* pp. 196–198.

119. Interview 7, February 9, 1995.

120. Ibid.

121. Shen Tong, *Almost a Revolution,* pp. 200–201.

122. Interview 10, February 23, 1995.

123. Interview 7, February 9, 1995, and ibid. See also Wang Chaohua, in *Huigu yu Fansi,* p. 44.

124. Interview 10, February 23, 1995.

125. Feng Congde, in *Huigu yu Fansi,* pp. 62–63.

126. Liu Yen, in ibid., pp. 65–66.

127. Interview 7, February 9, 1995.

128. Ibid.

129. Interview 10, February 23, 1995.

130. Ibid.

131. Interview 7, February 9, 1995.

132. Text of student dialogue with Yuan Mu; reprinted in Oksenberg et al., *Bejing Spring, 1989,* pp. 218–244.

133. One source explained this event to me as follows: "After the huge success on April 27, the student leaders were afraid to organize another huge demonstration on May 4. To stimulate student excitement and anger, Wang Dan and Wu'er Kaixi went into hiding for a few days. This wasn't completely trumped up, as they had heard that their names had been mentioned in a Politburo meeting. Plus, Wang had connections with Fang Lizhi, and Wu'er had connections with Liu Xiaobo. Thus, between the two of them, they represented all that the government feared and hated most. Anyway, this ploy worked. Wu'er had great prestige at Shida, and because of this, the students became very angry when they heard that he was in danger" (Interview 7, February 9, 1995).

134. Shen Tong, *Almost a Revolution,* p. 208. See also, Feng Congde, in *Huigu yu Fansi,* p. 68. This event was also discussed in Interview 7, February 9, 1995.

135. Feng Congde, in *Huigu yu Fansi,* p. 68.

136. Interview 10, February 23, 1995.

137. Apparently, this change in size was a concession to the numerous students who now wished to have a seat on the Standing Committee (see Wang Chaohua, in *Huigu yu Fansi,* pp. 73–74).

138. Feng Congde, in *Huigu yu Fansi,* p. 68.

139. Wang Chaohua, in ibid., p. 72.

140. Feng Congde, in ibid., p. 68.

141. Black and Munro, p. 164.

142. Ibid., p. 165.

143. *Xinhua* (Beijing; in English), May 4, 1989; FBIS, May 4, p. 1. Cited in Oksenberg et al., *Bejing Spring, 1989,* pp. 255. See also Brook, *Quelling the People,* p. 36.

144. Forty-seven schools had representatives in attendance.

145. Ibid., p. 69.

146. Shen Tong, *Almost a Revolution,* p. 221.

147. Interview 7, February 9, 1995. For the text of the declaration, see the Robin Munro Collection, Section XIII, Document 7.

148. Shen Tong, in *Almost a Revolution,* p. 221.

149. "Declaration," Beijing Gaoxiao Zizhi Lianhehui, reprinted in *Bajiu Zhong-guo Minyun Ziliao* (Hong Kong Chinese Language University Student Union, 1991), p. 154; Shen Tong, *Almost a Revolution,* p. 226.

150. Interview 7, February 9, 1995.

151. Ibid.

152. See, e.g., Wang Chaohua, in *Huigu yu Fansi,* p. 75; and Chai Ling, in *Huigu yu Fansi,* p. 88.

153. Shortly thereafter, Zhou decided to forsake involvement with students and became instrumental in founding the Beijing Workers' Autonomous Federation.

154. Wang Chaohua, in *Huigu yu Fansi,* p. 75.

155. Interview 11, March 3, 1995.

156. Ibid.

157. Ibid.

158. Shen Tong, *Almost a Revolution,* pp. 223–224.

159. Ibid., p. 223.

160. Interview 11, March 3, 1995. See also Shen Tong, *Almost a Revolution,* p. 224.

161. Reprinted in *Bajiu Zhongguo Minyun Ziliao,* pp. 148–149.

162. Interview 11, March 3, 1995.

163. Shen Tong, *Almost a Revolution,* p. 225.

164. Interview 11, March 3, 1995.

165. Shen Tong, *Almost a Revolution,* p. 229.

166. Interview 7, February 9, 1995.

Chapter 4

1. For earlier discussions of this radicalizing trend, see Craig Calhoun, *Neither Gods Nor Emperors* (Berkeley: University of California Press, 1994), pp. 183–185; Liu Xiaobo, "That Holy Word, 'Revolution,' " in Elizabeth Perry and Jeffrey Wasserstrom, eds., *Popular Protest and Political Culture in Modern China,* 2d ed. (Boulder, CO: Westview Press, 1994); and George Black and Robin Munro, *Black Hands of Beijing: Lives of Defiance in China's Democracy Movement* (New York: John Wiley and Sons, 1993), pp. 208–209.

2. Apparently, the idea was previously put forth in many different arenas. For example, it is reported that on May 9 some graduate students in Building no. 46 at Beida displayed a poster calling for a hunger strike (Feng Congde, in *Huigu yu Fansi* [Essen, Germany: German Rhine Writers' Association 1989 Student Research Group, 1993], p. 124). In addition, Zhang Boli had earlier suggested an on-campus hunger strike, noting that in this way protestors could actually "sneak" some food in campus bathrooms (Chai Ling, in ibid., p. 89). Further, on May 8, Wu'er Kaixi made a speech to the chemistry department at Shida in which he expressed his desire to begin a hunger strike (Liang Er, in ibid., p. 127).

3. Liu Yan, in *Huigu yu Fansi,* p. 123.

4. Chai Ling, in ibid., p. 89.

5. Interview 12, March 4, 1995.

6. Chang Jin, in *Huigu yu Fansi,* p. 93.

7. Ibid.

8. Chai Ling, in *Huigu yu Fansi,* p. 89.

9. Shen Tong, *Almost a Revolution* (Boston: Houghton-Mifflin, 1990), p. 235.

10. Ibid., p. 237. See also Interview 12, March 4, 1995.

11. Interview 12, March 4, 1995; see also Chai Ling, in *Huigu yu Fansi,* p. 92.

12. Yang Chaohui, as quoted in *Huigu yu Fansi,* pp. 94–95.

13. Wang Chaohua, in ibid., p. 95.

14. Chai Ling, in ibid., p. 90.

15. Zheng Xuguang, as quoted in ibid., p. 95.

16. Liang Er, in ibid., p. 97.

17. Interview 10, February 23, 1995; Interview 7, February 9, 1995.

18. Interview 10, February 23, 1995.

19. *Xinwen Daobao* (printed at Tiananmen Square), May 12, 1989; reprinted in *Zhongguo Zhichun* (New York) 75 (August 1989): 11–12.

20. "Hunger Strike Statement," Tiananmen Archive, Columbia University, Document H-18.

21. Shen Tong, *Almost a Revolution,* pp. 238–239.

22. Wang Chaohua, in *Huigu yu Fansi,* p. 99.

23. Feng Congde, in *Huigu yu Fansi,* p. 130.

24. Interview 12, March 4, 1995. See also Chai Ling, in *Huigu yu Fansi,* p. 104.

25. Feng Congde, in *Huigu yu Fansi,* p. 130.

26. Chai Ling, in ibid., p. 104.

27. Ibid., p. 126.

28. Ibid., p. 131.

29. Interview 12, March 4, 1995.

30. Interview 11, March 3, 1995. See also Wang Chaohua, in *Huigu yu Fansi,* p. 99; Shen Tong, *Almost a Revolution,* pp. 239–240.

31. Wang Chaohua, in *Huigu yu Fansi,* p. 100; Shen Tong, *Almost a Revolution,* p. 240.

32. Shen Tong, *Almost a Revolution,* p. 241.

33. Wang Chaohua, in *Huigu yu Fansi,* p. 100.

34. Shen Tong, *Almost a Revolution,* p. 242.

35. Interview 11, March 3, 1995.

36. Ibid.

37. Shen Tong, *Almost a Revolution,* p. 242.

38. Ibid., p. 246.

39. Interview 11, March 3, 1995; Interview 7, February 9, 1995; and Chai Ling, in *Huigu yu Fansi,* p. 144.

40. Interview 11, March 3, 1995.

41. Li Lu, in *Huigu yu Fansi,* p. 135.

42. Chai Ling, in ibid., p. 131.

43. Wang Chaohua, in ibid., p. 134.

44. Chai Ling, in ibid., p. 133.

45. Ibid., 131.

46. Wang Chaohua, in *Huigu yu Fansi,* p. 155.

47. Shen Tong, *Almost a Revolution,* p. 257.

48. Timothy Cheek, "From Priests to Professionals: Intellectuals and the State under the CCP," in Perry and Wasserstrom, eds., *Popular Protest and Political Culture in Modern China,* p. 41.

49. Ibid., p. 44.

50. Ibid., pp. 44–45.

51. Li Lu, in *Huigu yu Fansi,* p. 175.

52. Li claims that he purposely did not bring his student identification card because he planned to travel to Beijing by sneaking on a train (ibid.).

53. Chai Ling, in *Huigu yu Fansi,* p. 145. It is not entirely clear why Chai Ling was so quick to place her trust in Li. However, as the movement progressed, their relationship became quite close, and possibly romantic. At the same time, Chai Ling's relationship with Feng Congde grew increasingly estranged; indeed, not long after the movement ended, the two divorced.

54. Ibid., p. 144.

55. Ibid.; Li Lu, in *Huigu yu Fansi,* p. 171.

56. This was not the only time that self-immolation was considered. For example, on the night of May 8, a history student at Shida made this suggestion, and at a press conference on May 15 an unnamed student stated that he wished to burn himself to death to protest government intransigence (Li Lu and Liang Er, in *Huigu yu Fansi,* pp. 173–174).

57. Chai Ling, in *Huigu yu Fansi,* p. 144.

58. Li Lu, in ibid., p. 136.

59. Ibid., p. 171.

60. Ibid., p. 136.

61. Ibid., p. 171.

62. Ibid., p. 137.

63. Ibid.

64. Feng Congde, in *Huigu yu Fansi,* p. 151. See also Chang Jin, in ibid., p. 107.

65. Feng Congde, in ibid., p. 153.

66. Ibid., p. 133.

67. Chai Ling, in ibid., p. 147.

68. Ibid., p. 148.

69. Interview 16, March 15, 1995.

70. Chai Ling, in *Huigu yu Fansi,* p. 148.

71. Ibid.

72. Interview 16, March 15, 1995.

73. Li Lu, in *Huigu yu Fansi,* p. 137.

74. Ibid.

75. Chai Ling, in *Huigu yu Fansi,* p. 149.

76. Li Lu, in ibid., p. 140. See also Shen Tong, *Almost a Revolution,* p. 266.

77. Chai Ling collapsed on the morning of May 16 and at noon on May 17; Wu'er Kaixi collapsed on the afternoon of May 16; and Li Lu collapsed on the afternoon of May 17 (Chai Ling, in *Huigu yu Fansi*, pp. 148–149; Li Lu, in ibid., p. 140).

78. Li Lu, in ibid., p. 141.

79. Shen Tong, *Almost a Revolution*, p. 281. See also Wang Chaohua, in *Huigu yu Fansi*, pp. 157–158.

80. "Letter to Compatriots of the Nation," Beijing City Workers' Union, May 17, 1989; *Zhongguo Minyun Yuan Ziliao Jingxuan*, vol. 1, June 25, 1989, p. 28. This group used various titles throughout its existence (e.g., Capital Workers' Autonomous Union), yet all refer to the same group.

81. Chai Ling, in *Huigu yu Fansi*, p. 146.

82. Ibid., p. 147.

83. Ibid.

84. Li Lu, in *Huigu yu Fansi*, p. 142.

85. Ibid.

86. Interview 12, March 4, 1995.

87. Wang Chaohua, in *Huigu yu Fansi*, p. 160.

88. Ibid., p. 159.

89. Interview 10, February 23, 1995.

90. Wang Chaohua, in *Huigu yu Fansi*, pp. 192–193.

91. Ibid., pp. 158–159.

92. Liang Er, in *Huigu yu Fansi*, p. 193.

93. Chang Jin, in ibid., p. 177. See also Wang Chaohua, in ibid., p. 159.

94. Feng Congde, in ibid., p. 153.

95. Ibid.

96. Ibid.

97. Li Lu, in *Huigu yu Fansi*, p. 160.

98. Feng Congde, in ibid., p. 153.

99. Wang Chaohua, in ibid., p. 159.

100. Li Lu, in ibid., p. 160.

101. Wang Chaohua, in ibid., p. 159. Indeed, Wang claims that as a result of this situation she had to appeal to the Shida Autonomous Union for funds.

102. Interview 12, March 4, 1995.

103. Ibid.

104. This stand was located in front of the Museum of History so as to maintain an appropriate distance from the hunger-striking students.

105. By May 16, over two thousand Beida students were working in this capacity at the square. On May 17, these security workers were reorganized into an hierarchical system. Each position in the system was assigned a number to be displayed by its incumbent. Regardless of changes in personnel, the same position would always be designated by the same number. Chang Jin, in *Huigu yu Fansi*, pp. 176–177.

106. Ibid., p. 179; Interview 12, March 4, 1995.

107. Interview 12, March 4, 1995.

108. Interview 13, March 4, 1995.

109. Interview 12, March 4, 1995.

110. Interview 13, March 4, 1995.

111. Interview 12, March 4, 1995.

112. Wang Chaohua, in *Huigu yu Fansi,* p. 157.

113. Li Lu, in ibid., p. 140

114. It is not clear exactly who attended this meeting, though it is certain that Wang Dan and some BSAF representatives were there.

115. Shen Tong, *Almost a Revolution,* p. 282. It is interesting to note that this new organization did not introduce any new demands that differed from those of the BSAF.

116. Ibid., p. 279.

117. Shen Tong, in *Huigu yu Fansi,* p. 186.

118. Shen Tong, *Almost a Revolution,* p. 279.

119. Wang Chaohua, in *Huigu yu Fansi,* p. 162.

120. Feng Congde, in ibid., p. 194.

121. The student delegation included Wu'er Kaixi, Wang Dan, Wang Chaohua, Xiong Yan, Wang Zhixin, Zhen Songyu, and Shao Jiang. The names of the other four students who attended the meeting have not been recorded. *Renmin Ribao,* May 19, 1989, pp. 1, 4.

122. Wang Chaohua, in *Huigu yu Fansi,* p. 162.

123. Xinhua News Agency report, May 18, 1995. Reprinted in *Bajiu Zhongguo Minyun Ziliao* (Hong Kong Chinese Language University Student Association, 1991), p. 272.

124. Ibid.

125. Ibid., p. 273.

126. Beijing Television Service, May 18, 1989. Transcribed and translated in Michael Oksenberg, Lawrence R. Sullivan, and Marc Lambert, eds., *Beijing Spring, 1989: Confrontation and Conflict; The Basic Documents* (Armonk, NY: M. E. Sharpe, 1990), pp. 270–280.

127. Xinhua News Agency report, May 19, 1989. Reprinted in *Bajiu Zhongguo Minyun Jishi,* p. 295.

128. Lao Mu, in *Huigu yu Fansi,* pp. 198–199.

129. Liu Yan, in ibid., pp. 201–202.

130. Zhang Boli, in ibid., p. 196; Li Lu, in ibid., p. 169.

131. It is reported that 208 votes were cast, with 173 wishing to end the hunger strike, 28 opposing this view, and 7 abstaining (Zhang Boli, in *Huigu yu Fansi,* p. 196). However, these numbers must be called into question, as it would have been physically impossible for 208 persons to attend a meeting on the bus, and at no time were messengers sent out of the bus to gather other votes.

132. Ibid.

133. Xin Ku, in ibid., p. 205.

134. Zhang Boli, in ibid., p. 196.

135. Feng Congde, in ibid., p. 204.

136. Ibid.

137. Zhang Boli, in *Huigu yu Fansi*, p. 197.

138. Wang Chaohua, in ibid., p. 205. Wang claims that this announcement was made with no knowledge of Wu'er Kaixi's meeting with Yan Mingfu, or of Feng Congde's contestation of the Hunger Strike Command's original decision to end the strike.

139. Chai Ling, in *Huigu yu Fansi*, pp. 200–201.

140. In the words of Zhang Boli, "After martial law was announced, the Hunger Strike Command had basically completed its historical mission" (Zhang Boli, in ibid., p. 207).

141. Chai Ling, in ibid., p. 224; Zhang Boli, in ibid., p. 207.

142. Wang Chaohua, in ibid., pp. 212–213.

143. Xin Ku, in ibid., p. 213.

144. Wang Chaohua, in ibid., pp. 213–214.

145. Interview 15, March 9, 1995.

146. W. K. Tang, "The Story of a Non-Governmental Reformist Research Institute in China," *A Changing China* (sponsored by the North American Coalition for Chinese Democracy) (Winter 1991).

147. Interview 15, March 9, 1995.

148. For example, one interviewee noted that Liu Gang had a particularly strong influence on Wang Dan (ibid.).

149. Ibid.

150. The group nominally was responsible for the production of the movement newsletter entitled, "Express News" ("Xinwen Kuaixun"), but in actuality Lao Mu individually managed its production (Lao Mu, in *Huigu yu Fansi*, p. 234).

151. Interview 16, March 15, 1995.

152. Chai Ling, in *Huigu yu Fansi*, p. 107.

153. Zhang Lun, in ibid., pp. 231–232; Lao Mu, in ibid., p. 233.

154. Zhang Lun, in ibid., p. 232.

155. Lao Mu, in ibid.

156. Zhang Lun, in ibid., p. 233.

157. Interview 7, February 9, 1995.

158. Interview 17, March 16, 1995.

159. The following day, the name of this group was changed to the "Headquarters to Protect Tiananmen Square."

160. Bai Meng, in *Huigu yu Fansi*, p. 268.

161. Zhang Boli, in ibid., pp. 209–210. See also Chai Ling, in ibid., p. 224.

162. Lao Mu, in ibid., p. 233.

163. Wang Chaohua, in ibid., p. 277.

164. Ibid., p. 266.

165. Liang Er, in ibid., p. 266.

166. Li Lu, in ibid., p. 238.

167. Ibid., p. 266.

168. Ibid., p. 219.

169. Although Wang Chaohua had been appointed to the standing committee of the Temporary Command, she soon resigned from the position. Explaining this decision, Wang states, "[In the Temporary Command], I had many opinions but was never given the opportunity to express them. So I resigned" (Wang Chaohua, in *Huigu yu Fansi,* p. 270).

170. Li Lu, in ibid., p. 223.

171. Zhang Lun, in ibid., p. 280.

172. Li Lu, in ibid., p. 281.

173. See Chai Ling and Liang Er, in ibid., p. 279; Liang Er and Li Lu, in ibid., p. 281; and Bai Meng, in ibid., p. 287.

174. Bai Meng, in ibid., p. 287.

175. Interview 7, February 9, 1995. See also, Feng Congde, in *Huigu yu Fansi,* p. 271.

176. Interview 7, February 9, 1995.

177. Feng Congde, in *Huigu yu Fansi,* pp. 238–239.

178. Ibid., p. 239. Concurrently, Zhang Boli began to work toward the establishment of a Democracy University, hoping to hold "classes" at the square until June 20, and afterward relocate to Beida (Interview 16, March 15, 1995).

179. Interview 7, February 9, 1995.

180. Ibid.

181. "Beijing Workers' Autonomous Federation Preparatory Committee Emergency Message" (Beijing Workers' Autonomous Federation Preparatory Committee Notice, May 30, 1989), Robin Munro Collection, Document XIV.4.

182. "Emergency—Workers' Autonomous Union Preparatory Committee goes to Public Security Bureau to exchange opinions regarding Shen Yinghan's detainment" (Workers' Autonomous Union Preparatory Committee Notice, not dated), Robin Munro Collection, Document XIV.2.

183. Han Minzhu and Hua Sheng, eds., *Cries for Democracy: Writings and Speeches from the 1989 Chinese Democracy Movement* (Princeton, NJ: Princeton University Press, 1990), p. 349. The group included Liu Xiaobo, Zhou Duo, Gao Xin, and Taiwan rock star Hou Dejian.

184. Li Lu, in *Huigu yu Fansi*, pp. 305–306.

185. Ibid., p. 305.

186. Li Lu, in *Huigu yu Fansi,* p. 306.

187. Ibid., p. 309.

188. Feng Congde, in ibid., p. 318.

189. Ibid.

190. "Recognize the Essence of Turmoil and the Necessity of Martial Law," *Renmin Ribao,* June 3, 1989, pp. 1–2.

191. Yuan Mu (news conference), Beijing Television Service, June 6, 1989; FBIS, June 7, p. 12.

192. Chen Xitong, "Report on Checking Turmoil and Quelling the Counter-Revolutionary Rebellion," June 30, 1989 (Beijing: New Star Publishers, 1989), p. 3.

193. Interview 5, February 6, 1995.

194. Interview 3, January 15, 1995.

195. Interview 4, February 6, 1995.

196. Interview 6, February 7, 1995.

197. Of course, interviewees had an interest in downplaying any elitist reasoning that also might have supported this strategy. In addition, they may have been simply unaware of their own elitism. Yet, had this sort of attitude been the primary reason for this strategy choice, one would expect at least some indication of disdain toward workers during lengthy interviews. Further, given the current bitterness that exists among many prominent leaders of the movement of 1989, as well as widespread accusations of student elitism in many analyses of it, one might expect interviewees to accuse their antagonists of such attitudes. However, none of those whom I interviewed made any such claims. Moreover, interviewees from Taiwan also did not make any statements of this nature. Thus, although elitism certainly may have influenced the students' decision-making process, student statements and student-produced documents provide no clear evidence that this was the primary cause of their choice of strategy.

198. Most notably, in interviews with Andrew Walder and Gong Xiaoxia, two individuals involved in the Beijing Workers' Autonomous Federation's claim that student leaders wanted no ties with city workers (Walder and Gong [1993]). Similarly, in interviews with Anita Chan and Jonathan Unger, a junior faculty member from Chongqing reports that students there were greatly embarrassed when it was discovered that the two persons they had elected as their leaders were not students but private entrepreneurs (*getihu*). Anita Chan and Jonathan Unger, "Voices from the Protest Movement in Chongqing: Class Accents and Class Tensions," in Jonathan Unger, ed., *The Pro-Democracy Protests in China: Reports from the Provinces* (New York: M. E. Sharpe, 1991).

199. Interview 4, February 6, 1995.

200. Interview 10, February 23, 1995. For a similar account of these activities, see Liang Er, in *Huigu yu Fansi,* p. 33.

201. "Xinwen Kuaixun," May 31, 1989, p. 5, Robin Munro Collection, Document XXIII.1.

202. Beida pamphlet (undated), Robin Munro Collection, Document II.4.

203. "Courageously Stand Up, Working Brothers," Beida leaflet (undated), Robin Munro Collection, Document II.29.

204. All-Beijing City Students' Autonomous Federation flyer, May 31, 1989, Robin Munro Collection, Document XIII.1.

205. See, for example, Shen Tong, *Almost a Revolution,* p. 277; and Liang Er, in *Huigu yu Fansi,* p. 298.

206. See also Andrew Walder and Gong Xiaoxia, "Workers in the Tiananmen

Protests: The Politics of the Beijing Workers' Autonomous Federation," *The Australian Journal of Chinese Affairs* (January 1993), p. 7.

207. Ibid., p. 6.

Chapter 5

1. For a more detailed history of student dissent in Taiwan, see Teresa Wright, "Student Mobilization in Taiwan: Civil Society and Its Discontents," *Asian Survey* (November/December 1999), pp. 986–1008.

2. These islands are known as the Senkaku in Japanese.

3. Chen Guuying, "The Reform Movement among Intellectuals in Taiwan since 1970," *Bulletin of Concerned Asian Scholars* (July–September 1982), p. 35.

4. Deng Piyun, *Bashi Niandai* (Taipei: Taiwan Yanjiu Jijinhui, 1990), p. 4.

5. For examples, see ibid., p. 15.

6. Editorial: "Student Movement: Forever the Road of Rebellion," *Zhongxing Fashang Formosa,* April 1990; reprinted in Fan Yun, ed., *Xinshengdai de Ziwo Zhuixun* (Taipei: Taiwan Yanjiu Jijinhui, 1991), p. 314.

7. Fan Yun, ed., *Xinshengdai de Ziwo Zhuixun,* p. 382; He Jinshan, Guan Hongzhi, Zhuang Lijia, and Guo Chenqi, *Taibei Xueyun* (Taipei: China Times Publications, 1990), p. 22.

8. He et al., *Taibei Xueyun,* p. 22.

9. Fan Yun, ed., *Xinshengdai de Ziwo Zhuixun,* pp. 382, 385. The two other schools with the most activity at this time were Tung-hai University and Tung-wu University.

10. Interview 21a, November 11, 1993.

11. Ibid.; Deng, *Bashi Niandai,* pp. 33–34.

12. Interview 21a, November 11, 1993.

13. Deng, *Bashi Niandai,* p. 35.

14. Ziyou Zhiai editing group, *Taida Xuesheng 'Ziyou Zhiai' Yundong Jishi* (Taipei: Nanfang), pp. 4, 43–44; Deng, *Bashi Niandai,* pp. 47–48.

15. These journals included Taida's *Love of Freedom (Ziyou Zhiai);* Chengchih University's *Wildfire (Yehuo);* Chung-hsing Fa-shang University's *Spring Thunder (Chunlei);* Central University's *Angry Wave (Nutao);* Tung-hai University's *East Tide (Dongchao);* and the Taipei Medical Institute's *Antibody (Kangti).* Editorial: "Student Movement: Forever the Road of Rebellion," in *Zhongxing Fashang Formosa,* April 1990; reprinted in Fan Yun, ed., *Xinshengdai de Ziwo Zhuixun,* p. 315. See also He et al., *Taibei Xueyun,* pp. 22–23.

16. Interview 21a, November 11, 1993. See also Fan Yun, ed., *Xinshengdai de Ziwo Zhuixun,* p. 388. The DPP was formed by *dangwai* activists in September 1986. The party subsequently was allowed to contest elections for local offices, the Legislative Yuan, and the National Assembly.

17. Deng, *Bashi Niandai,* pp. 96–99.

18. Interview 21a, November 11, 1993. See also "Student Movement: Forever the Road of Rebellion," reprinted in Fan Yun, ed., *Xinshengdai de Ziwo Zhuixun,* p. 315; and He et al., *Taibei Xueyun,* p. 22.

19. Interview 21a, November 11, 1993.

20. Deng, *Bashi Niandai,* pp. 134–135.

21. Ibid.

22. Fan Yun, ed., *Xinshengdai de Ziwo Zhuixun,* p. 316.

23. Deng, *Bashi Niandai,* pp. 219–220.

24. See Fan Yun, ed., *Xinshengdai de Ziwo Zhuixun,* pp. 382–398.

25. Wu Jianmin, in "Hope for a Domestic Student Movement," *Zhongguo Luntan,* May 10, 1990, p. 30.

26. Interview 25, December 9, 1993; Fan Yun, ed., *Xinshengdai de Ziwo Zhuixun,* pp. 394, 398.

27. These professors included He Te-fen, Ch'u Hai-yuen, and Chang Ch'ung-tung.

28. Interview 25, December 9, 1993.

29. He et al., *Taibei Xueyun,* p. 32. Some of the more prominent groups attending this meeting were the the Taiwan Environmental Protection Union, the local Farmers' Association, and the Taiwan Professors' Association. The last group was formed in early 1990, as a successor to Chenshe, the first autonomous professors' group in Taiwan, founded in 1989 at Taida. The two groups utilized slightly different tactics, however; Chenshe focused mainly on written and spoken dissent, whereas the Taiwan Professors' Association was more action-oriented (Interview 35, January 11, 1994).

30. Interview 42, June 23, 1998.

31. Deng, *Bashi Niandai,* p. 304.

32. Interview 21b, December 6, 1993.

33. *Jiushi Niandai* (April 1990), p. 37; *Zhongyang Ribao,* March 12, 1990. Cited in Peter Moody, Jr., *Political Change on Taiwan: A Study of Ruling Party Adaptability* (New York: Praeger Publishers, 1992), p. 174.

34. Deng, *Bashi Niandai,* pp. 304–305.

35. He et al., *Taibei Xueyun,* p. 34.

36. Ibid.

37. Deng, *Bashi Niandai,* p. 305.

38. He et al., *Taibei Xueyun,* p. 32.

39. Deng, *Bashi Niandai,* p. 306.

40. Interview 21a, November 11, 1993.

41. He et al., *Taibei Xueyun,* p. 34. For the text of the statement, see Fan Yun, ed., *Xinshengdai de Ziwo Zhuixun,* pp. 293–295.

42. He et al., *Taibei Xueyun,* p. 34. See also, Deng, *Bashi Niandai,* p. 306.

43. See Map 3 in Chapter 5.

44. "Taida Students Protest, Surrounded by Police," *Zili Wanbao,* March 14,

1990, p. 5; *Xin Xinwen,* March 26–April 1, 1990, p. 28; He et al., *Taibei Xueyun,* p. 34.

45. Deng, *Bashi Niandai,* p. 306; Interview 42, June 23, 1998.

46. "Taida Students Demand the Dissolution of the National Assembly," *Ziyou Shibao,* March 15, 1990, p. 1.

47. "Taida Students Protest, Surrounded by Police," *Zili Wanbao,* March 14, 1990, p. 5; "Taida Students Take to the Streets," *Zhonghua Ribao,* March 15, 1990, p. 4.

48. Deng, *Bashi Niandai,* p. 307.

49. The two friends were He Chung-hsien and Yang Hung-jen.

50. Interview 56, August 7, 1998.

51. Interview 42, June 23, 1998; Interview 56, August 7, 1998.

52. He et al., *Taibei Xueyun,* p. 36; Interview 30, December 20, 1993; Interview 56, August 7, 1998.

53. This is a reference to the seven hundred-odd elderly members of the National Assembly.

54. Fan Yun, ed., *Xinshengdai de Ziwo Zhuixun,* p. 404. See also "Indignant White Lily," *Xin Xinwen,* March 26–April 1, 1990, p. 22.

55. Interview 42, June 23, 1998; Interview 56, August 7, 1998.

56. Interview 42, June 23, 1998; Interview 56, August 7, 1998. See also Deng, *Bashi Niandai,* p. 309.

57. Fan Yun, ed., *Xinshengdai de Ziwo Zhuixun,* p. 406.

58. He et al., *Taibei Xueyun,* p. 37.

59. Ibid.

60. Fan Yun, ed., *Xinshengdai de Ziwo Zhuixun,* p. 404.

61. He et al., *Taibei Xueyun,* p. 40.

62. The members were: Chou Ke-jen, Fan Yun, and Lu Ming-chou (Taiwan Medical School); Ch'en Shang-chih (Chung-hsing Fa-shang University); Liao Su-chen (Fu-jen University); Lin Te-hsun (Wen-hua University); and Kuo Chi-chou (Tung-hai University). A representative from Tung-wu University also was originally chosen, but he almost immediately withdrew from the group (Fan Yun, ed., *Xinshengdai de Ziwo Zhuixun,* p. 406).

63. "Square Bulletin No. 1," March 18, 1990, 8:30 A.M. Reprinted in Lin Meina, ed., *Fennu de Yebaihe* (Taipei: Jianwang Chubanshe, 1990), pp. 92–93.

64. Interview 24, December 9, 1993 (italics added).

65. Deng, *Bashi Niandai,* p. 311.

66. "Fennu de Yebaihe," *Xin Xinwen,* March 26–April 1, 1990, p. 23.

67. He et al., *Taibei Xueyun,* p. 37.

68. Fan Yun, ed., *Xinshengdai de Ziwo Zhuixun,* p. 407.

69. Deng, *Bashi Niandai,* p. 311. See also Fan Yun, ed., *Xinshengdai de Ziwo Zhuixun,* p. 407.

70. Fan Yun, ed., *Xinshengdai de Ziwo Zhuixun,* p. 408.

71. Ibid., p. 405.

72. Deng, *Bashi Niandai,* p. 310.

73. Fan Yun, ed., *Xinshengdai de Ziwo Zhuixun,* p. 405.

74. Ibid., pp. 408, 410; "Square Bulletin No. 1," March 18, 1990, 8:30 A.M, reprinted in Lin Meina, ed., *Fennu de Yebaihe,* p. 93.

75. He Tung-hong, as quoted in "Fennu de Yebaihe," *Xin Xinwen,* March 26–April 1, 1990, p. 24.

76. Liao Su-chen, as quoted in ibid. This article incorrectly names Liao; see Fan Yun, ed., *Xinshengdai de Ziwo Zhuixun,* p. 410.

77. "Square Bulletin No. 1," March 18, 1990, 8:30 A.M; reprinted in Lin Meina, ed., *Fennu de Yebaihe,* pp. 92–92.

78. Deng, *Bashi Niandai,* p. 314.

79. Interviews 29, December 17, 1993, and 23, December 9, 1993.

80. "Fennu de Yebaihe," *Xin Xinwen,* March 26–April 1, 1990, p. 25; Fan Yun, ed., *Xinshengdai de Ziwo Zhuixun,* p. 410.

81. *Zhongguo Shibao,* March 19, 1990, pp. 1–2.

82. "Taipei Municipal Police Announce Principle: Don't Interfere with the Student Action, But Continue to Protect Student Safety," *Zhongguo Shibao,* March 20, 1990, p. 4.

83. Fan Yun, ed., *Xinshengdai de Ziwo Zhuixun,* p. 410.

84. Interview 29, December 17, 1993.

85. Interview 42, June 23, 1998.

86. The group also agreed that delegates to the conference would be allocated on the basis of proportional representation (Fan Yun, ed., *Xinshengdai de Ziwo Zhuixun,* p. 410).

87. Ibid.; "Square Bulletin No. 2," March 19, 1990. Reprinted in Lin Meina, ed., *Fennu de Yebaihe,* pp. 99–101.

88. Fan Yun, ed., *Xinshengdai de Ziwo Zhuixun,* p. 410.

89. Ibid., p. 412.

90. Deng, *Bashi Niandai,* p. 313.

91. Ibid., p. 314. In the account of this meeting presented in Fan Yun, ed., *Xinshengdai de Ziwo Zhuixun* (p. 411), it is also claimed that at the meeting Lee expressed his wish to personally visit the students but was dissuaded by other meeting attendees.

92. Liao Jinzhu, "Waili Shentou, Jiaoshou Yuxin," *Xin Xinwen,* March 26–April 1, 1990, p. 68.

93. Interview 27, December 9, 1993.

94. Deng, *Bashi Niandai,* p. 318.

95. Fan Yun, ed., *Xinshengdai de Ziwo Zhuixun,* pp. 412, 414.

96. Deng, *Bashi Niandai,* p. 315.

97. Fan Yun, ed., *Xinshengdai de Ziwo Zhuixun,* p. 414.

98. Lin Meina, ed., *Fennu de Yebaihe,* pp. 97–98.

99. Interview 29, December 17, 1993; Interview 32, December 28, 1993; and Interview 35, January 11, 1994.

100. Interview 21b, December 6, 1993; Interview 28, December 13, 1993; and Interview 35, January 11, 1994.

101. Interview 21b, December 6, 1993.

102. Interview 28, December 13, 1993, and Interview 29, December 17, 1993.

103. Interview 28, December 13, 1993.

104. Deng, *Bashi Niandai*, pp. 318–319. Despite this great increase in student participants, the vast majority of the newcomers did not join the hunger strike; indeed, by nightfall, only thirty-one students had begun to fast (Fan Yun, ed., *Xinshengdai de Ziwo Zhuixun*, p. 416).

105. Deng, *Bashi Niandai*, p. 318.

106. Fan Yun, ed., *Xinshengdai de Ziwo Zhuixun*, p. 414.

107. Deng, *Bashi Niandai*, p. 319.

108. "Student Sit-in Instructions," (Flyer) General Secretary Group, March 20, 1990, reprinted in Lin Meina, ed., *Fennu de Yebaihe*, p. 103; Deng, *Bashi Niandai*, p. 319.

109. Deng, *Bashi Niandai*, p. 414.

110. Ibid.

111. Ibid.

112. This group included Zheng Wencan, Wang Pingyun, He Dongchang, Peng Jianzhi, Lin Zhiping, Zeng Ruoyu, and Ding Yongyan (Fan Yun, ed., *Xinshengdai de Ziwo Zhuixun*, p. 418).

113. Deng, *Bashi Niandai*, p. 321; Fan Yun, ed., *Xinshengdai de Ziwo Zhuixun*, p. 418.

114. Fan Yun, ed., *Xinshengdai de Ziwo Zhuixun*, p. 416.

115. Interview 21b, December 6, 1993.

116. Fan Yun, ed., *Xinshengdai de Ziwo Zhuixun*, p. 418.

117. Ibid., p. 420.

118. Huang Huijuan, *"Guangchangshang Yanchu Zhongshan Chuanqi," Xin Xinwen*, March 26–April 1, 1990, p. 32.

119. Chi Huangfu, "Disturbances behind 'Compromise' within the KMT," *Da Gong Bao* (Hong Kong), March 18, 1990, p. 4. Of course, Lee did not keep his promise of retiring. In addition, he slighted his promise to Lee Huan, appointing Hao Po-ts'un to replace Lee Huan as party premier in May 1990.

120. Fan Yun, ed., *Xinshengdai de Ziwo Zhuixun*, p. 420.

121. Interview 25, December 9, 1993.

122. Deng, *Bashi Niandai*, p. 327. As some of the Policy Group members had actually fallen asleep by this point, the professors and graduate students wrote the bulk of the statement (Interview 35, January 11, 1994).

123. Fan Yun, ed., *Xinshengdai de Ziwo Zhuixun*, p. 424; Deng, *Bashi Niandai*, pp. 326–327.

124. Lee received 95.96 percent of the votes. "Taiwan's Political Farce Winds Down," *Jiushi Niandai* (April 1990), p. 33.

125. Fan Yun, ed., *Xinshengdai de Ziwo Zhuixun*, p. 424; Deng, *Bashi Niandai*, pp. 328–329.

126. Despite this public act of contrition, these students did not completely retreat from organizational activities. Indeed, all the members of the Policy Group attended the dialogue with Lee Teng-hui.

127. In the only other substantive revision of the original three points, the second point was altered to demand that the National Affairs Conference be held within a month of the presidential inauguration (Deng, *Bashi Niandai*, pp. 329–330).

128. Fan Yun, ed., *Xinshengdai de Ziwo Zhuixun*, pp. 424, 426; Deng, *Bashi Niandai*, p. 330.

129. Ibid.

130. "President Faces Students, Presidential Office Becomes Site of Negotiations" (transcription of dialogue), *Xin Xinwen*, March 26–April 1, 1990, p. 72.

131. Lee said the word "absolute" in Taiwanese, evoking loud applause from the student contingent.

132. "President Faces Students," *Xin Xinwen*, March 26–April 1, 1990, pp. 72–73.

133. Ibid., p. 73.

134. Ibid., pp. 74–74.

135. Ibid., pp. 72–76.

136. Fan Yun, ed., *Xinshengdai de Ziwo Zhuixun*, p. 426.

137. Deng, *Bashi Niandai*, p. 331.

138. Ibid.; Fan Yun, ed., *Xinshengdai de Ziwo Zhuixun*, p. 426.

139. In the final tally, thirty-two voted for the proposal, one opposed, and four abstained (Deng, *Bashi Niandai*, p. 331; Fan Yun, ed., *Xinshengdai de Ziwo Zhuixun*, p. 428).

140. Fan Yun, ed., *Xinshengdai de Ziwo Zhuixun*, p. 426.

141. See, for example, the statements of Wen-hua University, Yang-min Medical Institute, Chiao-feng University, China Medical Institute, Taiwan Shen Institute, Feng-chia University, and Taipei Medical Institute. Reprinted in Deng, *Bashi Niandai*, pp. 332–336.

142. See, for example, statements from Chung-hsing Fa-shang University, Yang-min Medical Institute, Fu-jen University, Chung-yuen University, and Feng-chia University (ibid.).

143. See, for example, statements from Chung-hsing Fa-shang University, Fu-jen University, and Chung-yuen University (ibid.).

144. "Yang-min Medical School Three-Part Statement," reprinted in Deng, *Bashi Niandai*, pp. 332–333. It is not clear to whom this criticism refers. It may be surmised, however, that it was Fan Yun, as she was the most prominent student leader during these last few days of the movement.

145. "China Medical Institute" (withdrawal statement), ibid., p. 334.

146. Tan-chiang University was the one school in opposition.

147. "Statement of All Protesting Students at the Chiang Kai-shek Memorial" March 22, 1990; reprinted in Fan Yun, ed., *Xinshengdai de Ziwo Zhuixun,* pp. 304–305.

148. Fan Yun, ed., *Xinshengdai de Ziwo Zhuixun,* p. 428.

149. Deng, *Bashi Niandai,* p. 336.

150. In actuality, this never came to pass (Interview 35, January 11, 1994).

151. Fan Yun, ed., *Xinshengdai de Ziwo Zhuixun,* p. 428.

152. "Fennu de Yebaihe," *Xin Xinwen,* March 26–April 1, 1990, p. 35.

153. Interview 31, December 28, 1993.

154. Interview 30, December 20, 1993.

155. Interview 23, December 9, 1993. This statement was repeated almost verbatim in Interview 30, December 20, 1993.

156. Interview 21b, December 6, 1993; Interview 22, December 8, 1993; Interview 23, December 9, 1993; and Interview 29, December 17, 1993.

157. In 1977, a riot erupted in the city of Chung-li on election day, as charges of voting abnormalities were leveled against the KMT. The race had been contested by former KMT member Hsu Hsin-liang, who ran (and won) as an independent candidate. Hsu later became a prominent member of the DPP. In 1979, a large-scale demonstration organized by the *dangwai*-affiliated journal *Formosa* culminated in a clash with police and the extended imprisonment of many notable *dangwai* leaders. For a detailed account of the latter, see John Kaplan, *The Court-Martial of the Kaohsiung Defendants* (Berkeley: Institute of East Asian Studies, University of California, 1981).

158. "Dissidents Clash with Police in Taipei," *South China Morning Post,* August 30, 1988.

159. "Double Tenth Marked with Street Clashes and Prison Protest," *Hong Kong Standard,* October 11, 1989; "Kuomintang Faces Challenge over Detention of Dissident," *South China Morning Post,* October 11, 1989.

160. "Democrat Candidate Charged over Riot," *Hong Kong Standard,* January 7, 1990; "Police Ordered to Take Tough Stand on Riots," *South China Morning Post,* February 22, 1990; "Taiwan's Age War," *Asiaweek,* March 9, 1990.

161. Interview 24, December 9, 1993. See also Interview 30, December 20, 1993.

162. *Zhonghua Ribao,* March 14, 1990, p. 1.

163. *Zhongguo Shibao,* March 17, 1990, p. 1, and March 18, 1990, pp. 2–3.

164. Ibid., March 19, 1990, pp. 1–2.

Chapter 6

1. Charles Tilly, *The Contentious French* (Cambridge, MA: Belknap Press, 1986).

2. Doug McAdam, *Political Process and the Development of Black Insurgency, 1930–1970* (Chicago: University of Chicago Press, 1982).

3. Sidney Tarrow, *Power in Movement: Social Movements, Collective Action, and Politics,* 2d ed. (New York: Cambridge University Press, 1998).

4. See, for example, Charles D. Brockett, "The Structure of Political Opportunities and Peasant Mobilization in Central America," *Comparative Politics,* April 1991, pp. 253–274; Lynn Kamenitsa, "The Process of Political Marginalization: East German Social Movements after the Wall," *Comparative Politics,* April 1998, pp. 313–333; Karl Dieter-Opp and Christiane Gern, "Dissident Groups, Personal Networks, and Spontaneous Cooperation: The East-German Revolution of 1989," *American Sociological Review* 58 (October 1993), pp. 659–680; Michael Bratton and Nicolas van de Walle, "Popular Protest and Political Reform in Africa," *Comparative Politics,* July 1992, pp. 419–442; Donatella della Porta, *Social Movements, Political Violence, and the State* (Cambridge: Cambridge University Press, 1995); and Peter P. Houtzager and Marcus J. Kurtz, "The Institutional Roots of Popular Mobilization: State Transformation and Rural Politics in Brazil and Chile, 1960–1995," *Comparative Studies in Society and History.*

5. See, for example, Woei Lien Chong, "Petitioners, Popperians, and Hunger Strikers: The Uncoordinated Efforts of the 1989 Chinese Democratic Movement," in Tony Saich, ed., *The Chinese People's Movement: Perspectives on Spring 1989* (Armonk, NY: M. E. Sharpe, 1990); Josephine M. T. Khu, "Student Organization in the Movement," in Roger Des Forges, Luo Ning, and Wu Yenbo, eds., *Chinese Democracy and the Crisis of 1989* (Albany: State University of New York Press, 1993); and Lee Feigon, *China Rising: The Meaning of Tiananmen* (Chicago: Ivan R. Dee, 1990), pp. 134–136. A unique counterassessment of this salon-centered approach can be found in Jeffrey Wasserstrom and Liu Xingyun, "Student Associations and Mass Movements," in Deborah Davis, Richard Kraus, Barry Naughton, and Elizabeth Perry, eds., *Urban Spaces in Contemporary China* (New York: Woodrow Wilson Center Press and Cambridge University Press, 1995).

6. See, for example, Andrew Walder and Gong Xiaoxia, "Workers in the Tiananmen Protests: The Politics of the Beijing Workers' Autonomous Federation," *The Australian Journal of Chinese Affairs* (January 1993), pp. 1–29; and Elizabeth Perry, "Casting a Chinese 'Democracy' Movement: The Roles of Students, Workers, and Entrepreneurs," in Elizabeth Perry and Jeffrey Wasserstrom, eds., *Popular Protest and Political Culture in Modern China: Learning from 1989,* 2d ed. (Boulder, CO: Westview Press, 1994).

7. Anita Chan and Jonathan Unger, "Voices from the Protest Movement in Chongqing: Class Accents and Class Tensions"; Roy Forward, "Letter from Shanghai"; and Shelley Warner, "Shanghai's Response to the Deluge"; all in Jonathan Unger, ed., *The Pro-Democracy Protests in China: Reports from the Provinces* (Armonk, NY: M. E. Sharpe, 1991).

8. Tang Boqiao, *Anthems of Defeat: Crackdown in Hunan Province 1989–1992* (New York: Asia Watch, 1992), pp. 7–8.

9. For example, workers reportedly joined students in a hunger strike on May 16, and on May 24 the Changsha Students' Autonomous Federation organized a

mass demonstration in conjunction with the Changsha Workers' Autonomous Federation (Tang, *Anthems of Defeat*, pp. 10–15).

10. See, for example, Jeffrey Wasserstrom, *Student Protests in Twentieth-Century China* (Stanford, CA: Stanford University Press, 1991), p. 137.

11. See Suzanne Pepper, *Civil War in China* (Berkeley: University of California Press, 1978), pp. 42–90.

12. Ibid., p. 43.

13. See Wasserstrom, *Student Protests in Twentieth-Century China*, and Pepper, *Civil War in China*.

14. This phrase was coined by Guillermo O'Donnell and Cecilia Galli in reference to Argentina. See Guillermo O'Donnell, "La cosecha del miedo," *Nexos* (Mexico City) 6, no. 6 (1983). Similar statements are found in: Brockett, "The Structure of Political Opportunities and Peasant Mobilization in Central America"; Dieter-Opp and Gern, "Dissident Groups, Personal Networks, and Spontaneous Cooperation: The East German Revolution of 1989"; and Bratton and van de Walle, "Popular Protest and Political Reform in Africa."

15. Juan E. Corradi, Patricia Weiss Fagen, and Manuel Antonio Garreton, eds., *Fear at the Edge: State Terror and Resistance in Latin America* (Berkeley: University of California Press, 1992), p. 2.

16. Ibid.

17. Ibid.

18. Norbert Lechner, "Some People Die of Fear: Fear as a Political Problem," in Corradi et al., eds., *Fear at the Edge*, p. 29.

19. Patricia Weiss Fagen, "Repression and State Security," in ibid., p. 67.

20. Maria Helena Moreira Alves, "Cultures of Fear, Cultures of Resistance," in ibid., p. 190.

21. See William Gamson, *The Strategy of Social Protest*, 2d ed. (Belmont, CA: Wadsworth Publishing Co., 1990), p. 172. This point has been raised in numerous works, including David Snow, Louis Zurcher, and Sheldon Eckland-Olson, "Social Networks and Social Movements: A Microstructural Approach to Differential Recruitment," *American Sociological Review* 46 (1980), pp. 787–801, and Doug McAdam, "Recruitment to High-Risk Activism: The Case of Freedom Summer," *American Journal of Sociology*, July 1986, pp. 64–90.

22. Dieter Opp and Gern, "Dissident Groups, Personal Networks, and Spontaneous Cooperation: The East German Revolution of 1989," pp. 673–674. An intriguing study of the budding women's movement in post-Communist Russia also finds a substantial correlation between organizational growth and friendship ties. See Valerie Sperling, *Organizing Women in Contemporary Russia: Engendering Transition* (Cambridge: Cambridge University Press, 1999).

23. Lynn Kamenitsa, "The Process of Political Marginalization: East German Social Movements after the Wall," *Comparative Politics*, April 1998, pp. 324–325. Dieter Opp and Gern reach a similar conclusion in, "Dissident Groups, Personal Networks, and Spontaneous Cooperation: The East German Revolution of 1989."

24. See, for example, Craig Calhoun, *Neither Gods Nor Emperors* (Berkeley: University of California Press, 1994), p. 183.

25. Juan E. Corradi, "Toward Societies without Fear," in Corradi et al., eds., *Fear at the Edge*, p. 279.

26. Javier Martinez, "Fear of the State, Fear of Society: On the Opposition Protests in Chile," in Corradi et al., eds., *Fear at the Edge*, p. 146.

27. Ibid.

28. Wonmo Dong, "Student Activism and the Presidential Politics of 1987 in South Korea," in Ilpyong J. Kim and Young Whan Kihl, eds., *Political Change in South Korea* (New York: The Korean PWPA, 1988), p. 175.

29. Josef Silverstein, "Students in Southeast Asian Politics," *Pacific Affairs* (Summer 1979), p. 211.

30. Carina Perelli, "Youth, Politics, and Dictatorship in Uruguay," in Corradi et al., eds., *Fear at the Edge*, p. 239.

31. Brockett, "The Structure of Political Opportunities and Peasant Mobilization in Central America," p. 262. See also Bratton and van de Walle, "Popular Protest and Political Reform in Africa," p. 430.

32. Kamenitsa, "The Process of Political Marginalization: East German Social Movements after the Wall," p. 315.

33. Ross Prizzia and Narong Sinsawasdi, *Thailand: Student Activism and Political Change* (Bangkok: Allied Printers, 1974), p. 52.

34. Ibid., p. 56.

35. Silverstein, "Students in Southeast Asian Politics," p. 202.

36. Ibid., p. 204.

Bibliography

Alves, Maria Helena Moreira. "Cultures of Fear, Cultures of Resistance." In Juan E. Corradi, Patricia Weiss Fagen, and Manuel Antonio Garreton, *Fear at the Edge: State Terror and Resistance in Latin America*. Berkeley: University of California Press, 1992.

Bajiu Zhongguo Minyun Ziliao (Data from the Chinese People's Movement of 1989). Hong Kong: Hong Kong Chinese Language University Student Union, 1991.

Barme, Geremie. "Traveling Heavy: The Intellectual Baggage of the Chinese Diaspora." *Problems of Communism* (January–April 1991): 94–112.

Bermeo, Nancy. "Myths of Moderation: Confrontation and Conflict during Democratic Transitions." *Comparative Politics* (April 1997): 305–322.

Black, George, and Robin Munro. *Black Hands of Beijing: Lives of Defiance in China's Democracy Movement*. New York: John Wiley and Sons, 1993.

Bratton, Michael, and Nicolas van de Walle. "Popular Protest and Political Reform in Africa." *Comparative Politics* (July 1992): 419–442.

Brockett, Charles. "The Structure of Political Opportunities and Peasant Mobilization in Central America." *Comparative Politics* (April 1991): 253–274.

Brook, Timothy. *Quelling the People*. New York: Oxford University Press, 1992.

Calhoun, Craig. *Neither Gods Nor Emperors*. Berkeley: University of California Press, 1994.

Chan, Anita, and Jonathan Unger. "Voices from the Protest Movement in Chongqing: Class Accents and Class Tensions." In Jonathan Unger, ed., *The Pro-Democracy Protests in China: Reports from the Provinces*. Armonk, NY: M. E. Sharpe, 1991.

Chao, Linda, and Ramon Myers. "The First Chinese Democracy." *Asian Survey* (March 1994): 213–230.

Cheek, Timothy. "From Priests to Professionals: Intellectuals and the State under the CCP." In Elizabeth Perry and Jeffrey Wasserstrom, eds., *Popular Protest and Political Culture in Modern China: Learning from 1989*. Boulder, CO: Westview Press, 1992.

Chen, Edward I-hsin. "Current Debates over Marxist Theory in the PRC." In Ramon Myers, ed., *Two Societies in Opposition: The Republic of China and the People's Republic of China after Forty Years*. Stanford, CA: Hoover Institution Press, 1991.

Chen Guuying. "The Reform Movement among Intellectuals in Taiwan since 1970." *Bulletin of Concerned Asian Scholars* (July–September 1982).

Chen Xitong. *Report on Checking the Turmoil and Quelling the Counter-Revolutionary Rebellion.* Beijing: New Star Publishers, 1989.

Cheng, Tun-jen. "Democratizing the Quasi-Leninist Regime in Taiwan." *World Politics* 41, no. 4 (July 1989): 471–499.

Chiou, C. L. *Democratizing Oriental Despotism: China from 4 May 1919 to 4 June 1989 and Taiwan from 28 February 1947 to June 1990.* New York: St. Martin's Press, 1995.

Chong Woei Lien. "Petitioners, Popperians, and Hunger Strikers: The Uncoordinated Efforts of the 1989 Chinese Democratic Movement." In Tony Saich, ed., *The Chinese People's Movement: Perspectives on Spring 1989.* Armonk, NY: M. E. Sharpe, 1990.

Chou, Yansun, and Andrew Nathan. "Democratizing Transition in Taiwan." *Asian Survey* (March 1987): 277–299.

Copper, John. *A Quiet Revolution.* Lanham, MD: Ethics and Public Policy Center, University Press of America, 1988.

Corradi, Juan E. "Fear of the State, Fear of Society." In Juan E. Corradi, Patricia Weiss Fagen, and Manuel Antonio Garreton, *Fear at the Edge: State Terror and Resistance in Latin America.* Berkeley: University of California Press, 1992.

Crowley, Stephen. *Hot Coal, Cold Steel.* Ann Arbor: University of Michigan Press, 1997.

della Porta, Donatella. *Social Movements, Political Violence and the State.* Cambridge: Cambridge University Press, 1995.

———. "Social Movements and the State: Thoughts on the Policing of Protest." In Doug McAdam, John McCarthy, and Mayer Zald, eds., *Comparative Perspectives on Social Movements.* Cambridge: Cambridge University Press, 1996.

Deng Piyun. *Bashi Niandai* (The eighties). Taipei: Taiwan Yanjiu Jijinhui, 1990.

Dittmer, Lowell. *China's Continuous Revolution: The Post-Liberation Epoch, 1949–1981.* Berkeley: University of California Press, 1987.

———. "The Tiananmen Massacre." *Problems of Communism* 38, no. 5 (September–October 1989): 2–15.

Domes, Jurgen. "Political Differentiation in Taiwan: Group Formation within the Ruling Party and the Opposition Circles, 1979–1980." *Asian Survey* (October 1987).

———. "The 13th Party Congress of the Kuomintang: Towards Political Competition?" *China Quarterly* (June 1989): 345–359.

Dong, Wonmo. "Student Activism and the Presidential Politics of 1987 in South Korea." In Ilpyong J. Kim and Young Whan Kihl, eds., *Political Change in South Korea.* New York: The Korean PWPA, 1988.

Epstein, Erwin H., and Wei-fan Kuo. "Higher Education." In Douglas C. Smith, ed., *The Confucian Continuum: Educational Modernization in Taiwan.* New York: Praeger, 1991.

Esherick, Joseph, and Jeffrey Wasserstrom. "Acting Out Democracy: Political Theater in Modern China." In Elizabeth Perry and Jeffrey Wasserstrom, eds., *Popular Protest and Political Culture in Modern China: Learning from 1989*. 2d ed. Boulder, CO: Westview Press, 1994.

Fagen, Patricia Weiss. "Repression and State Security." In Juan E. Corradi, Patricia Weiss Fagen, and Manuel Antonio Garreton, *Fear at the Edge: State Terror and Resistance in Latin America*. Berkeley: University of California Press, 1992.

Fan Yun, ed. *Xin Sheng Dai de Ziwo Zhuixun* (Self-reflections on the new era). Taipei, 1991.

Fang Yangzhong et al. "Fennu de Yebaihe" (Indignant white lily). *Xin Xinwen* (The journalist) (March 26–April 1, 1990): 20–35.

Feffer, John. *Shock Waves: Eastern Europe after the Revolutions*. Boston: South End Press, 1992.

Francis, Corrina-Barbara. "The Progress of Protest in China." *Asian Survey* 29, no. 9 (September 1989): 898–915.

Gamson, William. *Power and Discontent*. Homewood, IL: Dorsey Press, 1968.

———. *The Strategy of Social Protest*. 2d ed. Belmont, CA: Wadsworth Publishing Co., 1990.

Gamson, William, and David Meyer. "Framing Political Opportunity." In Doug McAdam, John McCarthy, and Mayer Zald, eds., *Comparative Perspectives on Social Movements*. Cambridge: Cambridge University Press, 1996.

The Gate of Heavenly Peace. Documentary film. Long Bow Group, 1995.

Gati, Charles. *The Bloc That Failed*. Bloomington: Indiana University Press and the Center for Strategic and International Studies, 1990.

German Rhine Writers' Association 1989 Student Research Group. *Huigu yu Fansi* (Review and reflect). Essen, Germany, 1993.

Giugni, Marco G., Doug McAdam, and Charles Tilly, eds. *From Contention to Democracy*. New York: Rowman and Littlefield, 1998.

Gregor, A. James, and Maria Hsia Chang. "The Thought of Sun Yat-sen in Comparative Perspective." In Chu-yuan Cheng, ed., *Sun Yat-sen's Doctrine in the Modern World*. Boulder, CO: Westview Press, 1989.

Han Minzhu and Hua Sheng, eds. *Cries for Democracy: Writings and Speeches from the 1989 Chinese Democracy Movement*. Princeton, NJ: Princeton University Press, 1990.

Hartford, Kathleen. "The Political Economy behind the Beijing Spring." In Tony Saich, ed., *Perspectives on the Chinese People's Movement: Spring 1989*. Armonk, NY: M. E. Sharpe, 1990.

Hayhoe, Ruth. *China's Universities and the Open Door*. New York: M. E. Sharpe, 1989.

———. *Education and Modernization: The Chinese Experience*. New York: Pergamon Press, 1992.

———. *China's Universities 1895–1995: A Century of Cultural Conflict*. New York: Garland Publishing, 1996.

He Jinshan, Guan Hongzhi, Zhuang Lijia, and Guo Chengqi. *Taipei Xueyun* (Taipei student movement). Taipei: Zhongguo Shibao Chubanshe, 1990.

Henze, Jurgen. "The Formal Education System and Modernization: An Analysis of Developments since 1978." In Ruth Hayhoe, ed., *Education and Modernization: The Chinese Experience*. New York: Pergamon Press, 1992.

"Hope for a Domestic Student Movement." *Zhongguo Luntan* (China forum), May 10, 1990.

Houtzager, Peter, and Marcus Kurtz. "The Institutional Roots of Popular Mobilization: State Transformation and Rural Politics in Brazil and Chile, 1960–1995." *Comparative Studies in Society and History* (April 2000).

Huang Huijian. "Guangchangshang Yanchu Zhongshan Chuanqi" (Legend of Zhongshan performed at square). *Xin Xinwen* (The journalist), March 26–April 1, 1990, p. 32.

Huntington, Samuel P. "Will More Countries Become Democratic?" *Political Science Quarterly* (Summer 1984): 193–218.

———. *The Third Wave: Democratization in the Late Twentieth Century*. Norman: University of Oklahoma Press, 1991.

Jenkins, J. Craig, and Bert Klandermans, eds. *The Politics of Social Protest: Comparative Perspectives on States and Social Movements*. Minneapolis: University of Minnesota Press, 1995.

Kamensita, Lynn. "The Process of Political Marginalization: East German Social Movements after the Wall." *Comparative Politics* (April 1998): 313–333.

Kaplan, John. *The Court Martial of the Kaohsiung Defendants*. Berkeley: Institute of East Asian Studies, 1981.

Kelliher, Daniel. "Keeping Democracy Safe from the Masses: Intellectuals and Elitism in the Chinese Protest Movement." *Comparative Politics* (July 1993): 379–396.

Khu, Josephine M. T. "Student Organization in the Movement." In Roger Des Forges, ed., *Chinese Democracy and the Crisis of 1989*. Albany: State University of New York Press, 1993.

Kriesi, Hanspeter, et al. "New Social Movements and Political Opportunities in Western Europe." *European Journal of Political Research* 22 (1992): 219–244.

Kuofu Chuanchi (The complete works of Sun Yat-sen). Vol. 1. 2d ed. Taipei: Committee on Party History, Central Committee of the KMT, 1981.

Lechner, Norbert. "Some People Die of Fear: Fear as a Political Problem." In Juan E. Corradi, Patricia Weiss Fagen, and Manuel Antonio Garreton, *Fear at the Edge: State Terror and Resistance in Latin America*. Berkeley: University of California Press, 1992.

Lee Chin-chuan. "Sparking a Fire: The Press and the Ferment of Democratic Change in Taiwan." *Journalism Monographs* (April 1993).

Lee Feigon. *China Rising: The Meaning of Tiananmen*. Chicago: Ivan R. Dee, 1990.

Leng, Xhao-chuan, and Cheng-yi Lin. "Political Change on Taiwan: Transition to Democracy?" *China Quarterly* (December 1993): 805–839.

Liao Jinzhu. "Waili Shentou, Jiaoshou Yuxin" (Outside forces infiltrate, professors worried). *Xin Xinwen* (The journalist) (March 26–April 1, 1990): 68.

Lieberthal, Kenneth. *Governing China*. New York: W. W. Norton and Co., 1995.

Li Lu. *Moving the Mountain*. London: Macmillan, 1990.

Lin Meina, ed. *Fennu de Yebaihe* (Indignant white lily). Taipei: Jianwang Chubanshe, 1990.

Linz, Juan J. "An Authoritarian Regime: Spain." In Erik Allart and Stein Rokkan, eds., *Mass Politics: Studies in Political Sociology*. New York: Free Press, 1970.

Linz, Juan J., and Alfred Stepan. *Problems of Democratic Transition and Consolidation: Southern Europe, South America, and Post-Communist Europe*. Baltimore: Johns Hopkins University Press, 1996.

Lipset, Seymour. *Political Man: The Social Bases of Politics*. London: Heinemann, 1983.

Liu Xiaobo. "The Inspiration of New York: Meditations of an Iconoclast." *Problems of Communism* (January–April 1991): 113–118.

———. "That Holy Word, 'Revolution.' " In Elizabeth Perry and Jeffrey Wasserstrom, eds., *Popular Protest and Political Culture in Modern China*. 2d ed. Boulder, CO: Westview Press, 1994.

Maier, John H. "Tienanmen: The View from Shanghai." *Issues and Studies* 26, no. 6 (June 1990): 44–63.

Mao Zedong. *Selected Readings from the Works of Mao Zedong*. Peking: Foreign Language Press, 1971.

Martinez, Javier. "Fear of the State, Fear of Society: On the Opposition Protests in Chile." In Juan E. Corradi, Patricia Weiss Fagen, and Manuel Antonio Garreton, *Fear at the Edge: State Terror and Resistance in Latin America*. Berkeley: University of California Press, 1992.

McAdam, Doug. *Political Process and the Development of Black Insurgency, 1930–1970*. Chicago: University of Chicago Press, 1982.

———. "Recruitment to High-Risk Activism: The Case of Freedom Summer." *American Journal of Sociology* 92, no. 1 (July 1986): 64–90.

McAdam, Doug, John McCarthy, and Mayer Zald. "Social Movements." In Neil Smelser, ed., *Handbook of Sociology*. London: Sage Publications, 1988.

McAdam, Doug, Sidney Tarrow, and Charles Tilly. "Toward an Integrated Perspective on Social Movements and Revolution." In Mark Irving Lichbach and Alan S. Zuckerman, eds., *Comparative Politics: Rationality, Culture, and Structure*. Cambridge: Cambridge University Press, 1997.

McCarthy, J. D., and M. N. Zald. "Resource Mobilization and Social Movements: A Partial Theory." *American Journal of Sociology* 82, no. 6 (May 1977): 1212–1241.

———. *The Trends of Social Movements in America: Professionalization and Resource Mobilization*. Morristown, NJ: General Learning Press, 1973.

Mill, John Stuart. *A System of Logic*. New York: Longmans, 1965.

Moody, Peter. *Political Change on Taiwan: A Study of Ruling Party Adaptability*. New York: Praeger, 1992.

Morey, Ann I., and Zhou Nanzhao. "Higher Education in Mainland China: An Overview." *Issues and Studies* 26, no. 5 (May 1990).

Morris, Aldon, and Cedric Herring. "Theory and Research in Social Movements: A Critical Review." In Samuel Long, ed., *Annual Review of Political Science,* vol. 2. Norwood, NJ: Ablex Publishing Corp.

Nathan, Andrew. *Chinese Democracy.* Berkeley: University of California Press, 1985.

———. "Chinese Democracy in 1989: Continuity and Change." *Problems of Communism* 38, no. 5 (September–October 1989): 16–29.

Oberschall, Anthony. *Social Conflict and Social Movements.* Englewood Cliffs, NJ: Prentice-Hall, 1973.

———. "Opportunities and Framing in the East European Revolts of 1989." In McAdam, McCarthy, and Zald, eds., *Comparative Perspectives on Social Movements.* Cambridge: Cambridge University Press, 1996.

O'Donnell, Guillermo. "La cosecha del miedo." *Nexos* (Mexico City), no. 6 (1983).

O'Donnell, Guillermo, and Philippe Schmitter. *Transitions from Authoritarian Rule: Tentative Conclusions about Uncertain Democracies.* Baltimore: Johns Hopkins University Press, 1986.

O'Donnell, Guillermo, Philippe Schmitter, and Lynn Whitehead, eds. *Transitions from Authoritarian Rule: Comparative Perspectives.* Baltimore: Johns Hopkins University Press, 1986.

Oksenberg, Michel, Lawrence R. Sullivan, and Marc Lambert. *Beijing Spring, 1989; Confrontation and Conflict; The Basic Documents.* Armonk, NY: M. E. Sharpe, 1990.

Opp, Karl-Dieter, and Christiane Gern. "Dissident Groups, Personal Networks, and Spontaneous Cooperation: The East-German Revolution of 1989." *American Sociological Review* 58, no. 5 (October 1993): 659–680.

Pepper, Suzanne. *Civil War in China.* Berkeley: University of California Press, 1978.

———. *China's Education Reform in the 1980's.* Berkeley: Institute of East Asian Studies, 1990.

Perelli, Carina. "Youth, Politics, and Dictatorship in Uruguay." In Juan E. Corradi, Patricia Weiss Fagen, and Manuel Antonio Garreton. *Fear at the Edge: State Terror and Resistance in Latin America.* Berkeley: University of California Press, 1992.

Perry, Elizabeth. "Casting a Chinese 'Democracy' Movement: The Roles of Students, Workers, and Entrepreneurs." In Elizabeth Perry and Jeffrey Wasserstrom, eds., *Popular Protest and Political Culture in Modern China: Learning from 1989.* 2d ed. Boulder, CO: Westview Press, 1994.

———. "Trends in the Study of Chinese Politics: State–Society Relations." *China Quarterly* (September 1994): 704–713.

Price, Ronald. "Moral-Political Education and Modernization." In Ruth Hayhoe, ed., *Education and Modernization: The Chinese Experience.* New York: Pergamon Press, 1992.

Prizzia, Ross, and Narong Sinsawasdi. *Thailand: Student Activism and Political Change.* Bangkok: Allied Printers, 1974.

"Rationality and Morality: Interview with Wu'er Kaixi." *Beijing Spring* (June 1995).

Rucht, Dieter. "The Impact of National Contexts on Social Movement Structures: A Cross-Movement and Cross-National Comparison." In Doug McAdam, John McCarthy, and Mayer Zald, eds., *Comparative Perspectives on Social Movements*. Cambridge: Cambridge University Press, 1996.

Saich, Tony, ed. *Perspectives on the Chinese People's Movement: Spring 1989*. Armonk, NY: M. E. Sharpe, 1990.

Schell, Orville. *Mandate of Heaven*. New York: Simon and Schuster, 1994.

Schwarcz, Vera. "Memory and Commemoration: The Chinese Search for a Livable Past." In Elizabeth Perry and Jeffrey Wasserstrom, eds., *Popular Protest and Political Culture in Modern China: Learning from 1989*. Boulder, CO: Westview Press, 1992.

Shen Tong. *Almost a Revolution*. Boston: Houghton-Mifflin, 1990.

Silverstein, Josef. "Students in Southeast Asian Politics." *Pacific Affairs* 49, no. 2 (Summer 1976): 189–212.

Simmie, Scott, and Bob Nixon. *Tiananmen Square*. Seattle: University of Washington Press, 1989.

Simons, Herbert W., and Elizabeth W. Mechling. "The Rhetoric of Political Movements." In Dan D. Nimmo and Keith R. Sanders, eds., *Handbook of Political Communication*. London: Sage Publications, 1981.

Smelser, Neil, ed. *Handbook of Sociology*. London: Sage Publications, 1988.

Snow, David, Louis Zurcher, and Sheldon Eckland-Olson. "Social Networks and Social Movements: A Microstructural Approach to Differential Recruitment." *American Sociological Review* 45, no. 5 (October 1980): 787–801.

Sperling, Valerie. *Organizing Women in Contemporary Russia: Engendering Transition*. Cambridge: Cambridge University Press, 1999.

"Student Movement: Forever the Road of Rebellion." *Zhongxing Fashang Formosa* (April 1990).

"Summary of Deng Xiaoping's March 1979 Speech at a Discussion of Theoretical Issues." *Guang Jiao Jing* (Hong Kong) 85 (Nov. 16, 1979): 4–10.

"Taiwan's Age War." *Asiaweek,* March 9, 1990.

"Taiwan's Political Farce Winds Down." *Jiushi Niandai* (April 1990): 33.

Tang, W. K. "The Story of a Non-Governmental Reformist Research Institute in China." *A Changing China* 1, no. 1 (Winter 1991): 3–6.

Tang Boqiao. *Anthems of Defeat: Crackdown in Hunan Province 1989–1992*. New York: Asia Watch, 1992.

Tarrow, Sidney. *Democracy and Disorder: Protest and Politics in Italy, 1965–1975*. New York: Oxford University Press, 1989.

———. "Mentalities, Political Cultures and Collective Action Frames: Constructing Meanings through Action." In Aldon D. Morris and Carol McClurg Mueller, eds., *Frontiers in Social Movement Theory*. New Haven, CT: Yale University Press, 1990.

———. *Power in Movement: Social Movements, Collective Action, and Politics*. 2d ed. New York: Cambridge University Press, 1998.

Tilly, Charles. *From Mobilization to Revolution*. Reading, MA: Addison-Wesley, 1978.

——. *The Contentious French*. Cambridge, MA: Belknap Press, 1986.

Unger, Jonathan, ed. *The Pro-Democracy Protests in China: Reports from the Provinces*. Armonk, NY: M. E. Sharpe, 1991.

Wakeman, Frederic. "The June 4 Movement in China." *Items* 3. New York: Social Science Research Council.

Walder, Andrew. "The Political Sociology of the Beijing Upheaval of 1989." *Problems of Communism* 38, no. 5 (September–October 1989): 30–40.

Walder, Andrew, and Gong Xiaoxia. "Workers in the Tiananmen Protests: The Politics of the Beijing Workers' Autonomous Federation." *The Australian Journal of Chinese Affairs* 29 (January 1993): 1–29.

Wang Guobao. "Beijing Xueyun Qinghua Jianwen" (Account of events at Qinghua University during the Beijing student movement). *Tansuo* (Exploration) 66 (June 1989): 61–64.

Wasserstrom, Jeffrey. *Student Protests in Twentieth-Century China*. Stanford, CA: Stanford University Press, 1991.

Wasserstrom, Jeffrey, and Liu Xingyun. "Student Associations and Mass Movements." In Deborah S. Davis, Richard Kraus, Barry Naughton, and Elizabeth Perry, eds., *Urban Spaces in Contemporary China*. New York: Woodrow Wilson Center Press and Cambridge University Press, 1995.

Weber, Max. *The Theory of Social and Economic Organization*. New York: The Free Press, 1947.

Weigle, Marcia A., and Jim Butterfield. "Civil Society in Reforming Communist Regimes: The Logic of Emergence." *Comparative Politics* (October 1992): 1–23.

Wright, Teresa. "Student Mobilization in Taiwan: Civil Society and Its Discontents." *Asian Survey* 39, no. 6 (November–December 1999): 986–1008.

Wu, Hongda Harry. *Laogai: The Chinese Gulag*. Boulder, CO: Westview Press, 1992.

Wu, Hongda Harry, and Carolyn Wakeman. *Bitter Winds: A Memoir of My Years in China's Gulag*. New York: J. Wiley, 1994.

Wu Moren, Ni Peihua, Wang Zingjia, Yan Jiaqi, Wu'er Kaixi, Bao Minghui, and Ni Peimin, eds. *Bajiu Zhongguo Minyun Jishi* (Daily reports on the movement for democracy in China, April 15–June 24, 1989). New York: 1989.

Xie, Weizhi. "The Semihierarchical Totalitarian Nature of Chinese Politics." *Comparative Politics* (April 1993): 313–330.

"Xinwen Daobao" (News report). *Zhongguo Zhichun* (China spring) (New York) 75 (August 1989): 11–12.

Xin Xinwen editorial department. "Da Zongtong Miandui Daxuesheng, Zongtongfu Biancheng Tanpanchang" (President Faces Students, Presidential House Becomes Site of Negotiations). *Xin Xinwen* (The journalist) (March 26–April 1, 1990): 72.

Yu Yu-lin. "Change and Continuity in the CCP's Power Structure since Its 13th National Congress." In Ramon Myers, ed., *Two Societies in Opposition: The Republic of China and the People's Republic of China after Forty Years.* Stanford, CA: Hoover Institution Press, 1991.

Newspapers and News Services

Dagongbao (Hong Kong): March 21, 1989; March 18, 1990.
FBIS: May 4, 1989; May 31, 1989; June 7, 1989.
Hong Kong Standard: October 11, 1989; January 7, 1990.
The New York Times, May 11, 1995.
The New York Times (International Edition), April 30, 1995.
Renmin Ribao (Beijing): November 4, 1987; May 19, 1989; April 26, 1989; June 1, 1989; June 3, 1989.
Shijie Jingji Daobao (Shanghai), no. 426.
Shoudu Zaobao (Taipei), March 21, 1990.
South China Morning Post (Hong Kong): August 30, 1988; October 11, 1989; February 22, 1990; May 31, 1989.
Wenhuibao (Hong Kong), January 17, 1989.
Xinhua (Bejing): May 4, 1989; May 18, 1989; May 19, 1989.
Zhongguo Shibao (Taipei): March 17, 1990; March 18, 1990; March 19, 1990; March 20, 1990.
Zhonghua Ribao (Taipei): March 14, 1990; March 15, 1990.
Zhongyang Ribao (Taipei): February 3, 1990; February 28, 1990; March 5, 1990; March 12, 1990; March 14, 1990; March 26, 1990.
Zili Wanbao (Taipei), March 14, 1990.
Zili Zaobao (Taipei), March 21, 1990.
Ziyou Shibao (Taipei), March 15, 1990.

Archives

Robin Munro Collection. Documents II.4; II.29; XIII.1; XIV.2; XIV.4; XXIII.1. University of California, Berkeley, Center for Chinese Studies.
Tiananmen Archive. Columbia University, New York. Document H-18.

Index

About the Author

Teresa Wright received her doctoral degree in political science from the University of California, Berkeley. She is currently an assistant professor of political science at California State University, Long Beach. Her research interests focus on comparative social movements and democratization in East Asia. Professor Wright's articles on student protest in China and Taiwan have appeared in *China Quarterly* and *Asian Survey. The Perils of Protest* is her first book.